Telling an
American Horror Story

Telling an *American Horror Story*

Essays on History, Place and Identity in the Series

Edited by
CAMERON WILLIAMS CRAWFORD
and LEVERETT BUTTS

McFarland & Company, Inc., Publishers
Jefferson, North Carolina

ALSO OF INTEREST

*H.P. Lovecraft: Selected Works,
Critical Perspectives and Interviews on His Influence*
(H.P. Lovecraft, Edited by Leverett Butts, McFarland, 2018)

LIBRARY OF CONGRESS CATALOGUING-IN-PUBLICATION DATA

Names: Crawford, Cameron Williams, 1985– editor. | Butts, Leverett, editor.
Title: Telling an American horror story : essays on history, place and identity in the series / edited by Cameron Williams Crawford and Leverett Butts.
Description: Jefferson, North Carolina : McFarland & Company, Inc., Publishers, 2021 | Includes bibliographical references and index.
Identifiers: LCCN 2021001039 | ISBN 9781476680613 (paperback : acid free paper) ∞
ISBN 9781476641775 (ebook)
Subjects: LCSH: American horror story (Television program)
Classification: LCC PN1992.77.A5255 T45 2021 | DDC 791.45/72—dc23
LC record available at https://lccn.loc.gov/2021001039

BRITISH LIBRARY CATALOGUING DATA ARE AVAILABLE

ISBN (print) 978-1-4766-8061-3
ISBN (ebook) 978-1-4766-4177-5

© 2021 Cameron Williams Crawford and Leverett Butts. All rights reserved

No part of this book may be reproduced or transmitted in any form or by any means, electronic or mechanical, including photocopying or recording, or by any information storage and retrieval system, without permission in writing from the publisher.

Front cover image © 2021 Shutterstock

Printed in the United States of America

*McFarland & Company, Inc., Publishers
Box 611, Jefferson, North Carolina 28640
www.mcfarlandpub.com*

Acknowledgments

The editors wish to thank the contributors to this volume. Without their unique insight and dedication, this project would not exist.

Table of Contents

Acknowledgments v

Introduction
    CAMERON WILLIAMS CRAWFORD *and* LEVERETT BUTTS 1

Part I. History and Folklore

Asylum: Taboos and Transgressions in U.S. History
    ERIN GUYDISH BUCHHOLZ 8

Where Myth Meets History: Discursive Haunting
and the Resurrection of Marie Laveau in *Coven*
    RITA MOOKERJEE 26

Coven's LaLaurie and Laveau: Contemporary
Narratives of Southern Gothicism, Folklore
and Nineteenth-Century New Orleans
    TAMMIE JENKINS 39

Apocalypse and the Devil We Are
    LEVERETT BUTTS 54

Part II. Space and Place

Derridean Hauntology as Cultural Praxis: The Strange
Case of *Murder House*
    JONATHAN GREENAWAY 66

The Psychiatric Clinic in Horror Cinema and TV: *Asylum*
    ANTONIO SANNA 81

The Swampy Boundaries of "Otherness" in *Freak Show*
and *Roanoke*
    CAMERON WILLIAMS CRAWFORD 100

The Meta-Carnival: Monsters and Mothers in *Freak Show*
 JENNIFER K. COX   112

Part III. Identity Politics

The Mother-Witch and Witch as Mother in *Coven*
 SARAH FOUST VINSON   134

Wear Something Black: Fashion and Fierce Femininity in the Witch Drag of *Coven*
 MICHELLE L. PRIBBERNOW   148

Destructive Leadership in *Coven*, *Freak Show* and *Cult*
 CORRINE E. HINTON   164

The Lesbian Gothic in *Asylum* and *Hotel*
 TOSHA R. TAYLOR   189

Appendix I. List of Episodes   207
Appendix II. List of Major Characters   212
About the Contributors   217
Index   219

Introduction

CAMERON WILLIAMS CRAWFORD
and LEVERETT BUTTS

On October 5, 2011, American television experienced a major shift in prime-time programming. A new supernatural drama premiered that quite literally revolutionized our expectations of weekly evening scheduling. *American Horror Story* introduced 21st-century mainstream audiences to the anthology television format. Created by Ryan Murphy and Brad Falchuk, the series now comprises nine seasons—*Murder House, Asylum, Coven, Freak Show, Hotel, Roanoke, Cult, Apocalypse,* and *1984*. Each season of the show is self-contained, featuring different (though sometimes overlapping) storylines, characters, settings, and time periods.

Admittedly, anthology series have been a fairly common presence in prime-time television before this: during the early days of television, such classic programs as *Alfred Hitchcock Presents* (1955–1965) and *The Twilight Zone* (1959–1964), along with lesser-known series such as the Western *Dick Powell's Zane Grey Theatre* (1956–1961) and drama series such as *General Electric Theater* (1953–1962), showed that telling a brand new story each week with new characters and a rotating cast could prove a successful format. Audiences liked them because they did not have to feel obligated to catch every episode every week, producers approved of the format because the rotating casts kept production costs low (through not having to negotiate ever-increasing salaries as the series grew more popular), and the anthology format allowed syndicators to air the series in no particular order.

As television matured, the anthology format gradually became less common but remained fairly popular throughout the 1970s and into the 1980s. Rod Serling followed up his science fiction series, *The Twilight Zone*, with a horror anthology series, *Night Gallery* (1970–1973). *The Twilight Zone* has been revived three times since its ending in 1964: once from 1985 to 1989, again from 2002 to 2003, and since 2019, a new series hosted by

2   Introduction

Jordan Peele has been part of CBS' streaming channel. Two more anthology series found popularity during the 1980s as well: *Alfred Hitchcock Presents* was revived from 1985 to 1989 and Steven Spielberg's fantasy adventure series, *Amazing Stories*, ran from 1985 to 1987. Each of these programs proved popular with audiences and have retained a kind of cult status into the present day.

Thus, when *American Horror Story* (*AHS*) debuted, the anthology format had been a staple of American television since the medium's inception. What this new show did differently, however, was to tell a single, coherent story over a single season and then, using mostly the same cast as new characters, tell a new story over the course of the next season. This was similar to the format sometimes (though not always) used by PBS' *Masterpiece Theatre* (1971–present), in which stories may cover multiple episodes but rarely entire seasons. However, while *Masterpiece Theatre* is produced by WGBH in Boston, much of its actual presentations are originally UK productions.

Since its premiere, *AHS* has spawned a plethora of stylistic (and equally successful) clones. Ryan Murphy and Brad Falchuk followed their success with *AHS* by creating two new and successful anthology series: *American Crime Story* (2016–present), which focuses each season on dramatically retelling true crime stories from American history, and *Feud* (2017–present), chronicling season-long stories of famous feuds such as that between Bette Davis and Joan Crawford (Season 1) and Prince Charles and Princess Diana (Season 2). Others have followed with their successful season-spanning anthology series, such as Nick Pizzolatto's hard-boiled mystery series *True Detective* (2014–present) and Noah Hawley's *Fargo* (2014–present), loosely based on the Coen brothers' film of the same name. It has also helped renew the public's waning interest in the traditional anthology format, paving the way for such anthologies as Netflix's Serlingesque *Black Mirror* (2011–present), BBC's dark comedy series *Inside No. 9* (2014–present), CBBC's horror anthology *Creeped Out* (2017–present), and Netflix's *The Haunting of Hill House* (2018–present).

But *AHS* is much more than simply a new style of anthology series. That alone would hardly be enough justification for a scholarly treatment. The series has proven to be both a popular and critical success; since its premiere, *AHS* continues to score an impressive viewership and has been nominated for nearly 300 awards, of which it has received over 70, among them more than a dozen Emmy Awards and two Golden Globes.

In addition to cementing its place in television history, *AHS* has been lauded for how it blends and bends elements of the horror genre with true events in American history. Take for example the seventh season, *Cult*, which imagines a dystopian version of America following the contentious 2016 election. The season employs classic horror tropes—most notably a sect of gruesome, murderous clowns that terrorizes residents of a seemingly peaceful Michigan neighborhood—to confront the real-life anxieties felt by many Americans in the face of Trumpism. "It doesn't take much to infer that this season is a commentary on Mr. Trump's political rise," writes *New York Times* critic John Koblin; yet, as Murphy himself explains, *Cult*'s commentary extends even further: "It is trying to poke fun and make jokes at the expense of—but also examine and portray—how truly irrational people are when they stop listening to each other and when they begin acting out of fear instead of any rational thought or debate."

The horror genre has long been used as a tool for social commentary, and *AHS* is no exception to this. In fact, it is one of the reasons for the series' profound cultural significance. Take away the killer clowns, the ghosts, or the witches, and *AHS* tells a different story; it holds a mirror up to our society and forces viewers to reckon with some very real "American" horrors, from our troubling history of medical and mental health treatment (*Murder House, Asylum, Freak Show, Hotel*), to the lingering legacy of slavery and racism (*Coven, Roanoke*), or to our singularly American problem with gun violence and mass shootings (*Murder House, Freak Show, Cult*). Each season also tackles timely and sometimes uncomfortable topics, like how we deal with difference or with other civil rights issues regarding race, gender, sexuality, or ability. In so doing, *AHS* has sparked ongoing, important conversations about our popular media and our entertainment, but perhaps more pointedly, about our collective American culture.

It is because of this continuing critical debate that the series necessitates further scholarly attentions. This book collects new critical essays from established and up-and-coming scholars that interrogate the many ways the series explores the nuances of our American culture. The essays in this collection apply a cultural criticism/studies framework to examine how *AHS* engages, critiques, and illuminates our contemporary culture—particularly its history, ideology, and social policies.

We have divided our volume into three separate yet overlapping categories that all in some way analyze how *AHS* asks its audiences to reckon with our American cultural practices and social politics. Our collection begins in Part I: History and Folklore, which places *AHS* within the historical context(s) it evokes and traces the ways in which it carefully blurs the boundaries between fact and fiction. In "*Asylum:* Taboos and Transgressions in U.S. History," Erin Guydish Buchholz argues that critically watching *Asylum* places it within a larger U.S. historical structure and invites the audience to reconsider the way the past and present have been developed; in so doing, Buchholz interrogates the connection between historical past and present that surfaces in the narratives surrounding Lena's homosexuality, the season's representation of mental health patients and treatment, Kidd's and Grace's experiences of the U.S. justice system and government, and the role media plays in establishing a U.S. culture and history. Rita Mookerjee, in "Where Myth Meets History: Discursive Haunting and the Resurrection of Marie Laveau in *Coven*," examines the third season's representation of the historical "Vodou practitioner" as an early agent of black/Creole southern feminist discourse, arguing that *Coven*'s interpretation brings Laveau to life as part-myth, part-historiography. Tammie Jenkins also looks at the third season's representation of historical women. In "*Coven*'s LaLaurie and Laveau: Contemporary Narratives of Southern Gothicism, Folklore and Nineteenth-Century New Orleans," Jenkins explores the characters of Marie Laveau and Madame Marie Delphine LaLaurie as they provide audiences with unparalleled (re)imagining of the facts, fictions, and mysteries surrounding the lives and deaths of these women. Drawing on James Porter's description of intertextuality as "the bits and pieces of text which writers or speakers borrow and sew together to create new discourses," Jenkins considers the ways that these women's lives have been (re)imagined through their fictional portrayals. Leverett Butts closes out this section by examining the eighth season, *Apocalypse*, through the lens of Jeffrey Burton Russell's five-volume history of evil—*The Devil, Satan, Lucifer, Mephistopheles*, and *The Prince of Darkness*—to illustrate the ways in which the show's personification of the Antichrist reflects modern fears of youth culture.

In Part II: Space and Place, our lens narrows, concentrating on the show's treatment of the particular spaces and places that are part of each season's historical/cultural settings. In "Derridean Hauntology as Cultural Praxis: The Strange Case of *Murder House*," Jonathan Greenaway applies a close reading of Derrida's *Specters of Marx* to argue that the cultural hauntology of *Murder House*—the series and the titular house—reveals not only the depth of our entanglement with the ghosts of the past, but also the sheer scale of our responsibility towards them, finishing with the liberatory and ethical potential that ghosts bring into the cultural discourse of the present and future, where justice towards the individual, the Other, and the family can once again be rethought, reworked and recreated. Antonio Sanna looks at the setting of the series' second season in the essay, "The Psychiatric Clinic in Horror Cinema and TV: *Asylum*," which illustrates the history of psychiatric clinics and places *Asylum* in the tradition of horror that depicts the "madhouse" as part of a series of thematic concerns and visual techniques that emphasize the suffering of the characters, the deranged status of the human psyche, and the claustrophobic and macabre appearance of the clinic itself. In "The Swampy Boundaries of 'Otherness' in *Freak Show* and *Roanoke*," Cameron Williams Crawford analyzes the discursive function of "the swamp" in southern literary and cultural history in order to illuminate the ways in which *Freak Show* and *Roanoke* use "freakishness" as a metaphor for "difference" and, in so doing, confront southern regional—and indeed, national—anxieties about otherness and difference. Jennifer K. Cox's "The Meta-Carnival: Monsters and Mothers in *Freak Show*" also looks at the setting of *Freak Show*; using Mikhail Bakhtin's "carnivalesque" and Julia Kristeva's "abject" to construct a theoretical frame, this essay examines how the season uses a carnival setting to challenge social norms and measure identity formation with mothers and monsters as benchmarks.

We continue to narrow our scope in our concluding section, Part III: Identity Politics, which examines how the series confronts notions of individual representation. Sarah Foust Vinson's essay, "The Mother-Witch and Witch as Mother in *Coven*," engages E. Ann Kaplan's concept of a "'master' mother-discourse" that depicts mothers as angels or witches and suggests that any new discourses of motherhood must contend with or respond to such archetypal versions of the mother-witch and mother-angel. This essay then explores how *Coven* challenges the archetypal mother-witch figure through its play on the mother as actual witch. Michelle L. Pribbernow offers another perspective on the third season in "Wear Something Black: Fashion and Fierce Femininity in the Witch Drag of *Coven*." Pribbernow's essay makes the case that costumes in *Coven* reference diverse pop culture images of American witches, from the Puritans to Stevie Nicks and the occult-inspired fashion of the early 1970s to the goth-clad witches of the 1990s. This essay explores what these "witch wear" references suggest about the version of female power portrayed in the show and its potential for a subversive version of femininity. Corrine E. Hinton's "Destructive Leadership in *Coven*, *Freak Show* and *Cult*" interprets the varied and complex discursive strategies at work in order to understand how the characters Fiona, Cordelia, and Elsa demonstrate their community orientation, position themselves as leaders, influence their members, and unify or divide the communities they serve. This essay also looks at the show's seventh season, *Cult*, and how Kai Anderson contributes to and complicates fictionalized leaders as we witness the formation, rise, and downfall of his community. Lastly, Tosha R. Taylor's essay, "The Lesbian Gothic in *Asylum* and *Hotel*," places the second and fifth seasons within the historical discourses of queerness pertaining to what we may consider the "lesbian Gothic." Taylor analyzes how both *Asylum* and *Hotel* specifically speak to the positioning of the queer woman as belonging to a Gothic space or engaging in practices associated with Gothic monstrosity.

The essays in this collection reveal the ways in which *AHS* grapples with a wide range of issues, each essay interrogating how *AHS* asks its audience to confront parts of our own contemporary culture. The series, which has been renewed for at least thirteen seasons, continues to draw in viewers and proves to be a new cornerstone of modern television horror. Perhaps more importantly, as this book asserts, it continues to prompt vital discussions about our American time and place.

Part I
History and Folklore

Asylum

Taboos and Transgressions in U.S. History

Erin Guydish Buchholz

Introduction

History repeats itself, or so we are told. But what if it doesn't? *American Horror Story: Asylum* captivates its audience with a combination of pathological character development familiar to the viewer from shows such as *Criminal Minds* and over-the-top plot twists and paranormal events reminiscent of *The X-Files* that are unbelievable yet leave the viewer pondering its plausibility. In these ways, nineteenth- and twentieth-century mental illness taboos are critically examined to reveal the distance society has from mental health policies today. *Asylum* uses psychological, historical, and literary landmarks to make a statement on past American perspectives on mental illness as well as contemporary judgments. This series explores social opinions of mental illness paralleling Nellie Bly's and Bill Baldini's exposés; the former and continued classification and treatment of homosexuality[1]; and the role media plays in developing history and social morals. Critically aware viewers can locate significant historical and social critiques in *Asylum*, making this season more than just an entertaining contribution to the anthology series.

The taboos associated with mental illness and treatment are reexamined critically as institutions such as the Church and science-driven sanatoriums battle over appropriate treatment methods. *Asylum* uses a recently valued genre called "historical fantasy" to provide "a mode of historical engagement that is distinct from other affective postures that dominate the commemorative landscape [of historical memory]" (Elliott 137). Michael Elliott assumes an interdisciplinary approach to researching U.S. representations in public spaces. His work explains that historical fiction and fantasy can explore culture through historical alternatives (plausibilities) rather than solely revisionist or propagandized versions of realities. While his focus is counter-factual narratives, he does open the door to the consequences of "what-if" storylines, which will be prioritized here. Additionally, Elliott recognizes connections and distinctions when studying filmed or written mediums. These are crucial components to acknowledge when working with various cultural narratives. However, this piece will focus largely on interpreting plot points, allusions to historical events, and the implicit critiques of U.S. social circumstances. As such, the medium will be treated secondary to the investigation of the storyline and its use of cultural markers. In this sense, the show attends to the ambiguous relationship between science and religion in the medical and mental health fields. There is no final judgment passed determining which institution is correct and which is a failure. Instead, this work, through characters such as Lana, Sister Jude, Kit, and others, reveals a complex history of incapacitation and treatment of patients. Critical viewers will take the time to step back from the sensational entertainment value of the work to analyze the potential commentary within the plot and characters of the piece.

The layering of time periods in this season foregrounds its simultaneous cultural critique of the past and present. Furthermore, it also emphasizes the way history is constructed by the media. The series reveals its analysis as it follows historical fantasy conventions by "including overt speculation on the nature of the historical narrative itself" (Elliott 147). This becomes highly apparent in a few instances throughout the myriad historical explorations. One of the most explicit occurrences are in Anne Frank's appearance at Briarcliff. In "I Am Anne Frank (Part 1)," Anne Frank surfaces at Briarcliff to reveal Dr. Arden's Nazi history. Her identity is later explained away as an unconscious digestion of World War II research by a woman suffering from post-partum depression (2:4). However, the what ifs of Anne's possible survival and its consequences challenge the faith often placed in media (Anne Frank's *Diary* in this case) and its position as an omnipotent force. Anne explains her survival saying that she was too weak to say who she was and "who would have asked?" Eventually she justifies her self-silencing by describing it as a self-sacrifice for the greater good of social morality. She argues that if she survived and went public with it that her existence would diminish the evil of World War II and the Nazis (2:4). Her survival would frustrate the humanization of World War II victims that her diary and the media promote. So even as *Asylum* contests histories, it demonstrates how powerful laying bare and re-encountering well-established (or media-promoted) histories can be. Anne's inability to correct a historically significant account of quashed innocence leading to global moral formation alludes to the power media and history possess when they work together. By maintaining such a storyline, *Asylum* metatextually presents its argument in order to draw attention to the histories it is reexamining.

In addition to explicit critiques of social narratives, this season is invested in the connection between history and narrative presentation. Hayden White, a well-known scholar, explains the connection between history, literature, and presentation: "The historian arranges events in the chronicle into a hierarchy of significance by assigning events different functions as story elements in such a way as to disclose the formal coherence of a whole set of events considered as a comprehensible process with a discernible beginning, middle, and end" (7). White's point reflects hidden manipulations of history and narrative, such as the media's authoritative versions of social and cultural records. The writers of the series choose the events within and the presentation of them to promote a particular understanding of the time period depicted along with a commentary on the viewer's contemporary epistemology and institutions. One article explains, "He [Ryan Murphy] is more than happy to admit that his shows are political, and that their mission is to educate as much as entertain. 'There is not a lot of LGBTQ history out there; I grew up knowing nothing'" (Mulkerrins). Murphy's comment reveals intentionality in both subject and projected political statements within the series. In the case of Anne Frank, viewers are asked to question the media and history (past and present), researched perspectives on society (in individuals such as Dr. Arden), and ethical norms (the good of the self-weighed against the well-being of society). These poignant and purposeful framings of plot events and characters continue throughout *Asylum* to encourage inquiries by the audience introspectively and socially/culturally.

Paradigms of Mental Health

Early on in the series, the contentious relationship between science and religion is established. A young man and his parents arrive at Briarcliff seeking aid because his behaviors towards animals and other people are troubling in "Tricks and Treats." Sister Jude and the Monsignor advocate for an exorcism while Dr. Thredson wants to use Western medicine. The result is the death of the boy, despite both methods of treatment being used (2:2). This failure sets up a theme continued for the rest of the season, which Murphy describes as being about "sanity and tackling real life horrors" (Andreeva). The foundation has been laid for the discussion of historical treatment (and its representations) of marginalized communities (such as LGBTQIA, women, mental illness sufferers, and convicts). Neither the "sane" practice of Western medicine nor the faith in good could stop the "real life horror" of a young death. The boy's demise lays the groundwork for the traditionally antagonistic debate, as well as for the recognition of more implicit similarities between scientific and religious belief that astute viewers may observe as the season continues.

Scientific and religious ethics' similarities and differences continue to be established in another early episode when Lana and Thredson discuss her "homosexuality" as an illness. Lana accuses Thredson and his profession: "According to your Bible, the diagnostical and statistical manual of disorders, I'm sick" (2:4). Lana creates a concrete metaphor between the religious judgments and those of scientists by calling their reference book their Bible. She doesn't just allude to the problem of an ill-informed mental health classification. Instead, her comment reveals the problem of having blind faith in any sort of paradigm. Lana's comment is just as pertinent to the mid-twentieth century setting of *Asylum* as to the environment of contemporary viewers where debates concerning the legalization of gay marriage and outlawing of conversion/aversion therapies are ongoing. In an examination of the history and contemporary practice of conversion therapies, one group of scholars explains, "Despite the fact that homosexuality has been declassified as a mental disorder for 30 years and despite various professional organizations' rejection of CT as an unethical, harmful, and empirically invalid practice, conversion or reparative techniques continue to receive both scholarly and clinical support" (Cramer et al. 94). The continued practice of conversion therapy reveals the saliency of the paradigmatic thought-process Lana critiques. In order for a treatment to be given, it must be in response to an affliction. So, while Thredson's "Bible" no longer outlines homosexuality as an illness, it advocates that sort of classification through the continued support of such therapy. The inferences often drawn by radicals of religious texts is mimicked here by a scientific practice as *Asylum* makes a statement about past and present social injustice simultaneously through explorations of historical narratives and representations.

Exploration of the blurriness of morals and mental illness as dictated by religion versus those advocated for through scientific inquiry reappear as the season references literary events and contemporary circumstances. Murphy's desire to explore political and social histories merge with Elliott's explorations of cultural materials (in this case institutions) to illuminate ways various communities experience and cope with grand cultural narratives. For example, a paradox of the definition of mental illness applied to women versus men arises in Fanny Fern's historically and literarily significant newspaper column on August 28, 1858, when she chastises society for its double standard. The writer laments the status of prostitutes as society deems them "unfit to live, as unfit to die; *they*, the weaker party, while their partners in sin, for whom you claim greater mental superiority, and who, by your own finding, should be much better able to learn and *to teach* the lesson of self-control—to them you extend perfect absolution" (307). Fern's comments come after her observation of these women being paraded at Blackwell's Island. They are sent there for their crimes, while their partners are left unmolested. Similarly, in *Ten Days in a Madhouse*, Nellie Bly, who is one of the earliest exposé journalists in the U.S., critiques morally corrupt lines of reasoning. When Bly is getting admitted to Blackwell's, "The nurses questioned me unceasingly about my home, and all seemed to have an idea that I had a lover who had cast me forth on the world and wrecked my brain" (Bly). The insinuation here is that Bly would, reasonably, be admitted due to a mental illness caused by an immoral relationship that failed to come to fruition in a legitimate (matrimonial) manner. Fern's and Bly's commentaries are echoed in multiple ways throughout the season, specifically through implicit analyses of such gender-normed thought-processes. While the writers of *Asylum* may not have explicitly referenced these instances of cultural marginalization, their discussions and references to lived experiences indicates the problematics of ignoring history, individuality, and prejudices in creating cultural histories.

In the same way that nineteenth-century women were committed for moral transgressions, women in the twentieth and twenty-first centuries are still judged as deviant when they are seductive but not submissive. This season presents two explicit incidences critiquing this social taboo. The first instance discusses this idea metatextually. In the opening scene of "Welcome to Briarcliff," the two honeymooning characters flirtatiously talk about female desire and society's judgment of it. After reading some details about Briarcliff the newlywed bride asks, "What are we gonna tell the kids about the honeymoon?" Her husband responds, "We'll tell them the truth. We visited the 12 most haunted places in America and screwed our brains out in every single one." However, she retorts with "Or that Mommy's a horror freak and Daddy lives to make Mommy happy?" (2:1). This exchange is significant in two ways. One, it establishes the idea that past social/cultural norms need to be challenged for individuals and society to progress. In addition, the bride's final remark insinuates the need for female sexuality to be claimed, appreciated, and accepted not as risqué, a mental condition, or a deviance from a social norm. Having this scene and statement early on invites viewers to question historical connotations and contemporary social critiques of individuals and groups. Furthermore, this critique positions the later introduced character of Shelley as a complex female, not a simple characterization of a blonde-haired, blue-eyed whore. Shelley is the second instance of this social and moral critique. Shelley narrates her own story, explaining that after running away, she married and became her husband's property. When she steps out of her marriage (as her husband has done) and he discovers it, he commits her. She justifies her behavior, arguing she doesn't enjoy sex, but pleasure. However, her problem with her incarceration is that "they [authority figures] let him do it" knowing the circumstances under which she was being committed (2:2). Shelley's story, preceded by the bride's explicit commentary and the historically aware viewer's understanding of past mental illness and morality definitions, draws attention to the way critiques of female sexuality were and are meted out. *Asylum* takes its critique one step further than many other cultural productions. Rather than simply focusing on feminine presentation, sexuality, and taboo, it focuses on commentary concerning society's reactions to feminine seduction, power, and mental capability.

The themes, such as feminine sexuality and its social position or the value of patients' lives and ethics of experimentation, raised in *Asylum* are as important as the mindsets that allow judgmental norms to perpetuate. The critically cognizant audience will see past the shock value of Dr. Arden's experiments and the ill treatment of patients to the show's references to real-life instances where justifications for these activities were accepted. In an interview with *TV Guide*, Murphy previewed the season saying, "The story [of season two] is a period piece in a mental institution based largely on truth and truth is always scarier than fiction" (Bryant and Abrams). Quite a few pieces document ill treatment of and experimentation on patients, along with the reasoning that permitted such atrocities. Murphy's comment is unclear as to exactly which historical or cultural truths may be referenced in this season. However, his insight to creation here insinuates that the purpose of this season is to get viewers to reflect on social and historical norms, their development, and their unquestioning acceptance. The problematic definition of mental illness and its derivative treatment surfaces in this season as well as historically (although not always publicly recognized). Early on in her writings, Bly documents this in a caregiver's rough comments after a cold, cruel, dirty bath. The nurse tells her, "This is charity, and you should be grateful for what you get" (Bly). The gruesome details of patients sharing dirty water, being sent to bed wet, and ill patients being forced to take ice cold baths is shocking in and of itself. However, Bly's documentation of the commentary connects to Murphy's focus in *Asylum* of demonstrating the frightening non-fiction reality of socially normed judgments and values. Both works aim to address the lack of empathy, or even critical thought, when engaging with marginalized populations—and the horror that is ignored through these normed practices.

As the season continues, Dr. Arden's work and mistreatment of patients, along with their exposure, emphasizes the normalcy of some of the most commonplace horrors of society. "*The story* is horrifying," says

Murphy, but it is not just the grisly events that the viewer is offered (Bryant and Abrams). The pathology behind the characters' actions is presented and with their references to historical and cultural narratives, aware viewers are asked to reconsider morals, ethics, and mental illness as dismissively sure-footed. "The Origins of Monstrosity" reveals Dr. Arden conducting a range of experiments. The Monsignor approves a set of his experiments in hopes that it will provide benefits for human longevity (2:6). Once again, the shock value comes not just from the brutal experiments being conducted, but also from the mentality driving the brutality and the bending of moral lines. A historical comparison occurred at Willowbrook State School, an asylum for "retarded children," where Dr. McCollum and Dr. Krugman experimented with the effects of blood transfusions on hepatitis (Hevesi). According to Seymour B. Thaler, the experiments were eventually criticized for "using retarded children as human guinea pigs" (qtd. in Hevesi). Thaler's remark was later recanted, but as this season's historical play demonstrates, without knowing the motivation behind it, it's probable that the results of the research were seen as more valuable than the patients' lives (or quality of life). In both cases, while the experiments were problematic, what is judged even more harshly is the way in which they were conducted, or the ethical paradigm those individuals were working from to justify cruel treatment of patients, as in Bly's, Murphy's, and McCollum's narratives.

U.S. Justice System

In addition to questions of the value of patients' lives, another highly significant theme is the debate of nature versus nurture. However, the work implicitly critiques a nature versus nurture approach to justice as it details stories of various criminal, but not insane, characters. Two minor characters that test the nature versus nurture paradigm (and its presumptions of "good" character) are Pepper and Leigh (the Santa Claus killer). Pepper is a character who suffers from microcephaly (a condition in which a person's head is smaller than those of their peers and can sometimes be accompanied by developmental delays or intellectual disabilities). The severity of Pepper's disability is implied early on as she rarely speaks or often only replies with one-word answers. Due to her inability to communicate effectively, it is determined that she cannot comprehend morality (nature is privileged by her peers). Eventually in "The Name Game" (through a supernatural twist), Pepper gains the ability to speak and explains why she is in Briarcliff. She says her sister's husband killed their baby and blamed it on her. They believed him, and she was sent to Briarcliff. Her accusers and judge believed she was immoral due to her condition (2:10). Pepper's story shows the problem with judging individuals, particularly those who have difficulty communicating and who are aesthetically different, as she is called a "monster" and "pinhead." The idea of nature determining her character (as well as that of the free murderous husband) fails; however, it fails not just because the binary model is flimsy, but also because it does not take into consideration the people who use it to make judgments and how it is manipulated (basing intellectual abilities on physical appearances).

The nature-nurture model fails again in its application to two versions of the same character. Leigh is incarcerated for killing 18 people from 5 families in one night, which was a response to a Christmas when he was imprisoned for stealing a loaf of bread. His story is explained in "The Coat Hanger" when the jailors went caroling, and five prisoners held Leigh down and raped him. In response, when Leigh got out at Christmas, he felt empowered by taking on Santa's persona and determining "who was naughty and who was nice/who deserved to live and to die" (2:9). *Asylum*'s social critique is twofold here. In one way it critiques the nature versus nurture debate. Leigh is not inherently evil due to his nature nor is it due to his environment. While his violence is (self-admittedly) a reaction to his violent attack, his paralleling it with Santa Claus' work results in a crime grounded in socially sanctioned punishment rather than reward. As Pepper's story shows problems with ways judgments are formed, Leigh's narrative shows issues with that, as well as with the ways society judges itself and others. The punishment-based version of Santa that Leigh acts as demonstrates an issue with the way social reward and punishment systems are constructed. Ideas of good and evil, along with where those character traits arise from, are complicated in both Pepper and Leigh's narratives, as well as how society maintains its standards of the same. Elliott's concept of historical play and exaggeration is enacted to more deeply understand the implications of Santa Claus' naughty or nice list from the viewpoint of punishment instead of reward. Leigh follows the tradition of the Christmas Krampus (an oft-ignored cultural reference in the U.S.), doling out punishment instead of gifts using his personal framework for judgment (instead of society's behavioral norms). Leigh never explains what his definitions of innocence or guilt are, and as such with his backstory in mind, his narrative provides reflection on these ideas: Who is innocent? Who is guilty? Who has the ability to pass judgment? Who determines what the truth is?

Similar questions and presumptions are challenged by the work done by exposé journalists of the nineteenth and twentieth century. In Bly's narrative, she draws attention to the expendability of patients. She asks Dr. Ingram what a fire in the ward would mean for patients. He says the nurses would open the doors to get them out, but Bly insists they would not (remember, patients should expect nothing as they are "charity" cases). The doctor asks Bly how she would solve the problem, and she responds that there are locks that can open an entire block of cell doors at once. The doctor immediately becomes suspicious and asks where Bly had been before Blackwell's. She asserts she saw them at an institution she visited. The doctor does not believe her, responding, "There is only one place I know of where they have those locks ... and that is at Sing Sing" (Bly). His insinuation is that Bly must have been in one of the most sinister prisons in America, and not as a visitor as she asserts, but as an inmate. Bly laughs at the implication, but this incident describes a problematic judgment and evaluation system. First, the patients are unworthy. Their lives are expendable, as were Pepper's and Leigh's since they were discounted as defective according to social norms of character development. Here, because Bly is institutionalized, it is assumed she has previously been committed. Therefore, anything she has to say or do must be examined with the idea that she is not "normal" in mind. In other words, her "guilt" of being a social deviant is established before she is justly (or unjustly) committed/diagnosed.

The easy expense of individuals already branded as defective rings true in a later real-life exposé as well. In 1968, Bill Baldini conducted an exposé of the Pennhurst State School. The school was essentially a repository for intellectually disabled children. There are many similarities in Baldini's and Lana's exposés as they record the patients, staff, and administrators. In fact, multiple articles document connections between *Asylum* and Baldini's exposé. Lana's speech on screen during her return to Briarcliff paraphrases Baldini's and footage uses similar lighting as well as patient depictions (Greenwood; Fan Contributors). The significant similarity in the current discussion of patient value and expendability appears in Baldini's third episode of his five-minute exposé episodes. In a similar way to Bly's and *AHS*' (in general) predetermined judgments about good, evil, the risk of those individuals in society, and their lack of value within confines, Baldini performs a comparison that illustrates the problem with these normed ideals. He describes the conditions of Pennhurst residents while comparing it to conditions for large cats at zoos. While he narrates the visual flips between images of panthers within cages and residents of Pennhurst in a variety of squalorous and poorly lit places, Baldini lays out the facts of spacing and capacity for large cats and Pennhurst patients: the former are afforded much room within their confines and typically they have their own cages or habitats, while the latter live in a space made for 1,984 patients at most, packed in over the maximum with 2,800 students. From there he moves onto how much the state actually spends to maintain those lives. Zoos, Baldini explains, spend $7.15 per day per cat to upkeep and support their large cat collections. In contrast, Pennhurst spends $5.90

per day for each patient. However, he draws attention to the allocation of Pennhurst's money emphasizing that 80 percent of it goes to administrative costs. In total then, the value of each student is a meager $0.75 per day. Even at the inflation adjusted rates, this is a shameful value to equate with the upkeep of a human life. Moving healthcare as care to a business rewrites perspectives. Creating an alternate historical presentation where such discourse deserves condemnation emphasizes the experience of marginalized populations in a society that has normed and accepted such callous treatment. The same critique that Baldini performs here is seen earlier in Bly's questions about the values of patients' and inmates' lives (particularly as Sing Sing, a criminal prison, had fire-prepared cells, while Blackwell's, largely a poor house and women's asylum, did not), and later in *Asylum* by challenging preconceptions about inherent good and evil in mentally ill and non-normed characters.

While the previously mentioned critiques in this section focus particularly on values of life and absolute terms of evil and innocence, another significant critique raised in *Asylum* is invested in exploring whether abortion is murder. The earlier examples ask questions about the conduct of mental institutions, asylums, and their employees. This critique is still inquiring about justice, but instead, as historical fantasy does, asks "what ifs" about abortion and murder. Would Lana have been a murderer for aborting a fetus that later committed murders due to either an inherently evil character or a psychological identity-based break? Lana ironically complicates the answer to this question in "Spilt Milk" and "Madness Ends." The value of a life is established when Lana is laying on the table in a home of a doctor performing abortions when she stops saying "No more death." She explains her actions by saying that she simply "prayed really hard that someone else would give him the mothering I couldn't" (2:11; 2:13). Lana sees the value of a life, regardless of how it began. She decides that the life she carries deserves a chance. Pro-lifers rejoice at this victory, albeit short-lived. As the season continues to its climax, Lana's baby, Johnny, commits a series of murders eventually intending to culminate with Lana's. However, in a twist of poetic justice, Lana, at the height of danger, pulls the trigger and kills Johnny, point blank (2:13). She again is absolved of murder charges in light of self-defense under the circumstances. The effect of this plotline is to question the oft-used argument in many pro-life objections that a woman does not have the right to dictate who should live. In addition, it makes a farce of the argument "what if that abortion kills the person who...?" (insert as you like: cures cancer, is among the next U.S. Presidents, is the next Martin Luther King, Jr., etc.). Instead inquiring, "What if that abortion saves lives?" All the critiques in this section utilize alternate histories to reveal a deep investment in a similar concept, even as they get there in different ways: How are social justice systems, institutions, and legislation involved in the dehumanization of those with a dubious past or mental illness? What is the value of a life, and who determines that? What circumstances are considered in establishing that value?

Homosexuality

Along with challenging the ways that life value is established in society, one of the other most salient themes of *Asylum* is an implicit critique of the discrimination against LGB individuals (a theme that continues and eventually extends to T in later seasons). Deviant sexualities are something that has been both criminalized and tabooed as a mental illness for an extended period (perhaps since the conceptions of these labels). *Asylum* focuses most heavily on taboos and discrimination against lesbians via Lana's character and her circle of friends, but there are hints that Dr. Thredson is gay as well. (His disgust with females runs so deep that he can only impregnate Lana because he has intercourse with a dead Wendy.) Both characters and their sexual orientations offer critical insight concerning social perspectives on LGB individuals. With the series originally airing between 2012 and 2013, the discussion of Lana and her partner Wendy's living arrangements, as well as Dr. Thredson's avoidance of his sexuality, are particularly relevant. Same-sex marriage rights were hotly debated during these years. While some legislatures had voted to legalize same-sex marriage, 2012 was the first year that three states approved same-sex marriage laws through popular vote (Dimock and Staff). In addition, even as some popular votes rejected such laws, Barack Obama publicly announced his support of same-sex marriage (Dimock and Staff). Within this context, *Asylum* asks audiences if they will choose to move beyond the mid-twentieth-century frames of homophobia and persecution.

Some of the harshest critiques and praises about society's treatment of members of the LGBT community come about in the last episode through Lana's interview. Initially, April (the interviewer) says that Lana's partner (Marion) isn't allowed on camera. However, as Marion prepares to leave for an art event, she brings two glasses of white wine in for April and Lana. April reconsiders her position, perhaps to frustrate some taboos concerning queer relationships. April says Marion could do the "casual bringing the wine in thing" (2:13). Such an image has the potential to disarm some queer taboo by placing on screen a loving and caregiving relationship. However, it also has the potential to position the two lovers as friends through such an innocent act. Ultimately, Marion smiles and curtly dismisses herself, refusing to become a P.R. pawn for either side (2:13). However, even as the viewers of Lana's interview never see this interaction, *Asylum* viewers do. In addition, they also see Marion's response to the ploy which invites audiences to consider how much of their news and other media is framed to establish a particular perspective or ideology. It begs the question of how much of our world is accurately depicted versus how much is the media's or a P.R. director's construction. As such, media is critiqued here and a more aware audience position is advocated for. In this case, audiences are asked to be aware of how queer relationships are being characterized. Viewers should consider what is shown on screen, as well as why.

In addition to this timely critique, Lana's interview discusses the status of queer families and parenting. April asks Lana if she had ever considered having children. Lana explains that there was a lack of a way for gay families to have kids. Instead, she simply stayed close to her friends' and families' kids (2:13). This is an important depiction of LGB families within a 2012 context. Lana's statement implies that conditions have changed with times and LGB members can have families, which based on the Pew Research Center's timeline was true for those in about 11 U.S. states. These states provided recognition and protection of marriage rights, but parental rights were a vastly different story. Unless one parent was the biological parent, these rights could be contested (Dimock and Staff). The cautious standpoint on LGB rights is reinforced as Lana gestures towards the idea of growth in society's perspectives but is also reserved, considering she never entertained the idea, even as she grew older, became emerged in a more accepting society (especially considering her wealth), and was aware of the adoption process.

Arguably, one of the strongest cases made for a reevaluation of the status of the queer community and individuals as well as society's treatment of them comes about in the episode where Lana is subjected (willingly) to aversion/conversion therapy. The visceral depiction of aversion therapy evidences the irrationality behind ideas of one's *choice* of sexual orientation. A 2015 article by Christi R. McGeorge, Thomas Stone Carlson, and Russell B. Toomey explains that therapies of this type are based in the idea that "an LGB sexual attraction is not an actual sexual orientation, but rather a 'lifestyle choice' or set of 'sexual attractions' that can be changed or controlled through behavior therapy interventions" (43). The problem with such a perspective is the personal anguish such a "therapeutic" process can induce as it pushes patients to stigmatize and reject elements of their identities. In particular during Lana's aversion therapy, a personal photo of Wendy is projected on the wall. The viewer watches as Lana struggles with her desire to be "well" and her emotional attraction to Wendy (in her attempt to hold back her medicine-induced vomit) (2:4). Lana's character shows the viewer the damage that social stigmas, and their translation into various institutions (as with the examples in the previous section), can do. Furthermore, Lana's attachment to a thick tube filled with a yellowish fluid in a dingy room supervised by a too-eager-to-see-her-reaction Dr. Thredson indicates a sort of sadism in those willing to conduct this type of therapy. In the conversion portion of therapy, Dr. Thredson instructs Lana to masturbate. As such, two taboos are linked together ironically to get Lana to a socially accepted sexual orientation. However, while attempting to arouse herself using Daniel and her hand, Lana finds her release in vomiting, not an ecstasy-induced transformation. Arguably, this is a plot-device for trust-building on Dr. Thredson's part, but there is a greater weight to these moments in terms of social critique.

Lana's depression after the failed therapy session is indicative of a social critique deeper than the forward motion of the plot. After she is unable to demonstrate her ability to be heterosexual, Lana is despondent. The viewers see her in the common room, vastly disheveled, largely uninterested in what is going on around her, and completely having lost sight of her exposé purpose and escape (2:4). The result of society's rejection and her failure to live up to its norms reflect research conducted by the San Francisco State University. Researchers found LGBTQ people who were rejected by parents and/or caregivers (which could be a therapist) were "more than 8 times as likely to have attempted suicide, nearly 6 times as likely to report high levels of depression, more than 3 times as likely to use illegal drugs, and more than 3 times as likely to be at high risk for HIV and STDs" than those who were accepted (Human Rights Campaign Staff). The emphasis of these events are twofold: 1. It demonstrates the problem of devaluing individual and group identities and belittling them as disorders, and 2. The problematic outcomes of rejecting non-normed individuals from society are established. While conversion therapy is still debated, there is much more evidence advocating for its end due to its harmful impact on individuals and the damage it does to society through exclusions.

Along with raising awareness about social stigmas LGB individuals and communities are subject to, *Asylum* gives insight about inhumane and illegitimate "treatments" resulting from medical acceptance of social norms. Despite a myriad of organizational rejection of the use of conversion/aversion therapies (see the Human Rights Campaign's summary of "Organizational Positions on Reparative Therapy"), these types of treatments persist. Significantly, *Asylum* does exactly what some scholars have advocated for in the fight to end injustice in the contemporary world. Robert J. Cramer, Frank D. Golom, Charles T. LoPresto, and Shalene M. Kirkley call for "Respected scholars and practitioners to engage television programming, magazines, college campuses, and various other forums in order to reach a younger generation. These efforts may bring about a paradigmatic shift concerning LGB individuals, CT, and victims of prejudice" (110). *AHS*' development of storylines based on cultural narratives counter to majority histories (such as those told by heterosexual, scientifically, or socially sanctioned institutions) value minority and dismissed narratives without mainstreaming their stories or norms. Individuals aware of the clinical status of homosexuality, the treatments for it, and the affiliated social stigmas are likely to see *Asylum* working for this "paradigmatic shift concerning ... prejudice" for a variety of social groups, but most specifically here for the LGBTQIA community.

Alternative Histories/Media's Histories

In addition to the critiques of social paradigms, *Asylum* offers interrogations of the establishment of stereotypes and judgment/value systems in the U.S. A major way that social norms and cultural artefacts develop is through television programming. Metatextually, Lana explains television's power saying, "TV was the future," and that she needed an "angle, a hook ... and boy did I have a doozy" referring to her exposé of Briarcliff (2:13). Oppressed demographics, such as the mentally ill, have typically been ignored or are just silenced. News media, within *Asylum* and in real life, exposes those silenced groups and examines the truth (and/or lies) about them. As alluded to earlier, the grainy images and sickening treatment of patients used to display Lana's television exposé in *Asylum* are undeniably similar to the images appearing in Baldini's series "Suffer the Little Children." In addition, Baldini's work was aired on NBC, a television network, what Lana calls the "future." Undeniably then, parallels are being drawn between yet another historical American landmark in the treatment of the mentally ill within the show both in visual presentation, medium, and topic/purpose. If an American viewer is historically aware, they will likely recognize the bits of history and culture appearing here as well as those parts that are being rejected. These records are significant in a few ways: they establish contemporary paradigms, challenge those preconceptions, and create a preserved record of social growth and/or reservation.

The depictions of the press positions it as a heavily influential cultural factor. As such the press' responsibility to those who consume it is also stressed, offering a critical take on the "fluff" many "news sources" are accused of publishing today. Lana has two objects (in her exposé) that stress the need for documentation and "proof" in news stories: a taped confession and her file. Dr. Thredson threatens Kit to get at a tape of Thredson's confession for Bloody Face's murders. However, Lana, knowing its importance, stows it in a different place in hopes of being freed to report with proof (2:10). The second important piece of "proof" Lana leaves Briarcliff with is given to her by the Mother Superior (who helps Lana at Sister Jude's request). Mother Superior provides Lana with her file giving Lana documentation of her time at Briarcliff (2:11). These pieces of corroborative evidence allow Lana's story to have reliability and weight. Her work, moving from stories about domestic life (reflecting female journalists' transitions as far back as Bly's and Fern's) to more hard-hitting critiques, demonstrates the development of news media in a way that seems antithetical to the more socially driven, fluffy stories covered by major news companies today. In turn, these developments offer a critical perspective on the contemporary existence of media, the past formations of it, and the potential for future development.

This proof-based model of reporting is also critiqued as the storyline continues and alternate versions of histories are presented. Some of the most noticeable incidences include the version of Sister Jude's rescue by Lana, Lana's abortion, and the outcome of Sister Jude's accident for Missy. The most important part of these is that the viewer is presented stories that end in a clear manner: Sister Jude is rescued by Lana, Lana aborts the baby with a coat hanger, and Missy was murdered. However, after being presented with these moments, they are disregarded in "Continuum" because, as Lana says of her version of Sister Jude's saving, "it never happened" (2:12). The belief in these stories, that exist without proof, demonstrates the way truth can be manipulated, particularly by the media. Sister Jude's rescue is played out entirely in Lana's mind and narrative; Lana narrates the abortion of the baby and cleaning up the bloody mess; and Sister Jude receives newspaper clippings that show her the little girl's death. In these ways, reporters, or individuals, who are just telling stories are positioned to be critically examined. These invented narratives are developed to give a variety of poignant critiques of the media and its power. As one of the examinations of this season explains, "Our [the viewers'] fear is not of the past and what once was, nor of that which is unknown and seemingly impossible, but for what lies just around the corner" (Rosenberg and Rosenberg 10). The horror that this part of the season reveals is the power that storytellers (and/or story reporters) have and how uncritical examination can result in problematic paradigms and social injustices. On the flipside, this season also shows the potential for attention to those issues and the public's embrasure or rejection of them.

Hope

In all of the critical framework pertaining to Western social standards and perspectives, *Asylum* does not forget a crucial component to the horror story: an ending with closure. The story appears to wrap up neatly: Kit saves Sister Jude and gets his family (Alma, Grace, his kids), Dr. Thredson and his son are given due justice, and Briarcliff is sold then shut down thanks to Lana's reporting. There is hope towards the end of the season. While some of the wrap ups are cliché or too neat, parts of it continue to represent an investment in challenging social norms.

Sister Jude's rescue and the end of Briarcliff are two demonstrations of hopeful resolutions. Sister Jude is rescued by Kit after his wife, Alma, was committed to Briarcliff for murdering his other wife, Grace. While identifying Alma's body Kit sees Sister Jude. He visits her and helps her start to regain herself. Eventually Kit gets the Monsignor to discharge Sister Jude to him before the state takes over Briarcliff (2:13). Kit's actions demonstrate a cliché, but hopeful lesson: treat others as you would like to be treated. Even after Sister Jude was more often strict with him than not, Kit went back for her. The show advocates for a better treatment of each other despite all the brutality witnessed, ranging from Sister Jude's closet of whips and sticks to the arsenal of science-based "treatments" at Briarcliff. Instead of the more anticipated "an eye for an eye," Kit provides a model of good behavior for viewers.

Along the same lines, Kit acts as a moral compass for Lana when she is concerned with Hollywood, fame, and selling the rights to her story. It is during this meeting that Kit tells the story of Sister Jude and alludes to the problem of Lana failing to close the doors of Briarcliff as she set out to do (from before she even got committed) (2:13). Kit, unexpectedly, acts as one of the most moral characters after accusations of being Bloody Face for half the season, which sets him up as an unreliable narrator. Kit's urgings drive Lana to conduct her exposé instead of entering into a capitalist-driven endeavor. Her reports are reminiscent of Baldini's work as well as Geraldo Rivera's exposé on Willowbrook State School ("Willowbrook: The Last Great Disgrace"). The references to these real-life exposés and their call for social responsibility is paralleled by Kit's role in these instances. He provides an example of moral goodness and hope as time passes from the mid- to later–twentieth century.

Further evidence of hope for the contemporary generation arises in Kit's non-traditional family and Sister Jude's role in it. Dr. Thredson helps Kit and Grace be reunited with their baby because he feels it's important that children have their families. Alma reappears with Kit's daughter after Grace and their son move home (2:11). They live together for a time. Eventually disaster comes about, but out of losing his wives, Kit gains Sister Jude as a grandmother. In both instances, Kit's family is non-conventional. His families provide hope for the challenges contemporary families face as they vary from two-parent households. Viewers might see families they are familiar with—single parent households, step-family structures, and multiple generation families. These variant family structures become important as Sister Jude gives some advice to Kit's kids as she passes away. She tells Julia, "Don't ever let a man tell you who you are … it's 1970 and you can do anything you want," and demands that Thomas, "Never take a job just for the money. Find something that you love. Do something important" (2:13). Kit's family challenges conventions, but Sister Jude advocates for an awareness of social conventions and subversions of them. She encourages Julia to be bold and confident and tells Thomas to be sensitive. In short, she encourages them to be good *people*, not a good woman or man. Sister Jude's comments and Kit's non-conventional family serve as examples of U.S. social and cultural development expanding beyond heterosexual and gendered households and roles. These characters and storylines provide spaces for viewers to recognize themselves, their society, their history, and ways to change the future.

Conclusion

AHS is critical of both the past and present in its imagined presentation of American institutions based in Western ideologies that, while originally well-intentioned to keep society civil and well-ordered, results in corrupt and unjust cultural structures. The series does end with gestures towards hopeful developments for oppressed demographics and cultural norms. Historically and critically aware viewers are likely to see the potential critiques offered by the characters and storylines. The treatment of the mentally ill, preconceptions that inform social justice decisions, morality concerning sexual orientation and abortion, and finally hope for the future are all critiqued and analyzed through characters and plots in *Asylum*. Television is used effectively to perform social critiques. These critiques incorporate past historical and literary debates alongside contemporary concerns. Rather than being simply a campy, plot-twisting drama, *Asylum* dramatizes social and cultural issues that in some cases are considered to have been solved and in other cases have been and are still recognized as social problems. It provides situations where these issues can begin to be addressed as legitimate.

Notes

1. Homosexuality is used when referencing the presentation of sexual orientation within *Asylum* to emphasize the importance of addressing the topic and preserve its historical reception (as well as its changes). Because part of the aim is to explore past and present cultural

narratives regarding sexual orientation and its perceptions, LGBTQIA will be used regarding present discussions where cultural sensitivity is valued and recognized (as opposed to past rejection and stigmatization).

Works Cited

Andreeva, Nellie. "'American Horror Story' Sets Title for Second Cycle." *Deadline: Hollywood*, 1 Aug. 2012, deadline.com/2012/08/american-horror-story-sets-title-for-second-cycle-311394/. Accessed 7 Jan. 2017.
Baldini, Bill. "Suffer the Little Children." 1968. *Pennhurst Memorial & Preservation Alliance*, 2017, www.preservepennhurst.org/default.aspx?pg=26. Accessed 12 Dec. 2016.
Bly, Nellie. "Ten Days in a Mad-House." *A Celebration of Women Writers*, edited by Mary Mark Ockerbloom, Penn Libraries, 2012, digital.library.upenn.edu/women/bly/madhouse/madhouse.html. Accessed 12 Dec. 2016.
Bryant, Adam, and Natalie Abrams. "Mega Buzz: *Glee*'s New Love Interest, *Bones*' 'Torture' and *Diaries*' Transition." *TV Guide Today's News*, 24 Jul. 2012, www.tvguide.com/news/mega-buzz-glee-bones-spoilers-1050427/. Accessed 18 Dec. 2016.
Cramer, Robert J., et al. "Weighing the Evidence: Empirical Assessment and Ethical Implications of Conversion Therapy." *Ethics & Behavior*, vol. 18, no. 1, 2008, pp. 93–114.
Dimock, Michael, and Staff. "Same-Sex Marriage, State by State." *Pew Research Center*, 26 Jun. 2015, www.pewforum.org/2015/06/26/same-sex-marriage-state-by-state/. Accessed 15 Jan. 2017.
Elliott, Michael A. "Strangely Interested: The Work of Historical Fantasy." *American Literature*, vol. 87, no. 1, 2015, pp. 137–57.
Fan Contributors. "Trivia." *IMBD*, n.d., www.imdb.com/title/tt1844624/trivia. Accessed 19 Nov. 2019.
Fern, Fanny. *Ruth Hall and Other Writings*, edited by Joyce W. Warren, Rutgers UP, 2005.
Greenwood, Chelsea. "13 Surprising Things You Never Knew About *American Horror Story*." *Business Insider: Singapore*, 4 Oct. 2018, www.businessinsider.sg/american-horror-story-fun-facts-2018-10/. Accessed 31 Oct. 2019.
Hevesi, Dennis. "Robert W. McCollum, Who Studied Viral Diseases, Dies at 85." *The New York Times*, 25 Sep. 2010, www.nytimes.com/2010/09/26/education/26mccollum.html. Accessed 12 Dec. 2017.
Human Rights Campaign Staff. "The Lies and Dangers of Efforts to Change Sexual Orientation or Gender Identity." *Human Rights Campaign*, 2017, www.hrc.org/resources/the-lies-and-dangers-of-reparative-therapy. Accessed 15 Jan. 2017.
McGeorge, Christi R., et al. "An Exploration of Family Therapists' Beliefs About the Ethics of Conversion Therapy: The Influence of Negative Beliefs and Clinical Competence with Lesbian, Gay, and Bisexual Clients." *Journal of Marital and Family Therapy*, vol. 41, no. 1, Jan. 2015, pp. 42–56.
Mulkerrins, Jane. "'I Made Gay Sidekicks the Leads': How Ryan Murphy Changed TV Forever." *The Guardian*, 26 Oct. 2019, www.theguardian.com/tv-and-radio/2019/oct/26/ryan-murphy-american-horror-story-pose-politician-glee-nip-tuck. Accessed 10 Nov. 2019.
Rosenberg, Jessica, et. al. "American Horror Story: Asylum and the Power of the Mad Monster." *Inter-Disciplinary.net*, 2014, www.inter-disciplinary.net/at-the-interface/wp-content/uploads/2013/05/Rosenberg.pdf. Accessed 12 Dec. 2016.
White, Hayden. Introduction. *Metahistory: The Historical Imagination in Nineteenth-Century Europe*, Johns Hopkins UP, 1973, pp. 1–42.

Where Myth Meets History
Discursive Haunting and the Resurrection of Marie Laveau in Coven

Rita Mookerjee

Creole women are largely absent from narratives of American women's history with the exception of the semi-mythic, alleged Vodou queen, Marie Laveau. As historians like Carolyn Morrow Long have established, Laveau was, in fact, a real woman, but few historical records about her exist. *American Horror Story: Coven* includes a modern day, immortalized Marie Laveau character played by Angela Bassett. *Coven* offers portraits of two houses of witchcraft that are formidable in their own rights but divided by race in order to highlight the historical tensions that gripped the city during the Civil War and post–Emancipation. One of these houses is led by the famed Vodou queen herself. In the show, Bassett portrays Laveau as both a formidable sorceress and a peacekeeper of the city. This depiction of Laveau is imbued with ferocity and vengeance; *Coven*'s Marie avenges hate crimes, performs blood rituals, and summons an army of the dead straight out of the ground. While the real Marie Laveau's supernatural powers remain up for debate, it is clear that she spent her life serving as an advocate for people of color, not as a vigilante, but as an informal hand of justice with an impressive social network.

In "Speaking in Tongues," Mae Gwendolyn Henderson explains that, discursively, women of color must be engaged in a tradition of "revisionary methods of reading" so as not to continue the practice of "privileging one category of [self/identity] analysis at the expense of another" (349). This is salient in the case of Marie Laveau since depictions of her tend to be either saturated with blackness or whitewashed in the interest of focusing on her magic. For Henderson, "speaking in tongues" describes the practice of black[1] women's writing as it pertains to heteroglossia and glossolalia. She brings in Bakhtinian notions of dialogism to illustrate that every discursive community has a "social dialect" which encapsulates its own system of language containing ideological and perspectival properties (349). Henderson invokes Alice Walker to explain that in a theological sense, glossolalia is a sign of divinity and holy power. Glossolalia suggests "private, nonmediated language" whereas heteroglossia refers to the capacity to communicate in a multitude of known languages and "connotes public, differentiated, social, mediated, dialogic discourse" (353). Together, these two origins of speaking in tongues as a practice show the polyphony that is inherent within hybridized discourse. Using the Laveau legend in conjunction with sociocultural data about New Orleans, the legend's haunting of history via *Coven* is an example of speaking in tongues imbued with resonance. Therefore, the legend has the ability to reappear over time.

In an interview, Bassett described reading "Robert Tallant's novel 'The Voodoo Queen' and another nonfiction account of her famous character's life, and [had] met with a couple of voodoo experts, one of whom is a practitioner, [and visited] Laveau's presumed tomb to investigate the rites that occur there" (Walker). Thus, Bassett's depiction of the character was more informed by what we can term the Laveau legend than historical research. In *Coven*, Marie Laveau's status as a powerful, immortal woman who made a pact with the Vodou deity Papa Legba remains the focus of her story arc. Little to no attention is paid to her Creole subject positionality or even her mixed-race background, which would have been germane to the show since much of the season's conflict stems from black-white racial animosity.

There is no longer a need to treat history and myth as disparate entities. Even the dismissal of the Laveau legend itself has proven historically detrimental. Upon Laveau's death in 1894, Creole writer/lawyer Henry Castellanos authored "The Voudous: Their History, Mysteries, and Practices," which argued that Laveau was neither a conjuror or healer, but simply a matchmaker and amateur brothel madam. Castellanos maintained that Laveau's alleged social status was a product of her association with various people seeking sexual arrangements that she would then facilitate. He accused Laveau of fraud and of corrupting the Catholic community with blasphemous Vodou practices. While calling for the elimination of all Vodou practices in New Orleans, Castellanos claimed that all practitioners were "a mysterious sect of fanatics, imported from the jungles of Africa" and that "with the advances of our superior civilization it is to be hoped that the hour is not far distant when the last vestige of its degrading and dangerous influence will forever be wiped out of existence" (18). Since Castellanos' bigotry is evident, his commentary is not worth taking seriously in studying Marie Laveau's life or legend. Without access to community archives and special collections libraries, it remains difficult to learn anything about the real Marie Laveau. As such, *Coven*'s portrayal of Laveau can be treated as a supplementary text concerned with issues of agency, trauma, healing, and community for black and indigenous women and women of color writ large (hereto abbreviated as BIWOC). The writers craft a narrative of Laveau that allows her to interact with both fictional and historical characters. Apropos, the Laveau legend must not be discarded, but refined and elevated such that it reads as an integral part of her story and of Creole women's history. *Coven* and the various works of literature that have emerged are not efforts to martyr, fetishize, or defame Laveau, but rather to revive her story and resurrect her in different contexts.

This essay will not dismiss Laveau's silences nor will it ignore the lore that surrounds her. While scholars like Carolyn Morrow Long have dispelled many of the myths around this enigmatic and intriguing woman, this analysis of *Coven* will show how the haunting of historiographic research by the Laveau mythology is, in itself, a discourse that is unique to women's history and to the history of people of color in America. The role of mythos is not to dilute this analysis with contrived mysticism or to craft a fetishized metaphor for the sake of thematic unity. Rather, this is a study about liminality and the emergence of discourse from marginalized groups. While racist myths have been perpetuated about women of color for centuries, empowering myths work against them to reclaim and reimagine BIWOC's subjecthood, their triumphs, and their complexity of lived experiences. It is necessary to use the language of ghosts, the divine, and the occult along with historical data in order to detail the specific presence Laveau had as a public figure and has as a historic female icon of New Orleans. Normally, these sets of knowledge are critiqued by scholars as having limited ties to empirical or textual evidence. Here, they are appropriate because the *AHS* series revolves around the supernatural and the occult and because Laveau's history is intrinsically bound to folklore and hybridity. In literature and media, Vodou and magic work to shift viewers' worldviews by forcing them to reckon with a visual reality that would otherwise seem impossible.

Though efforts to retrieve the history of early New Orleans life and culture outside the region are uncommon, nineteenth-century New Orleans as a city can be read as America in microcosm. It has always been a hybrid space inhabited by hybrid bodies, Laveau being one of them. As Homi Bhabha asserts in *The Location of Culture*, hybrids have the potential to harness power and turn the oppressor's gaze onto itself in order to destabilize "the mimetic or narcissistic demands of colonial power but [reimplicate] its identifications in strategies of subversion" (112). In other words, Laveau acquired mobility as a Creole woman and made use of it; she amassed a substantial amount of money at one point and cultivated a largely white clientele (Long 84). Whether or not Laveau was a divine figure remains unproven, but *Coven*'s Marie shows how she could move between worlds while seeing, acting, and speaking beyond the present.

By assessing documents compiled by the Louisiana Writers' Project and several historical centers in Louisiana, scholars have been able to trace Marie Laveau through nineteenth-century New Orleans history. These local records speak to her strong presence in the city of New Orleans and some modicum of power. However, Laveau was not literate and left no diaries or notes about her life. She avoided press interviews to the extent that her evasion seemed deliberate. Since historical records of Marie Laveau range from sparse to inconsistent to nonexistent, and since the legend that surrounds her is largely speculative, it seems futile to try to analyze who the real Marie Laveau was and what sorts of agency she had as a nineteenth-century woman of mixed race. Still, in 1881, the *New York Times* ran an obituary entitled, "The Dead Voudou Queen—Marie Laveau's Place in the History of New Orleans—The Early Life of the Beautiful Young Creole—The Prominent Men Who Sought Her Advice and Society—Her Charitable Work—How She Became an Object of Mystery." Despite claims that the Laveau legend is untrue, this headline marks her death as an item of national significance. As a Creole woman, she was able to gain influence and assert herself as a public figure and made discursive and political contributions for free BIWOC in New Orleans. *Coven* fills in the gaps in this story and necessarily rebuilds her authority in the New Orleans of today.

Painting Marie: Issues of Representation

A stroll down modern-day Bourbon Street will often land visitors at Marie Laveau's House of Voodoo, a specialty shop for dolls, crystals, and books. The sign outside is a simple black circle with white bones spelling out the store's name. Admittedly, it is hard to imagine a connection between the powerful Vodou priestess and the assortment of logo beanies and mugs that comprises most of this shop's offerings. Though most of the goods are just kitschy souvenirs, the Marie Laveau prayer card sold here and elsewhere remains problematic. It features the most commonly referenced portrait of Laveau; she appears as a light-skinned woman with full lips in a simple dress and shawl, her hair tied up in a tignon.[2] It is alleged that George Catlin painted this piece in 1837; the whereabouts of the original are unknown, but a replica by Frank Schneider of the Louisiana State Museum was created between 1911 and 1922 (Long 57). The copy is currently on display at the same museum. Interviews conducted by the Louisiana Writers' Project in the early twentieth century deny that this painting resembles the real Marie Laveau who, according to her daughter Philomène

Glapion Legendre,[3] "never sat for an artist or allowed herself to be photographed" (56–57). Other circulated portraits depict Laveau as having dark skin, wearing more jewelry, her hair down in braids, etc. The painting as a cultural signifier relies on its antiquity to establish truth; people take the portrait at face value out of convenience. After all, a figure as mysterious as a mixed race Vodou priestess almost demands visual representation. The trouble is that the popular painting lacks any undeniable marker that the woman in question is Creole, much less Marie Laveau herself. The tignon remains the only exception as it has been historically associated with Creole women's styling in the nineteenth century. Without knowing the significance of this head scarf, it could be easy to misread the painted Laveau as mulatta, indigenous North American, Spanish, etc.

Conversely, it seems that other representations of Laveau are imbued with blackness in ways that teeter between gratuity and outright tokenization. Martha Ward's *Voodoo Queen: The Spirited Lives of Marie Laveau* stands as the first academic biography of its kind, yet it was not authored until 2002. Several writers have created works of fiction inspired by Marie Laveau, Francine Prose's novel being the most notable. Prose's 1977 *Marie Laveau* was well received, but it reads as more of a surrealist piece linking Marie Laveau to various powerful women of color. An excerpt from the end of the text reads:

> Marie Laveau has come back from the dead, her name is Zora Neale Hurston. Marie Laveau has come back from the dead. Her name is Sister Marie. She is an old lady in wartime Harlem with an evening reader-adviser business on the second floor of an office building on 125th Street. During the day, she works downtown as a maid. Marie Laveau has come back from the dead. Her name is Rosa Parks [...] After so many years, she's come back remembering the power of secrets and silence [370–374].

This type of amalgamation created by a white author threatens to essentialize BIWOC's experience to the point of essentialism. In "The Problem with 'Problematic,'" Prose claims that criticism aimed at white authors for writing the stories of BIWOC is a form of "censorship" and asks, "Doesn't fiction let the reader imagine what it might be like to be someone else? Or to enable us to consider what it means to be a human being—of another race, ethnicity, or gender?" This neocolonial attitude about storytelling is challenged by *Coven*'s intervention. As a living black actor, Bassett stands as the reanimated Marie which results in a far more holistic representation than anything a white writer could simply dream up.

Additionally, Prose imagines Laveau as the granddaughter of a Vodou priest. While several sources indicate that Laveau's mother and grandmother practiced Vodou, Prose's decision to situate Laveau's grandfather as the Vodou priest robs the narrative of a compelling womanist angle. Fortunately, *Coven* surrounds Marie with female apprentices, thereby recentering women within the narrative of power and conjure. In a 1977 review in the *New York Times*, Thomas Lask stated that Prose "conveys well that peculiar mixture of down-to-earth living and transcendental experience that marked New Orleans society of that time." Though it is reasonable to associate historic New Orleans with vibrancy and mysticism and *Coven* is saturated in this aesthetic, Lask irresponsibly romanticizes the reality of nineteenth-century Louisiana, especially for people of color. Simply put, "down to earth living" was not a choice, but a prescribed and enforced norm for freedmen and all people of color. In his study of Prose's work, Lask misses[4] the point entirely. Conversely, Jewell Parker Rhodes' 1993 *Voodoo Dreams* capitalizes on the folkloric aspects of the Laveau legend. Rhodes gives a mystical take on the life of Laveau, weaving in a romance plot and snapshots of nineteenth-century New Orleans. As a black woman writer, Rhodes takes far more care in the particulars of Laveau's life and times. Though Prose and Rhodes offer works of fiction (Rhodes' text being decidedly YA), readers readily conflate the account—full of secret powers, ritual sacrifices, and deathbed confessions—with the life of the real Marie Laveau.

Coven does not make the mistake of romanticizing the life and times of Marie Laveau. Marie spearheads community efforts to fight back and avenge wrongful killings of black people while going head-to-head with Supreme Fiona over turf rules. One of the most memorable of these scenes begins in "Fearful Pranks Ensue." It begins with a flashback to Henry, a young black boy riding a bicycle on a bright spring day in 1961. Suddenly, ominous music plays as a car full of white men pursues him. He tries to run down an alley to escape them, but he is cornered. Meanwhile, the boy's mother, Cora, works in Marie's salon. She explains that it is her son's first day at the previously white high school. Marie is suspicious of the newly integrated school and thinks it is risky to send black children there. The scene cuts to a horrific black and white frame of young Henry, now hanging from a noose in a tree. As his mother screams with grief, Marie watches with silent fury, eyes narrowed.

A dreamy, blurred sequence follows wherein Marie guts a snake and combines several ingredients in an urn as she performs a ritual. Her movements are fluid yet purposeful. As she crushes ingredients in her fists, corpses begin bursting through the earth at a graveyard nearby. The risen dead break into a shed where a circle of white men celebrate their crime with some beers. They are shocked when the animated corpses burst into the shed and futilely shoot them with guns. In a short time, the men are disemboweled and torn limb from limb (3:4).

The vindication of Henry by Marie cements her status as a powerful member of the black community. She acts in the name of justice, not for sport or personal gain. If history whitewashes Laveau, the impact she had as a mixed-race woman in an extremely specific geographical and social context is lost. Fortunately, *Coven*'s Marie is a far cry from this convoluted portrait; she sports long braids and African jewelry as she presides over her busy beauty salon in the black neighborhood of the Ninth Ward. Marie is frequently shown in candlelit scenes with lots of earth tones that accentuate her brown skin. During the episode "Boy Parts," Fiona excavates Delphine LaLaurie, a woman that Marie cursed with immortality for the torture of many house slaves including Marie's lover, Bastien. There is a compelling parallel here, since LaLaurie was a real debutante who resided in New Orleans during the nineteenth century. While there is historical evidence of LaLaurie's sadistic pursuits, her story is mythologized like Laveau's.

Fiona travels to Marie's salon to gloat, but Marie refuses to be intimidated and instead gives Fiona a lesson about the history of witchcraft. Marie explains that the white Salem witches only learned of their magic through Tituba, a slave girl. "We're more than just pins in dolls and seeing the future through chicken parts," Marie asserts while Fiona tries to dismiss the importance of African conjurers (3:2). This brief yet crucial scene underscores the white arrogance of the coven, but also gestures to the countless instances of white appropriation of black culture throughout American history. Fiona conceives of the black conjurers and shamans as primitive. Her contempt for them coupled with her racist attitude costs her the safety of her coven and wastes what is otherwise a powerful alliance.

In *Lovecidal: Walking with the Disappeared*, Trinh Minh-ha offers the property of resonance to describe what happens when "language meets its own edge" (7). Trinh explains that "[t]he present conveniently obliterates the past, but the latter keeps on returning to haunt the very consciousness that seeks to forget it" (131). While Trinh is speaking specifically about the Vietnam War here, this principle is integral in understanding why a woman about whom so little is definitively known keeps materializing in television and literature. While Laveau is touted for her social action and for providing counsel and healing to the community, she also embodies a fraught history of illegitimacy, taboo racial mixing, child marriages, and rape that America would certainly like to ignore if not willfully forget. Appearances of Laveau in a novel or film or history lesson or New Orleans tour are "events, both natural and manmade, [that] vibrate across times and places, tune in to one another, and deeply affect our life processes" (8). The sonic property of vibration and resonance is important in understanding Laveau and her lore, because it harkens back to epistemological oral traditions that are specific to people of color[5] in America. Laveau is famed for her social influence and Vodou powers; both concepts are contingent upon uttered speech. Much of the data compiled by the Louisiana Writers' Project comes from interviews with people who knew Laveau or her descendants. The fact remains that Marie Laveau on the page is often dissimilar from the Marie Laveau of history. In order to correct this, scholars and artists must wield the Laveau legend as *Coven* does—with a grain of salt, signaling the presence of mythology without removing it entirely.

Nineteenth-Century New Orleans

Today, New Orleans is understood as the point of convergence for the intersection of French and Spanish colonialism with the Caribbean, the latter often being historically mythologized as a locus of fortune and prosperity, not unlike Laveau herself. Prior to the Civil War, there were already legislative efforts to rob free people of color in New Orleans of their liberties, so by 1855, it was not possible for them to move into the city without some degree of harassment by white citizens or law enforcement (Long 85). During the Civil War, Louisiana troops left the city unprotected, and it was seized by Admiral David Farragut in 1862 (88). The Union did not lay siege to the city, but when the war ended in 1865, the "carefully-constructed three-tiered order of whites, free people of color [like Laveau], and slaves had been knocked to smithereens, and people of every color and station scrambled frantically to find their proper 'place' in the new society" (89). Subsequently, post–Emancipation New Orleans was a site of sociocultural chaos. The Anglo-American citizens who previously held power became increasingly suspicious of the Afro-Caribbean people of New Orleans, particularly with regard to religion. While it is evident that Santería, Haitian Vodou, and Candomblé[6] were blended with Roman Catholicism in the colonies, New Orleans Vodou was the only Afro-Catholic religion to take root anywhere in North America (93). The stigma around mixed-race people can be summarized in this context by a line from the *Historical Sketch Book and Guide to New Orleans and Environs* stating that "importation of the San Domingo negroes was forbidden by special edict [as being] too well acquainted with Voudouism and poison" (Coleman 95). This is certainly reiterated by the white coven's distaste for Marie and her community. As such, people marked by racial difference were treated with hostility, as they were believed to pose threats to the order of emergent American society. Women like Laveau, who was allegedly beautiful and maybe even white-passing, were viewed as harlots and targeted by white women who feared they would steal away their husbands with their exotic wiles. When free women of color sought avenues for social mobility, they were usually harassed by white citizens and ultimately silenced and halted in their efforts.

The Politics of Marie Laveau

As shown in *Coven*, it is alleged that Laveau worked as a hairdresser when she was young. In episodes like "Fearful Pranks Ensue," viewers see that Marie Laveau's salon is frequented by black women of all ages, suggesting that she has a strong reputation and even stronger ties to the community. In "The Dead," the young black witch Queenie pays a visit to Marie. Though Queenie resides with the white coven, Marie believes that she belongs in the Vodou community. As Queenie walks through the rooms of Marie's house, she sees many black people talking happily together. With a bucket of fish heads in hand, Marie disparages Queenie's life with the witches as she prepares to make a pot of gumbo. She feeds Queenie a taste from a wooden spoon (3:7). This act of tenderness shows Marie's desire to recruit Queenie, but it also points to her pride in black southern culture. The house full of people and steaming pot of food show that Marie's home is a place of refuge and nourishment.

The real Marie Laveau was also known to host gatherings and feed her community. In turn, people were drawn to her and eager to obtain her trust. She acquired vital personal information about important people in New Orleans (Long 83). Politicians and socialites sought her counsel and Vodou abilities. Though some say she gained power through blackmail, it is evident that she had the finances to influence the law and the community. Laveau pledged monetary assistance to free women of color who had been arrested for non-major crimes in New Orleans. An 1850 court document contains the following:

> On September 4th, 1850 [Laveau] guaranteed a security bond of $500 for her neighbor Julia Evans, who [...] was charged with "'grossly insulting abusing, and threatening' a white woman in violation of the Black Code, which mandated that free colored persons should not imagine themselves equal to whites; on the contrary, they are to defer to whites on every occasion and treat them with respect." Evans was arraigned and, despite her plea of not guilty, she was sentenced to one week's imprisonment and ordered to pay court costs [84].

Many similar accounts can be found in archives in Louisiana, all united by an effort to help women accused of petty crimes (mostly against white people). Perhaps Marie Laveau did not mind promising money to acquaintances in trouble, but the frequency with which she did so suggests a greater investment in the lives of freed women and a commitment to abolishing the Black Code and similar laws of oppression. The state of Laveau's finances around this time is unclear; her second husband Christophe Glapion died in 1855 with much debt and their home was reclaimed (84–85). Still, Laveau was sought out in the community and furnished relatively large sums of money for her clients.

Contrasting stories exist about Laveau's involvement with the parish prison and some of her more mythologized judicial efforts, like the ones seen in *Coven*. One of the most popular of these is the story that Laveau would bring a special bowl of poisoned gumbo to prisoners like Antoine Cambre as a satisfying last meal that would spare them from the gallows (Long 157). Long explains that toward the end of her life, Laveau was associated with Christianity and did charitable works through the church. Laveau's movement into a Christian community can be read as another discursive haunting. Often a haunting is marked by unpredictability or surprise. Thus, Laveau's seemingly abrupt departure from Vodou and adoption of Christian practice can be read as her refusal to be coded as the "voudou queen." There is also the possibility that she never cut ties with Vodou and self-styled as Christian toward the end of her life as a means of diverting unwanted publicity and general questions from the community.

Vodou Discourse

Coven offers instances of Marie being surrounded by snakes, chalking religious symbols on the ground, and crafting potions. In "Fearful Pranks Ensue," Marie can be seen drawing a vèvè, an often-symmetrical image meant to draw a chosen deity to a ceremony. Since New Orleans Vodoun was not traditionally learned through written texts, it remains difficult to determine what sorts of rituals and ceremonies might have constituted Laveau's brand of Vodou. Laveau is thought to have begun her practice in the 1820s under the priestesses Sanité Dédé and Marie Saloppé after the death of her first husband, Jacques Paris (Long 98). Alternately, some texts like the 1900 *Picayune's Guide to New Orleans* suggest that Laveau's mother and grandmother held Vodou ceremonies at Congo Square and that they indoctrinated young Marie into the practice at an early age (100). Either way, the gendered legacy of vodou in Laveau's life shows a discursive haunting that is also a survival strategy: women sharing secrets with women in order to protect, heal, and harm if the need arose.

Laveau hosted weekly *layouts* or *parterres* which were private ceremonies of mixed participants that began with the arranging of flowers, colored candles, food, and drink on a white cloth on the ground as an offering to the spirits (Long 110). The ceremony also contained a small chorus and an accordion player. Laveau would ask the attendees what they were seeking before anointing them with rum and dancing or convulsing. The Laveau legend often refers to a huge snake called Zombi and several interviewees from the Louisiana Writers' Project recall the presence of snakes in Laveau's public rituals. The wholly benevolent Marie Laveau seen in some works of fiction is fabricated; the real Laveau was rumored to have a concealed altar surrounded by animal statues in the back of her home where she crafted "charms to kill, to drive away, to break up love affairs, and to spread confusion" (109–110). This space can be seen in *Coven* whenever Marie performs a ritual. She stores all of her elements and relics in this room, and it is kept closed during the day. Marie's artifacts and altars contrast the unceremonious style of witchcraft practiced by the coven; though the white witches sometimes use herbs or charms, they mostly perform spells nonverbally and outside of a designated space. The ceremonies Laveau presided over were often described as orgiastic, with women possessed by spirits speaking in tongues and writhing in the nude. Most non-interview accounts of New Orleans Vodou proceedings are gleaned from city arrest records; Vodou was often associated with drunkenness, prostitution, assault, vagrancy, and unlawful assembly (103).

Until the rise of newspaper columns detailing local events in the 1840s, Vodou did not really have a presence in Louisiana news. The notion of secrecy is crucial here because while Laveau did seem to actively avoid the press, Vodou itself was invisibilized in the early nineteenth century. Laveau's *parterres* were small gatherings so as to avoid police intervention; this suggests a conscious decision to restrict her practice to a specific group of insiders, thereby inscribing a discourse and reifying a community that could not be penetrated by the white oppressors of New Orleans. Unlike in the show, it is noteworthy that the attendees of Laveau's ceremonies were of different racial groups since this shows that perhaps her hybridity as a Creole woman along with her social standing allowed her to access these various people. Chezia Thompson-Cager describes a similar quality of liminality in her analysis of Ntozake Shange's *Sassafrass, Cypress, and Indigo*. The character Indigo is a fictitious counterpart of Marie Laveau. Indigo exists as a "star child" and a "carrier," meaning she "lives in the space between known or defined realities/time dimensions" and is also "a child who inherits the responsibility of speaking with the voice of the ancestors" (594). The rituals she held dealt with the "power of the language of naming and unnaming, making and unmaking inherent in visual and performing art forms and alchemistical processes such as cooking and mixing herbs" (597). Whether or not she healed people, the act of restructuring had power. Simultaneously, Laveau's dark practices need not be dismissed as malicious and undeserved. In conceiving of hybrid discourse, hauntings, and trauma, it is justified that people who have been perpetually maligned with no hope of change must turn to alternate modes of exacting justice and protecting themselves.

Conclusion

The deficiency of historical documentation concerning figures like Laveau reflects only the lack of attention paid to mixed-race people, not a dearth of culture or complexity. Works like *Coven* supplement history with myth and legend, which resurrects the past so that new heuristic modes can be grounded in evidence that is not confined to dates and statistics. As Ishmael Reed has stated, in order to understand people and circumstances outside limited context, "you have to come up with new myths" (10). Two sites, the Widow Paris tomb and a wall vault nicknamed "the Wishing Vault" in St. Louis Cemetery No. 2, are frequented by followers and admirers of Marie Laveau. At both locations, visitors come and leave offerings of sweets and money; they also draw Xs in brick, "an African tradition symbolizing a point of concentrated power where the world of the living meets the world of the spirits" (Long 177). In *Coven*, Fiona even references this practice, pointing out the irony of leaving offerings to an immortal woman. Marie Laveau's two burial sites represent her resonating story and highlight the intersection of myth and reality that her narrative has produced. Her discursive haunting embodies both private and public multivocality and defies the constraints of space and time. A popular song for the beginning of traditional Vodou ceremonies goes, "l'uvri bayé pu mwé pu mwé pasé," meaning "remove the barrier for me so that I may pass through" (114). As in the case with *Coven*, the very mystery that makes her life and legacy unclear has imbued Marie Laveau with the power to disappear and reappear throughout history and literature.

Notes

1. Though Henderson is specifically discussing black women, her argument can be applied to a subject like Marie Laveau since blackness is inextricable from Creole identity. Here, the inclusion of theories of black women's discourse is not meant to homogenize women of color, but to instead link unifying discursive properties as points of access.

2. In Spanish colonies, the tignon was mandated by law. Women of color were not permitted to style their hair or beautify it with ornaments. The tignon was subverted, however, and the "scarf imported from Madras, India became a fashion statement" (Long 20–21). In America, Afro-Caribbean women continued to don the tignon. Marie Laveau was famous for wearing "a tignon with seven points [...] upturned to heaven" (21).

3. Of the nine children Marie Laveau had, two of her daughters were Marie Heloïse Euchariste Glapion and Marie Louise Glapion. Carolyn Morrow Long posits that some accounts of Laveau's life are actually in reference to one of her daughters with whom she shared a first name. The "second Marie" as she is dubbed was also an alleged conjuror.

4. The most egregious detail of Lask's review is the title of the review: "Tale of a Noble Blackmailer" which relegates Laveau to petty criminal status.

5. To clarify, this endeavor is not meant to essentialize Creole women or people of color who were not able to pen their own histories. Instead, the oral tradition serves as a reference point connected to textual history by way of discursive hauntings.

6. Candomblé comes from Bantu and Yoruba traditions and is most popular in Bahia where the most Brazilians of African descent reside. Candomblé contains a complex pantheon of *orixas* ruled over by *Oludumaré*, the all-powerful god. Dance and music figure greatly into the practice of Candomblé which literally means "to dance for the gods" (Selka 7).

Works Cited

Anderson, Jeffrey E. "The Voodoo Queen Unearthed: Three Recent Biographies of Marie Laveau." *Nova Religio: The Journal of Alternative and Emergent Religions*, vol. 13, no. 1, 2009, pp. 110–14. Accessed 11 Nov. 2019.
Bhabha, Homi. *The Location of Culture*. Routledge, 1994.
Castellanos, Henry. "The Voudous: Their History, Mysteries, and Practices." *Times-Democrat*. 24 June 1894.
Coleman, William Head. *Historical Sketch Book and Guide to New Orleans and Environs: With Map*. New Orleans Press, 1885.
Henderson, Gwendolyn Mae. "Speaking in Tongues: Dialogics and Dialectics and the Black Woman Writer's Literary Tradition." *African American Literary Theory: A Reader*, NYU Press, 2000, pp. 348–68.
Lask, Thomas. "Books: Tale of a Noble Blackmailer." Review of *Marie Laveau*. *The New York Times*, 15 Sep. 1977.
Long, Carolyn Morrow. *A New Orleans Voudou Priestess: The Legend and Reality of Marie Laveau*. U of Florida P, 2006.
Prose, Francine. *Marie Laveau*. Berkeley Publishing, 1977.
_____. "The Problem with 'Problematic.'" *The New York Review of Books*, 1 Nov. 2017, www.nybooks.com/daily/2017/11/01/the-problem-with-problematic/. Accessed 11 Nov. 2019.
Reed, Ishmael. "When State Magicians Fail: An Interview with Ishmael Reed." *Conversations with Ishmael Reed*, edited by Bruce Allen Dick and Amrijit Singh, UP of Mississippi, 1995, pp. 3–13.
Selka, Stephen. "Mediated Authenticity: Tradition, Modernity, and Postmodernity in Brazilian Candomblé." *Nova Religio: The Journal of Alternative and Emergent Religions*, vol. 11, no. 1, 2007, pp. 5–30. Accessed 11 Nov. 2019.
Thompson-Cager, Chezia. "Ntozake Shange's 'Sassafrass, Cypress and Indigo'": Resistance and Mystical Women of Power." *NWSA Journal*, vol. 1, no. 4, 1989, pp. 589–601. Accessed 11 Nov. 2019.
Trinh, Minh-ha. *Lovecidal: Walking with the Disappeared*. Fordham UP, 2016.
Walker, Dave. "Angela Bassett Is Getting to Know Marie Laveau, Her 'American Horror Story: Coven' Character." *The Times-Picayune*, 5 Aug. 2013, www.nola.com/entertainment_life/movies_tv/article_06d580a7-d2c3-513e-aa95-06d993dc795c.html. Accessed 11 Nov. 2019.

Coven's LaLaurie and Laveau
Contemporary Narratives of Southern Gothicism, Folklore and Nineteenth-Century New Orleans

TAMMIE JENKINS

The city of New Orleans has been an enigma since its colonization in 1718 by the French settlers. Originally named *La Nouvelle-Orléans* in honor of Philip II, Duke of Orléans, the city emerged as a strategic location for commerce and agricultural endeavors due to its proximity to the Mississippi River and Lake Pontchartrain. New Orleans was protected by a natural levee, which surrounded the land, making it easily defensible against seafaring enemies. Over time, New Orleans became a bustling city with many myths, legends, and folkloric tales embedded in the narratives of its people and places. These are stories that continue to perpetuate the infamy and popularity of two prominent female figures from the nineteenth century. They are Madame Marie Delphine LaLaurie and Marie Catherine Laveau. Flash-forward to 2013, to *American Horror Story: Coven*'s use of a revisionist historical approach to (re)imagine the narratives of LaLaurie and Laveau for the series' third season.

Using the city of New Orleans and two infamously, iconic, and historical women, *Coven* recontextualizes these older tales and redefines their taken-for-granted assumptions regarding the actions or behaviors of these women. For years, I had heard stories of Madame Delphine LaLaurie that accentuated her mental instability and physical cruelty towards her slaves. These accounts described LaLaurie as a depraved torturer, a criminal mastermind, and a serial killer whose former home, the LaLaurie Mansion, is allegedly haunted by the specters of LaLaurie and the enslaved persons she slaughtered. On the other hand, Marie Laveau's narratives depict a woman with divine gifts (e.g., clairvoyance, healing, jinxing) who used the African-derived spiritual practice of Vodou to expand her social status and to earn a living.

This essay employs *Coven* as a case study of the ways that intertextuality is used to connect historical facts and related fictions in a present-day context. This essay draws on James E. Porter's explanation of intertextuality as "the bits or pieces of texts which writers or speakers borrow and sew together to create new discourses" (34). I employ the following guiding questions: How are the narratives of LaLaurie and Laveau used to depict Southern Gothicism? What is the significance of space/place in (re)imagining New Orleans history and fantasy on *Coven*? In what ways is intertextuality used to connect the characters of LaLaurie and Laveau to one another and the larger society? In so doing, I consider the ways that these women's lives have been (re)imagined through their portrayals by Kathy Bates and Angela Bassett, respectively, on primetime television.

Madame LaLaurie and Marie Laveau: Portraits of Multiplicitous Lives

By the eighteenth century, New Orleans was a robust metropolis with identifiable cultural influences derived from its French, Spanish, African, Haitian, and Native American populations (Long 3). One of its appeals was its relaxed moral codes, which enabled groups that were normally separated by class and racial stratifications to interact with one another in public places. Prior to 1804, a larger concentration of the city were wealthy Creole families, enslaved persons, and free people of color, many of whom were quadroons. The latter were persons believed to possess one-fourth of their DNA from the European ruling class such as the French and later Spanish colonizers. Quadroon women were groomed at an early age to assume the role of non-legal wife to wealthy white gentlemen. These women attended an annual social gathering known as Quadroon Balls, which were like today's debutante balls, where the ladies were introduced to eligible suitors and their mothers negotiated their financial security (Ward 36). If a match was secured, the gentleman agreed to support his quadroon bride and any children produced during their union; however, many of these illegal marriages were dissolved when one died, or the man desired to have a legitimate family. The *placage* system was practiced by wealthy, white men and free women of color throughout New Orleans, while white, Creole women were products of their social status and cultural norms, which contributed to their marrying financially-secure men and procreating legal heirs. This group lacked many of the limitations of their black female counterparts, which afforded white Creole women more opportunities for becoming financially independent from their families and spouses over time.

One such woman became an influential socialite as well as an infamous nineteenth-century female New Orleans serial murderer and habitual slave torturer (Long 11; Love and Shannon 12). This woman was Marie Delphine McCathy LaLaurie, the daughter of Louis Barthelemy de McCarty, a highly respected plantation owner, and his wife, Marie-Jeanne L'Érable. Following the traditional expectations for women of her class, Madame Delphine LaLaurie entered her first marriage at the age of fourteen to a much older man named Don Ramon Lopez. He was a widower and an officer in the Spanish military. Their union was short-lived. At the age of eighteen, LaLaurie was a wealthy widow and single mother who lived on her own for the next seven years. She met Jacques Blanque, whom she married and with whom she had four children. He died expectantly, leaving LaLaurie a rich widow and single mother of five children.

By age forty-two, she had met and married her final husband, a doctor from France, named Dr. Leonard Louis LaLaurie, who was sixteen years her junior (Long 64; Love and Shannon 33). Their union produced one child. The couple's marriage was complicated by their drastic age difference and LaLaurie's strong will and ill-temper. Initially, Dr. LaLaurie moved to New Orleans from France in hopes of starting a medical practice; however, he married LaLaurie against his family's wishes and by 1834 the couple was living separately (Love and Shannon 37). Madame LaLaurie remained in the city while Dr. LaLaurie had relocated to Plaquemines Parish (34). She was the daughter of an affluent, white Creole plantation family, a status which enabled her to receive a rudimentary formal education. Like most women of her social class, LaLaurie was reared to marry well and to produce strong offspring.

The norms of her family's plantation life and their treatment of enslaved populations during her formative years may have played a pivotal role in her later mutilation, physical torment, and eventual murder of her slaves. Although the *Code Noir* (the Black Code) provided instruction for the humane treatment of slaves and outlined consequences for violations, even this legal document was not enough to detour LaLaurie from committing the atrocities to which she is forever connected (Brunage 123; Love and Shannon 13). She had the luck of influential relatives and friends as well as the wealth she inherited from the deaths of her first two husbands. This enabled her to buy her way out of trouble and later to escape New Orleans in the aftermath of the house fire. She traveled to Mandeville before setting sail for France with her third husband, Dr. LaLaurie, and her younger children. The LaLauries lived with relatives prior to settling in Paris in a chateau of their own. After a period of eight years, LaLaurie returned to New Orleans where she purchased a house near her former home in the French Quarter. She passed away in the mid-to-late 1850s and was buried in an undisclosed location (Love and Shannon 48). The absence of a gravesite bearing her name has led many scholars to speculate that LaLaurie was either interred in France or secretly buried under a pseudonym in New Orleans. Either way her legend, like that of Marie Laveau, lives on in the lore of the city.

Frequently, when I think about New Orleans and its myths or legends, the name of Marie Laveau often enters my mind and exits my lips. Her moniker is synonymous with the practice and commercial success of the African-derived spiritual practice known as Vodou. The premiere goddess of Louisiana mysticism and iconography is Marie Catherine Laveau. She was the illegitimate daughter of Charles Laveau (alias Charles Trudeau *dit* Laveau) and Marguerite D'Arcantel (also referred to as Marguerite Henry), both of whom were quadroons and free people of color (Fandrich 152; Ward 34). Laveau was born on September 10, 1794, and received the status of her mother. Her skills as a Vodouist began in childhood with training by her maternal grandmother, Catherine Henry (alias Catherine Pomet), and her mother Marguerite. Each taught Laveau the various uses of herbs and roots as well as how to care for an array of physical and mental ailments. At age seventeen, she married a Haitian immigrant and carpenter named Jacques Paris (Fandrich 155; Ward 34, 36). After her marriage, Laveau was given a house on Love Street by her father. The home was in the *Faubourg Marigny* neighborhood, which incidentally was near the LaLaurie Mansion on Royal Street.

Prior to his death, Paris, along with Sanite Dede, a Haitian refugee, and later Jean Montenet, a former slave from Senegal, indoctrinated Laveau into the spiritual practice of Vodou to which she added a New Orleans twist (Fandrich 135; Long 137; Ward 22, 32–33). After Paris died Laveau began earning a living as a beautician, where she developed an intricate network of supporters and Vodou practitioners who provided her with information that she may or may not have used to propel and to solidify her social standing in the community. According to local beliefs, Laveau had the ability to foretell the future, commune with the spirits, place or remove curses, as well as the gift of immortality. Although her final resting place has been in St. Louis Cemetery #1, it is widely believed that she is still alive, living in New Orleans and exercising her immense powers on behalf of those who visit her grave and leave three Xs on her tomb. Whereas the inability of scholars to locate LaLaurie's gravesite facilitated rumors of her immortality as tales of her haunting her former home began circulating (Brunage 129). Even though the paths taken by LaLaurie and Laveau were unconventional for women of nineteenth-century New Orleans, the choices that each made contributed to the myths and legends that have since defined their lives and existence. As a result, LaLaurie and Laveau through their actions defied larger societal expectations for women of their race and class in ways that enable *Coven* to retell these narratives using the Southern Gothic tradition.

Mastering Thematic Eccentricities and Resonant Characters

The history of Southern Gothicism (1940s–1960s) is a unique mixture of the culture, dichotomies, and characteristics embedded in its people, places, and narratives as evidenced in texts by Flannery O'Connor, William Faulkner, Henry Clay Lewis, and Mark Twain. These authors used their texts to deconstruct southern stereotypes by including flawed characters that contrasted against antiheroic characters with redemptive qualities. With origins in American Gothicism, European Gothicism, and European Romantic traditions, Southern Gothicism differs from these earlier versions in its use of "myths, legends, and folklore" (Botting 2) in order to retell older narratives using a modern lens (Tunc 80). According to Christopher J. Walsh, "the South has always been engaged in its own historical process of mythological construction" (19), which contributes to not only its "mysterious antiquity" (19) but also the cultural ambiguity of the region. The use of Southern Gothicism provides audiences with the underlying social narratives necessary to understand the interactions between characters and the larger society. Whereas both American and Southern Gothicism include depictions of violence in their renderings, Southern Gothicism expands its storylines and plot-points through representations of racism, slavery, and grotesque subject matter through its characters and settings.

Unlike American Gothicism, the Southern variety relies on history, fantasy, and real-life to (re)imagine traditional forms of storytelling while "preserv[ing] older traditions" (Botting 4). By integrating supernatural or spiritual elements such as Vodou, witchcraft, occultism, specters, cultural reappropriation, and inflated characterizations of people, places, or events in the tradition of the aforementioned cinematic offerings, *Coven* reinvents New Orleans folklore and mysticism through its renderings of the characters of Madame LaLaurie and Marie Laveau.

In addition, Southern Gothicism includes depictions of violence in its renderings to expand storylines and plot-points through the blending of grotesque subject matter, acts of betrayal, gratuitous violence, as well as depictions of decay (moral, architectural, landscape) as characters in its narratives (Tunc 80). *Coven*'s writers use Southern Gothicism to expose the hypocrisy that exists in the larger society and its institutional units by reflecting on the brokenness that exists in what is visually represented or suppressed. Their narratives are embedded with political, spatial, and environmental underpinnings which *Coven* deconstructs and (re)imagines from a revisionist historical perspective. Geographically situated in the southern half of the United States, Southern Gothicism on *Coven* is a method of storytelling that examines institutional racism and gender discrimination while subverting cultural tensions between black people and white people in a post-racial America.

Both LaLaurie and Laveau are used to represent fundamental attributes of Southern Gothicism that *Coven* extends to create alternative explanations for these women's selective morality and other communal graces to justify their over-arching acts of aggression, retribution, and reconciliation. In *Coven*, the fictionalized LaLaurie is an independent woman of means with enough collective bargaining power as well as political clout to avoid punishment for her heinous crimes and sadistic social graces. For instance, "Bitchcraft" shows LaLaurie hosting an elaborate Halloween party attended by the upper crust of New Orleans society in hopes of finding wealthy suitors for her three unwed daughters. Escorting Jacques, the governor's son, into her chambers of horrors, LaLaurie watches in relish as he is frightened by the contents of each kiosk and makes a hasty exit from her home. Although the other party guests present are equally horrified, they join LaLaurie in laughter and continue to enjoy the soirée (3:1; 3:5). While *Coven*'s Laveau lacks in financial sustainability, she more than makes up for it with her tenacity and pervasive powers of suggestion. This is evidenced by Laveau's entering a hospital's maternity ward and stealing a newborn. Upon exiting the facility, she sets the building on fire and leaves with the child in tow. She returns to Miss Robichaux's Academy where Fiona Goode, the Head Mistress, asks about the infant. Laveau declares that the neonate is hers and is a sacrifice for Papa Legba (3:10). However, she has a change of heart as she and Fiona decide on a different offering to make. Laveau's ability to save the life of the baby by convincing Papa Legba to accept an alternative victim signifies Laveau's ability to manipulate others and have him or her do her bidding (3:10). The overlapping narratives of LaLaurie and Laveau depict the lengths each employs to achieve her ultimate goals.

Drawing on nineteenth-century New Orleans and Southern Gothicism as points of departure, *Coven* mixes older LaLaurie and Laveau narratives with their twenty-first-century discourses through flashbacks and parallel flash-forwards that connect their factual and fictional pasts with that of their present-day realities. For the purposes of this essay, Southern Gothicism is operationally defined as a series of violent behaviors or immoral acts that includes but is not limited to the use of the supernatural and superstition as spaces of power and influence. Both LaLaurie and

Laveau depict the fundamental characteristics of Southern Gothicism, which *Coven* writers utilize to create alternative explanations for these women's use of selective morality and other communal graces to justify their overarching acts of retribution and reconciliation. However, *Coven* suggests that LaLaurie's and Laveau's race and social status governed their economic empowerment as well as their political influences in their communities.

Two Women, New Orleans and Southern Gothicism

The characters of Madame Delphine LaLaurie and Marie Laveau provide unparalleled (re)imaginings of the facts, fictions, and mysteries surrounding their lives and their deaths. LaLaurie and Laveau were notorious female figures of nineteenth-century New Orleans history and folklore whose accomplishments lend themselves beautifully to the retelling of their stories through a contemporary lens. The idea that these women engaged in behaviors deemed inappropriate or immoral based on their social statuses supplied the raw material necessary to re-envision these unfathomable tales across space and place as products of popular culture on television, in featured films, in books, and in music. However, the historical records associated with these extraordinary women are rarely integrated in modern retellings of their narratives. Instead, the lore surrounding LaLaurie and Laveau has been inundated with accounts of bloodlust, occult practices, supernatural abilities, and other forms of debauchery. Investigating uses of Southern Gothicism in texts by Mark Steadman, Molly Boyd found that the author used fragmentary revelations to provide alternative explanations for previously discussed events, phenomena, or stories. This includes the use of "narrative repetitions" (Banco 68), such as those that articulate the realistic underpinnings *Coven* employs to integrate the lived experiences of LaLaurie and Laveau into its storylines and plot-points while connecting them to one another, other characters, and the larger society.

For instance, *Coven* introduces the character of Delphine LaLaurie through flashbacks to 1833. She and her husband, Dr. LaLaurie, are hosting a party in hopes of finding suitable gentlemen for their daughters to marry. LaLaurie assumes the role typically occupied by the father. She presents each of her daughters and provides a tidbit of information to potential mates regarding her daughter's name, mannerisms, and skills. She begins with the oldest, Borquita (Marie Borja Delphine Lopez). Then, the middle daughter, Louise Marie Laure Blanque. Finally, the youngest Marie Louise Pauline Blanque, is announced with a disclaimer provided by LaLaurie. Her mother states that the talents of Pauline remain unknown currently. In an embarrassed attempt to save face, Pauline counters her mother's backhanded insult with a sexualized overture. Everyone engages in a bewildered chuckle, before the camera encircles a black male servant as if emphasizing the gaze placed upon him by LaLaurie's daughter, Pauline. Later that same evening, LaLaurie is interrupted from her nightly beauty ritual by her husband. She accompanies him only to find her daughter Pauline and Bastien, the male servant from the party, in Pauline's bedroom. Pauline admits to having intercourse with Bastien, who states that he was coerced. He adds that he belongs to another (3:1).

Upon hearing her daughter's admission, LaLaurie physically assaults her and instructs her to charge Bastien with rape. She orders Dr. LaLaurie to escort Bastien to her torture chamber. Later, a battered Bastien is shown chained to a wall as he awaits his cruel fate at the hands of LaLaurie. He is no longer attempting to plead his case and only protests when a young slave boy enters and places a hollowed bull's head upon his. At that moment, to LaLaurie's delight, Bastien becomes a Minotaur and she gets her revenge (3:1). This episode marks the beginning of the many encounters that LaLaurie will have with Laveau. Apparently, Laveau learns of the sadistic punishment Bastien, her lover, receives from LaLaurie and decides to avenge him. While LaLaurie is in her bedroom resuming her beauty regime, Laveau enters with a potion she states will control LaLaurie's husband's philandering and bring him emotionally back to her. After a brief discussion, LaLaurie takes the tonic from Laveau and drinks (3:6). Immediately LaLaurie convulses and falls to the floor. When she awakens, she witnesses an angry slave mob led by Laveau in the process of executing her husband and daughters. Although LaLaurie prays for death, she has been cursed with immortality by Laveau, who then buries LaLaurie alive. The reason for Laveau's punishment of LaLaurie is revealed in later episodes. Laveau was the woman to whom Bastien was betrothed (3:1; 3:3; 3:5; 3:6).

On *Coven*, the narratives of LaLaurie and Laveau are used to depict Southern Gothicism through representations of grotesque subject matters, acts of betrayal, gratuitous violence, and some form of decay. These actions overlap and are minutely distinguishable one from the other. For instance, the transformation of Bastien from man to beast borders on grotesque subject matter once he becomes a Minotaur. His conversion is the result of several acts of betrayal, gratuitous violence, and decay, which contributes to the chain of events that bring other characters into his narrative. After Bastien becomes a Minotaur, he is given the gift of immortality by Laveau. He is betrayed by both Pauline and LaLaurie for actions that he is forced to engage. His liaison with Pauline marks her decay as a daughter of a wealthy, white Creole family, which makes her unsuitable for marriage to a white man from a respectable family. Her punishment is physical assault and verbal aggression at the hands of her mother. The betrayal continues when Laveau learns of Bastien's fate and offers to help LaLaurie save her marriage. Instead, Laveau murders LaLaurie's husband and daughters, but spares Delphine and curses her with immortality. These actions contribute to Laveau's moral decay by demonstrating her ability to enact a ruthless level of human depravity in the name of justice.

The narratives of LaLaurie and Laveau, in *Coven*, situationally construct Southern Gothicism as thematic storylines and plot-points spanning across episodes. Through the use of alternative interpretations of these real-life figures' lived experiences, *Coven* transforms each into characters who challenge social norms for women of their time across intersections of race and class, hence, redefining Southern Gothicism as visual aesthetics and storied texts. This enables the creators and writers of *Coven* to use historical accounts and fictionalized versions of their lives and deaths to negotiate "spaces[s] marked by historical, symbolic, and social mediations" and to reappropriate physical spaces (e.g., LaLaurie Mansion; The French Quarter) (Giroux 347). By (re)imagining space/place in New Orleans history as fanciful reiterations, *Coven* recreates the lore and myths surrounding LaLaurie and Laveau as Southern Gothic narratives for contemporary audiences.

Dreaming Big: A Coven *Space/Place*

The return to nineteenth-century New Orleans on *Coven* removes the mysticism of the city from its historical foundation by placing it at the forefront of its storylines and plot-points. This transforms New Orleans from a space/place to that of a character with narratives of its own that interact with other characters as part of their overlapping discourses while remaining a distinctive locale portraying aspects of the Southern Gothic tradition. By (re)imagining the historical record regarding LaLaurie and Laveau, *Coven* depicts "Louisiana, and New Orléans in particular," as "sites [that] continue to play an important role in the Southern Gothic tradition" (Walsh 32) as past and present discourses. Using flashbacks and flash-forwards, the landscapes of New Orleans are continuously indistinguishable from the fantasy as each provides viewers with alternative visions and representations of this city. Each visit to the recent past "blends realism and grotesquery" (Boyd 41) while the present integrates "the murderous and the sublime" (Tunc 79), as physical, spiritual, and cultural aspects of New Orleans unremittingly evolve and adapt to *Coven*'s overlapping episodic narratives.

For instance, Madame LaLaurie arrives from Paris to New Orleans in 1830, accompanied by her husband, Dr. LaLaurie, and her three daughters. Once the family settles into their new dwelling, LaLaurie decides to cook chicken for dinner. She opts to slay the poultry herself and becomes entranced by the way that the blood vacates the body of the fowl. Her lust for blood is reignited when she finds an injured slave in her attic; pretending to offer him assistance LaLaurie allows him to bleed out until he loses consciousness. After he passes out, LaLaurie binds and gags the man in the attic, and beaming with delight at her conquest she states of her new home-place of New Orleans, "I think I'm going to like it here" (3:11).

The reinvention of the known lived experiences of LaLaurie on *Coven* removes her as a citizen of New Orleans by birth and replaces this fact by transplanting her and her family as French citizens seeking a new start in New Orleans. Although she appears to have no clear vision for her life in New Orleans, the audience becomes immediately privy to the underlying sinister reasons for LaLaurie's relocation to the new Americanized state of Louisiana. The return to nineteenth-century New Orleans on *Coven* removes the mysticism of the city from its historical foundation by locating it at the forefront of its storylines and plot-points. This transforms New Orleans from a space/place to that of a supporting character with narratives of its own that interact with other characters as part of their discourses while remaining a distinctive locale portraying traits of the Southern Gothic tradition, each of which contributes to the use of "grotesque characters, scenes, and situations" (Botting 79) marred by violence, betrayal, and decay (Tunc 80). This contributes to the flow of the show as flashbacks and flash-forwards are used to illustrate the significance of space/place in *Coven*'s (re)imagining of New Orleans history and fantasy through the characters of LaLaurie and Laveau.

Marie Laveau, a native daughter of New Orleans, became the reigning Queen of Vodou during the nineteenth century. She used her knowledge of Vodou to gain notoriety and considerable influence over many of the affluent families in the city. In addition to her thriving business, Laveau publicly performed Vodou ceremonial rites on Sundays in Congo Square and on Bayou St. Jean (Fandrich 196; Ward 34). Laveau is believed to have created a network of spies that provided her with sensitive information that she used as blackmail material. It is worth mentioning that LaLaurie and Laveau were parishioners of St. Louis Cathedral; therefore, a meeting between the two was possible, which brings their story full circle on *Coven* (Fandrich 104; Ward 20). For example, the flashback of Laveau entering LaLaurie's bedroom uninvited or announced suggests a certain degree of familiarity between these characters (3:1; 3:5; 3:6). The willingness of LaLaurie to accept assistance from Laveau implies that the former had knowledge or experiences with Laveau's gifts or ability to deliver on her promises. Both women were born in or near New Orleans and as adults each resided near one another. They frequented the same church for services and may have traveled to varying degrees in the same social circles. The consensus that *Coven* brings to the small screen is that Laveau shared much of the same political clout that LaLaurie did. It also suggests that each woman used their considerable influence to redefine space/place in New Orleans as both a physical and ideological location. Each of their narratives of lived experience intertextually redefined the landscape of nineteenth-century New Orleans by reclaiming or renaming the architecture surrounding the narratives of both LaLaurie and Laveau.

Intertextuality or Doubling: LaLaurie and Laveau

The statement that sometimes truth is stranger than fiction centralizes *Coven*'s use of intertextuality to connect the narratives of LaLaurie and Laveau to one another and the larger society. The writers of *Coven* use "bits and pieces" of the real lives and mythology of LaLaurie and Laveau to dramatize their history by stitching together alternative explanations for their actions on the television show (Porter 36). These women were towering figures of nineteenth-century New Orleans who were also pillars of their communities. Each employed a brand of retribution that contributed to their immortalization and their downfall. Kum Kum Sangari suggests that transverse perspectives are often employed to integrate fiction and reality using symbolism, metaphors, and other literary techniques to narratives. Such tales are used to facilitate discourses and to connect the lived experiences of individuals across time and space. In the case of LaLaurie, allegations of cruelty towards her slaves played a role, first in her slaves being taken and resold, then culminating with a fire at her residence, which exposed her depravity to the upper echelon of society.

Whereas the historical Laveau's commercialization of Vodou and her willingness to embrace practitioners of all races and classes made her a social pariah, *Coven* paints a different scenario by suggesting that LaLaurie and Laveau had been previously acquainted, but only to a superficial extent. The interactions between LaLaurie and Laveau are facilitated by the actions of LaLaurie's younger daughter, Pauline, the night of the party. The gala is in full swing as the camera pans the room and encircles Bastien. His inability to refuse the advances of Pauline set the narratives of LaLaurie and Laveau on a collision course that comes to a head in the twenty-first century. LaLaurie fled New Orleans s to France in 1834 but returned to the city in 1842 and lived in a home near the LaLaurie Mansion until her death in the 1850s (Love and Shannon 48). On *Coven*, she is portrayed as Cajun; however, she was in fact a white, Creole woman (21). The stories surrounding the treatment of her slaves have, over the years, been widely exaggerated; documentation of the actual torture, mutilation, and murder of her slaves has yet to be uncovered. For instance, Bastien was a real-life slave of LaLaurie (Long 114; Heinan 9). She inherited him upon the death of her second husband Jacques Blanque. He served in the LaLaurie home as coachman and houseman. It is believed that he was instrumental in saving LaLaurie from the wrath of the angry mob on April 10, 1834. There are accounts that state that Bastien was severely punished for his role in LaLaurie's escape. But archival records show that Bastien survived LaLaurie's desertion, and he was sold twice before being manumitted years later (Long 114).

Moreover, LaLaurie is portrayed as a robust, portly woman with a distinctly southern accent although she was reputed to have been French on *Coven*. Instead, she was a "gracefully built," thin woman of uncommon beauty (Long 173). She loved to throw elaborate parties and was extremely social. There are documents that she filed to manumit several of her slaves. She had five children by the time she met Dr. LaLaurie. She met her last husband through relatives, but they did not marry until after the birth of their son (53). Her husband, Dr. LaLaurie, is shown to be a much older man on *Coven*, when he was much younger than the twice-widowed LaLaurie. Additionally, LaLaurie was forty-two and Dr. LaLaurie a mere twenty-six. He is portrayed on *Coven* as a philanderer and the father of a child with a house-servant. Appalled by her husband's actions, LaLaurie murders the child and uses his blood to create her beauty balm. She invites the slain child's mother to her bedroom to assist her with her regimen. LaLaurie asks her to guess the ingredients, which the house-servant does. The servant realizes that the blood is that of her son and commits suicide (3:7). The correlating myth is that a ten-year-old girl named Leah was brushing LaLaurie's hair and inadvertently pulled a tangled strand. An enraged LaLaurie brandishing a whip gave chase which led to the girl's death (Love and Shannon 13). Over time, this tale has been retold with new and more elaborate details added as each generation placed their interpretation on the narratives of LaLaurie. Nonetheless, there is no evidence that Dr. LaLaurie engaged in such behavior while living in the home of LaLaurie.

A common thread linking LaLaurie and Laveau is Bastien; nevertheless, the reality is that Laveau helped slaves in a variety of ways such as ministering and care giving. But there is no definitive proof that she had taken one as her lover or sought to avenge their untimely deaths. Although, in *Coven*, Bastien is the lover of Laveau, there is no documentation or oral accounts of either knowing the other existed. The men who were known to have had a relationship with Laveau were her late husband Jacques Paris and her common-law spouse Christophe Glapion (Fandrich 155, 157). There were several women living in New Orleans with the name Marie Laveau (Fandrich 177). It is rumored that one of her surviving daughters used the name Marie Laveau to continue to cash in on the popularity of her mother. The tradition of naming daughters after their mother was popular during the nineteenth century and may have contributed to myths of Laveau's immortality. On the other hand, there were women who borrowed the name Marie Laveau for financial gain. Laveau has been describe as a statuesque, fair-complexioned woman with red undertones (Fandrich 154; Ward 19). She is reported to have had long, black hair which she kept covered by a *tignon* as per the law governing free women of color (Fandrich 186; Ward 19).

As stories of her immortality and reported sightings of Laveau, in the years following her death, began circulating, her hair texture became closely associated with that of her African ancestors and her complexion was darkened to deep brown. Her spiritual gifts and practice of Vodou were reappropriated to include elements of hoodoo, witchcraft, and other occult practices. Her appearance on *Coven* is comprised of long braids, modern clothing, and an attitude to match, as well as a (re)imagining of the story of "The Devil and Daniel Webster" (1937). In this short story, the protagonist (Jabez Stone) sold his soul to the Devil in exchange for seven years of material wealth. At the end of the contract, the Devil arrives to claim Mr. Stone's soul, but finds Mr. Webster. The story ends with the Devil leaving without the soul of Mr. Stone. Similarly, Laveau strikes a deal with Papa Legba, the Vodou *lwas* or deity of the spiritual crossroads. She is granted immortality in exchange for the sacrificial offering of innocent blood. If she fails or refuses to comply, Papa Legba receives her soul. It is this agreement with Papa Legba that gives her the ability to avenge Bastien, to punish LaLaurie, and to continue to live for over a century. But it is also Laveau's agreement with Papa Legba that leads to the death of her first-born child and her eternal damnation (3:10; 3:12). The use of intertextuality on *Coven* situates the narratives of LaLaurie and Laveau as a set of interrelated events that contribute to each taking the action they deem appropriate to the situation. The center of their conflict begins with Bastien and ends with Laveau breaking her contract with Papa Legba. Through their desire for revenge and the pleasure derived from inflicting punishment upon the other, both LaLaurie and Laveau create narratives on *Coven* that perpetuate the involvement of other characters as either their co-conspirator or cohort agitators.

Conclusion

Many of the events portrayed on *Coven* are rooted in the real-life narratives of Madame Delphine LaLaurie and Marie Laveau. Each was born in New Orleans and lived in the French Quarter at various points in their lives. Their myths and legends continue to fascinate new audiences and researchers, as each endeavor to piece together the lives and deaths of these remarkable women. Not only does *Coven* provide a contemporary retelling of the facts and fictions surrounding LaLaurie and Laveau, but it also opens possibilities for undocumented exchanges between these women. Drawing on Southern Gothicism, the writers of *Coven* create narratives that intertextually center New Orleans as the foundation for LaLaurie and Laveau's narratives by (re)imagining this city as an evolving space/place. The use of flashbacks and flash-forwards aid in the development of the backstories of LaLaurie and Laveau while presenting alternative explanations for their lived experiences. Their relationship begins with acts of betrayal and gratuitous violence coupled with grotesque actions and decay (moral, physical), as each relies on the cultural heritage and social customs of the nineteenth century to redefine their past and retell their present (Tunc 80).

The storylines and plot-points of *Coven* integrate pieces of LaLaurie's and Laveau's narratives that diverge from traditional retellings. LaLaurie's life is downplayed from that of a wealthy, independent, thrice-married woman with six children to that of a jealous, aging, and insecure woman with sadistic tendencies. She is further reduced from her former glory by an immortality curse placed upon her by Marie Laveau. Bassett's portrayal of Laveau creates a humanized version of a real-world woman whose stories of her extraordinary powers continue to lure individuals to her grave in hopes of divine intervention. Together, their blended tales on *Coven* provide alternative explanations for many of their publicized transgressions as well as their private internal conflicts.

WORKS CITED

Banco, Lindsey Michael. "The 'Peculiar Glare of Recognition': Drunkenness and the Southern Gothic in Flannery O'Conner's *The Violent Bear It Away*." *Gothic Studies Text*, vol. 11, no. 2, 2009, pp. 63–71.
Botting, Fred. *Gothic*. Routledge, 1996.
Boyd, Molly. "Rural Identity in the Southern Gothic Novels of Mark Steadman." *Studies in The Literary Imagination*, vol. 27, no. 2, 1994, pp. 41–56.
Brunage, W. Fitzhugh. "The Long Shadow of Torture in the American South." *The Oxford Handbook of Literature of the U.S. South*, edited by Fred Hobson and Barbara Ladd, Oxford UP, 2016, pp. 114–37.
Davison, Carol Margaret. "Haunted House/Haunted Heroine: Female Gothic Closets in 'The Yellow Wallpaper.'" *Women's Studies*, no. 33, 2004, pp. 47–75.
Fandrich, Ina J. *The Mysterious Voodoo Queen, Marie Laveaux: A Study of Powerful Female Leadership in Nineteenth Century New Orleans*. Routledge, 2005.
Giroux, Henry A. "Public Pedagogy as Cultural Politics: Stuart Hall and the Crisis of Culture." *Cultural Studies*, vol. 14, no. 2, 2000, pp. 341–60.

Heinan, T. R. *L'Immortalite: Madame LaLaurie and the Voodoo Queen*. Nonius LLC, 2012
Long, Carolyn Morrow. *A New Orleans Voudou Priestess: The Legend and Reality of Marie Laveau*. UP of Florida, 2006.
Love, Victoria Cosner, and Lorelei Shannon. *Mad Madame Lalaurie: New Orleans's Most Famous Murderess Revealed*. The History Press, 2011.
Milione, Anna. "Haunted Castles and Premature Burials: The Cure's *Faith*, Goth Subculture and the Gothic Literary Tradition." *The Gothic: Probing the Boundaries*, edited by Eoghain Hamilton, Oxford: Inter-Disciplinary Press, 2010, pp. 157–69.
Porter, James E. "Intertextuality and the Discourse Community." *Rhetoric Review*, vol. 5, no.1, 1986, pp. 34–47.
Sangari, Kum Kum. "The Politics of the Possible." *Cultural Critique*, no. 7, 1987, pp. 157–86.
Smith, Philip. "Re-visioning Romantic-Era Gothicism: An Introduction to Key Works and Themes in the Study of H. P. Lovecraft." *Literature Compass*, vol. 8, no. 11, 2011, pp. 830–39.
Tunc, Tanfer Emin. "Caroline Gordon's Ghosts: The Women on the Porch as Southern Gothic Literature." *The Southern Literary Journal*, vol. 46, no. 1, 2013, pp. 78–95.
Walsh, Christopher J. "'Dark Legacy': Gothic Ruptures in Southern Literature." *Critical Insights: Southern Gothic Literature*, edited by Jay Ellis, Salem Press, 2013, pp. 19–34.
Ward, Martha. *Voodoo Queen: The Spirited Lives of Marie Laveau*. UP of Mississippi, 2004.

Apocalypse and the Devil We Are

Leverett Butts

> "[I]f the Devil doesn't exist, but man has created him, he has created him in his own image and likeness."—Feodor Dostoevsky, The Brothers Karamazov

    American Horror Story's eighth season strays significantly from the anthology format it set up for its previous seasons. The stories of previous seasons remained separate from the others, despite the occasional crossover character (*Asylum*'s Pepper appearing in *Freak Show*, *Coven*'s Queenie checking into *Hotel*'s Hotel Cortez, and *Freak Show*'s Twisty the Clown appearing throughout *Cult*, just to name a few). However, by the end of the third episode, it becomes clear that *Apocalypse*, the eighth season's story, is a direct sequel to both the third season's story, *Coven*, and the final scene of first season's *Murder House*.

    The first three episodes of *Apocalypse* focus on the aftermath of a nuclear holocaust in 2021 that wipes out most of humanity and forces the survivors to either live in underground shelters or suffer the effects of radiation poisoning on the earth's surface. While this seems to follow the series' anthology pattern, it is clear by the end of the third episode that *Apocalypse* is, in fact, a direct sequel to *Coven*. The rest of the season flashes back to 2018 and follows the story of Michael Langdon—the son of *Murder House*'s Vivian Harmon and Tate Langdon born at the end of the first season—who discovers that he is the Antichrist, as he struggles to find his place in the world and discover how to end it. Meanwhile in New Orleans, Cordelia Goode, the Supreme witch, and her coven attempt to learn as much as possible about Michael and his weaknesses in order to either prevent the apocalypse or reverse it.

    Michael Langdon, himself, represents another departure from most of *AHS*' seasons in that he is the first monster based on a pre-existing literary text. *AHS* has had many archetypal monsters: ghosts, aliens, witches, serial killers, and vampires. However, none of these have been the creations of previous works. There may be vampires in *Hotel*, for instance, but none of them are Dracula or Elizabeth Bathory (though the Countess is almost certainly inspired by her), and while the ghosts of serial killers that gather every Halloween at the Hotel Cortez are indeed historical figures, they are neither major characters nor famous for being ghosts outside of the continuity of the television show. Similarly, *Coven* features a character, Kyle Spencer, created from the reanimated body parts of several dead fraternity brothers, but despite his resemblance to Mary Shelley's famous monster, he is clearly not the creation of Dr. Frankenstein.

Michael Langdon, though, is not simply a demon or an evil mastermind set on world domination, but the literal Antichrist. He is a curious choice, however, as he does not fit the typical portrayal of the Antichrist in either popular culture or literature. The usual depiction of the Antichrist involves a man (usually middle-aged or older) of extreme confidence, unquestionable power, and undeniable malevolence. He may, like *The Omen*'s Damien Thorne or Stephen King's Randall Flagg, appear charming on the surface, or, like Agares from James Blish's novel *The Devil's Day*, overtly sinister. Michael, on the other hand, is none of these things. Michael Langdon is a millennial Antichrist, struggling to find his way in the world and almost completely reliant on others. He is indecisive, constantly complaining that no one will tell him what to do next. Rather than evil, he is simply petty, harming only those whom he perceives as disrespecting or hurting him without consideration for any of the grand schemes one might expect from an Antichrist. He vacillates between wanting to be good and wishing to fulfill his destiny as the son of Satan. However, as a metaphor for modern day cultural problems, Michael perfectly exemplifies not only the negative stereotypes of younger generations, but the damage done by older generations when they minimize the concerns of the youth.

Many theologians link the Antichrist with "the beast that comes up from the abyss" as described in Revelations 11:7 ("Antichrist"). The most obvious indication that Michael is the Antichrist is that he literally transforms into such a beast when he loses control of himself. When Mallory, a witch who has been given a new personality to hide her nature from Michael, psychically attacks him during his interview with her in Outpost Three, Michael's face instantly transforms into a beastly visage resembling a mix of humanoid, simian, and canine features (8:3; 8:10). As a teenager, he transforms into this beast when he destroys the souls of the new residents of Murder House (8:6). He appears to Cordelia in this form during her apocalyptic vision, and the Warlock John Henry Moore witnesses Michael's beast form for just an instant after Michael receives the blessings of protection before testing his magical powers (8:5). Finally, he transforms in front of Mutt and Jeff, two robotics engineers, in order to convince them he is the Antichrist (8:8). There are, however, more significant signs of Michael's role as Antichrist.

The Antichrist appears in several places in the New Testament, primarily in the letters of St. John, where it is described as both a spiritual force and an individual that denies both God and Jesus (*The New International Version*, I John 4:3; II John 7). A similar figure, however, appears in the Gospel of Matthew as a one of many "false messiahs and false prophets [who] will appear and perform great signs and wonders" (Matt. 24:24). Finally, while no New Testament author other than John employs the term "Antichrist," most interpreters equate Paul's "man of lawlessness" who "will come to do the work of Satan with counterfeit power and signs and miracles" with both John's Antichrist and the aforementioned beast of Revelations (II Thes. 2:3–9).

During the first three episodes of *Apocalypse*, Michael certainly seems to fit the biblical portrayal of the Antichrist, the lawless man. Like the man of lawlessness who "will exalt himself over everything" (II Thes. 2:4), Michael arrives at Outpost Three, the underground fallout shelter that provides the primary setting, like a literal lord. He rides through the radiation-ravaged land in a Victorian carriage drawn by two black stallions. Beneath his radiation suit, Michael dresses like royalty wearing a royal purple frock coat and an imperial red ascot. While his clothing implies royalty, Michael's flowing hair suggests a specific line of kings, the long-haired Merovingians of medieval France. This dynasty of kings is particularly important here since, according to a conspiracy theory most famously elaborated by authors Michael Baigent, Richard Leigh, and Henry Lincoln in their two pseudo-historical books, *Holy Blood, Holy Grail* and *The Messianic Legacy*, and forming the central plot of Dan Brown's best-selling novel *The Da Vinci Code*, the Merovingians represent the living bloodline of Jesus Christ, being the descendants of His children by Mary Magdalene. Linking Michael Langdon to what many consider one of the most "magnificent" hoaxes of the twentieth century underscores his role as a false savior ("The Secret of the Priory of Sion").

That he has come to declare himself a savior of the elect is apparent from his first words. After informing Wilhemina Venable, the leader of Outpost Three, that half the outposts have been overrun by mutated scavengers and that the others are expected to fall soon, he announces that he has come "to evaluate the people here and select the ones most worthy of survival" (8:1). However, Michael's criteria for survival seem morally questionable at best as he uses his ability to "see in to the dark places people desperately try to keep hidden" to elicit the worst tendencies from those he interviews: he foments Mr. Gallant's anger toward his grandmother, manipulates him into killing her, and ultimately helps cover up her murder (8:2; 8:3). Similarly, he undermines Venable's authority and tacitly encourages Timothy and Emily to continue their illicit affair, referring to both this affair and Gallant's murder of his grandmother as "minor infractions" of frivolous rules before declaring all three "viable" candidates for salvation with "nothing to worry about" (8:3).

According to Matthew, another quality of the false messiah will be his performance of "great signs and wonders" (Matt. 24:24). The most obvious signs of Michael's role as Antichrist are the murder of crows that gathers around whichever house he inhabits, the "sweltering" heat that surrounds him, and his birthmark of three sixes behind his ear closely resembling and in the same place as the birthmark of Damien Thorne, perhaps the most famous cinematic Antichrist, in *The Omen* films (8:6). During the flashback episodes recounting Michael's rise, we see him perform many such "miracles." He kills a police officer with his mind, bringing him to the attention of The Hawthorne School for Exceptional Young Men, a school for warlocks and the male counterpart to Miss Robichaux's Academy for Exceptional Young Ladies; more importantly, during his trials here to determine whether he is as strong as the witches' Supreme, Michael astonishes his instructors when he not only locates a book hidden within a mirror, but also reaches into the mirror and retrieves it, effortlessly teleports about the examination room, and finally conjures a blizzard in the room, nearly killing one of the instructors (8:4).

Most importantly, though, is Michael's ability to complete The Seven Wonders, the ultimate test for witches to determine the next Supreme. The test of the Seven Wonders consists of seven feats of magic considered "so advanced, each pushes the boundaries of craft into art": Telekinesis, the ability to move objects with one's mind; Concilium, the ability to impose one's will on another; Pyrokinesis, the ability to create and control fire with one's mind; Divination, the ability to gain direct knowledge of an object, person, location, or event through means other than one's physical senses; Transmutation, the ability to move instantly from space to another without occupying the space between; Vitalum Vitalis, the ability to bring back the dead; and Descensum, the ability to descend to and return from the afterlife (3:12). During this trial, a witch must perform these seven most difficult acts of magic without perishing. Michael passes these trials easily. He even manages to outshine Cordelia Goode, the current Supreme, by saving her former students long since believed lost to her: rescuing Queenie from her imprisonment in Hotel Cortez and bringing Madison Montgomery back from the dead in order to prove to Cordelia he is capable of attempting the

Seven Wonders (8:4), and by returning Misty Day from Hell as part of his Descensum trial (8:5).

Further confirming Michael's role as Antichrist is the string of "unspeakable acts" he commits growing up: killing and mutilating innumerable insects and small animals before slitting his sitter's throat, attempting to strangle his grandmother, and finally slaughtering a priest brought in to intercede (8:6). As a teenager, he develops the ability to erase spirits from existence after murdering the two new owners of Murder House (8:6). After Madison Montgomery and the warlock Behold Chablis question the spirits of Murder House about Michael's history, and before Vivian Harmon, Michael's mother, tells of her failed attempt to destroy Michael, she directly links her son to the Antichrist. "What you are dealing with here is not just evil," she explains, "Michael is not just a bad witch for you to exterminate." By way of explanation, she then paraphrases Revelations 13:1–10: "Then I saw a beast with ten horns and seven heads rising out of the sea, and all who dwell upon the earth shall worship him."

Michael is, then, undoubtedly the Antichrist: he is clearly evil and surrounded by signs and portents of doom, he brings about the end of the world, and he sets himself up as a false savior. However, he is also, curiously, incompetent. Cordelia Goode even refers to him as "pathetic" and "a sad, scared little boy," and this seems not too far from the mark (8:10). Michael spends much of the years preceding the apocalypse bemoaning his own lack of direction and engaged in an ineffective quest to find someone to tell him how to be the Antichrist and what to do next. Without the assistance of a Satanic cult and two hedonistic robotics engineers, it seems unlikely that Michael, the literal son of Satan, would be able to accomplish the end of the world.

This seems a puzzling depiction of the Antichrist, a being that will not only succeed in destroying the world, but should arguably be the most fearsome embodiment of evil in Western literature. Perhaps historian Jeffrey Burton Russell can provide an explanation for this seemingly incongruous depiction. Russell is most well known for his five-volume history of the concept of the devil: *The Devil: Perceptions of Evil from Antiquity to Primitive Christianity*, *Satan: The Early Christian Tradition*, *Lucifer: The Devil in the Middle Ages*, *Mephistopheles: The Devil in the Modern World*, and *The Prince of Darkness: Radical Evil and the Power of Good in History*. Though ostensibly a history of the devil, Russell explains early in the first volume that he employs "the term 'the Devil,' as opposed to Satan, to designate the personification of evil found in a variety of cultures" (*The Devil* 34). His series, then, may also be read as an examination of the history of evil, as implied by Russell's quoting Jung: "If you regard the principle of evil as a reality you can just as well call it the devil" (33). Given that for many Christians, "the difference between Satan and the Antichrist is often blurred" and their respective roles "almost indistinguishable" (*Satan* 31, 88), one may learn just as much from a culture's representation of the former as the latter.

The study of each culture's image of the devil reveals much about what that culture fears most. In many early monist cultures, for example, evil and divinity were simply opposing sides of the same entity. "The study of the Devil," writes Russell, "indicates that historically, he is a manifestation of the divine, a part of the deity" (*The Devil* 31–32). This further implies both a love and a fear of god, who is responsible not only for the blessings of one's life but for the misfortunes, not simply the punishments for transgressions that one may expect from a parent-like god in its attempt to instruct its creation on right action, but also for the misfortunes of capricious fate, the evils that befall one for no reason.

Dualist cultures, such as the Judeo-Christian-Islam tradition, view evil as separate from divinity. Evil exists in opposition to, not complementary of, grace. It is with dualism, with its view of the devil as a separate entity from the god, that representations of evil become more complex, and more relevant to our purpose. Since Christianity is by its nature a dualist theology, each era's representation of evil, whether as devil or Antichrist, become significant to understanding that era's greatest fears. For example, in early Christian thought, the Antichrist is often depicted as a human tyrant, based "more specifically, upon more recent political enemies of the Jewish people, such as Antiochus Epiphanes, Nero, and Caligula" (243), implying here not only a distinction between divine good and worldly evil, but linking the ultimate image of evil to the tyranny of a currently invading political force.

By the Middle Ages, representations of the Antichrist begin to reflect prejudices more than political anxiety. Christian tradition of the fifth century depicted the Antichrist as the literal son of the devil and, along with the "Evil Spirit," part of an unholy "trinity of corruption" (*Satan* 116 n25), establishing a blood link between Satan and the Antichrist "with heretics, Jews, and other 'infidels'" (*The Devil* 257). Thus Chaucer, in "The Prioress' Tale," claims that the Antichrist will be "a Jew of the Tribe of Dan" (*Lucifer* 84), while many medieval Catholics consider the antipope Clement III as the Antichrist's "lackey" (161). During the Protestant Reformation, Martin Luther goes so far as to claim that the pope is the literal Antichrist: "I regard the see of Rome as possessed by Satan and as the throne of Antichrist" (qtd. in *Mephistopheles* 34). In short, from the Middle Ages and well into the Protestant Reformation, ultimate evil becomes a personification of the demographics, or at least the most negative qualities of the demographics, one despises.

More contemporary depictions of the Antichrist turn inward, making the Antichrist one of us and highlighting negative aspects of Western culture. Adolf Hitler is reincarnated as the Antichrist in Robert Van Kampen's 1997 novel, *The Fourth Reich*, bringing the medieval Christian bigotry that cast Jews as the Antichrist full circle by making that very racism the defining quality of the modern Antichrist. In Gore Vidal's 1953 novel, *Messiah*, the fictional religion known as Cavism, named after its founder John Cave, completely eradicates Christianity, thus suggesting that religion, or religious fervor, may itself be the Antichrist. Similarly, the ape Shift, from C.S. Lewis' *The Chronicles of Narnia*, who represents the Antichrist in Narnian cosmology, may also be read as a critique of totalitarian theocracy, which prevents man from exercising his God-given free will.

Perhaps the most famous of the modern depictions of the Antichrist is Damien Thorn, the antagonist of the first three films of *The Omen* franchise. Damien Thorn, adopted son of a former U.S. Ambassador to England and only living heir to, and CEO of, his uncle's company, Thorn Industries (having murdered or sanctioned the murder of his entire family), positions himself to be the new ambassador to England, where he believes the second Christ-child will soon be born and where he plans to kill the child and begin his own reign over the world, bringing about a permanent Armageddon by preventing Christ's return. Given Damien's role as both a businessman and a politician, one may thus read the Antichrist of *The Omen* as critiquing the dangers inherent in mixing private industrialism with politics.

If we accept that throughout history, depictions of evil, including the Antichrist, are meant to represent that culture or era's greatest dangers or fears, how does this relate to *AHS*' Michael Langdon? After all, for the bulk of *Apocalypse*, Michael seems more pitiable than perilous. Yes, he ultimately brings about the end of the world, but only through the assistance of more competent allies. He is clearly incapable of doing it alone. So what supposed societal ill does Michael represent?

Michael seems to encapsulate many of the negative stereotypes of the millennial generation. Technically Michael belongs to Generation Z, those born between the mid-nineties and the mid-2000s, having been born in 2011 and thus only ten years old at the time of *Apocalypse*. However, due to his demonic nature, he physically ages a decade over night, and thus appears to belong to the millennial generation (8:6). As an adult, Michael seems to embody most of the meme-worthy negative stereotypes lobbied against millennials: technology addiction, a sullen sense of entitlement, a lack of initiative, and an inability to act independently.

Michael seems tied to his technology. As an adolescent, Michael constantly plays video games; most notably, after murdering the priest, Michael returns to his gaming console and is happily playing when his grandmother, Constance, enters to discover the gruesome sight bleeding into the carpet next to him (8:6). In Outpost Three, Michael leaves his laptop on and open to his email server even when he is not in the room, implying that he wants the internet at his disposal without having to wait to boot his computer or log in, allowing two residents to read his confidential messages and instigate a rebellion (8:2). He hires two robotics engineers to recreate his slain mother figure/mentor, Miriam Mead, which he treats with as much love and admiration as he did her living counterpart (8:8).

Michael also seems to wallow in a kind of querulous entitlement. Whenever he faces negative consequences for his actions he seems to revert to a whining child and blames everyone but himself: when Constance commits suicide after Michael attempts to strangle her for telling him what to do and succeeds in murdering the priest, Michael weeps over the betrayal and adds her to the list of everyone who has ever, in his opinion, abandoned him (8:6). Indeed, his first action whenever he is faced with a setback is first to weep and whine. He weeps when he confronts Cordelia after Miriam Mead is burned at the stake and blames Cordelia for destroying the one person who ever loved him, without considering the reason Ms. Mead was executed (8:8).

More importantly, however, is Michael's lack of initiative and inability to think for himself. In the months between losing his mentor and instigating a nuclear holocaust, Michael wanders aimlessly about Southern California. While he knows he is the Antichrist and the son of Satan, he seems unable to act on his own to bring about prophecy. He spends four days in the forest begging his father to reveal himself and tell him what he needs to do next. "What do you want from me?" he whines into the air before falling to his knees and once again weeping, "What am I supposed to do? What the fuck am I supposed to do?" (8:8). Later, even after he reveals himself to be the Antichrist to a Satanic congregation, he loses patience with the members asking him for guidance: "Everyone keeps telling me I'm special, that I'm the only one who can bring about the end times, but nobody gave me a fucking instruction manual" (8:8).

This desire for external guidance is a recurring theme for Michael. When asked about his plan for world domination, Michael falls back on the plot of *The Omen III*: "I could start out as an ambassador and then I'd become one of the president's most trusted advisors" (8:9). When confronted with the idiocy of making plans based on 1970s horror movies, Michael grows frustrated: "Well, I don't know where else to look," he sighs. "It's not like there is a bunch of reference material on how to be the Antichrist" (8:9). It isn't until Mutt and Jeff introduce him to the Book of Revelations that Michael begins to find his way. Even here, though, Michael has not moved into any kind of self-motivation or personal sense of direction; he has simply found a better instruction manual than *The Omen*.

It would seem *AHS* is implying through its portrayal of the Antichrist in *Apocalypse* that the greatest evil facing the world today is the millennial. However, a closer look reveals something a little more problematic: Michael may not be truly evil. Throughout his life, he has tried to be good despite his demonic nature. Michael grows into his role, not because of his nature, but because those who undertake to nurture him either give up on him or use him toward their own ends. Constance admits to Behold and Madison that Michael was a "beautiful child with such a cheerful disposition" and that he left his kills for her as "presents, because he loved me" (8:6). Instead of teaching him better ways to express his love, Constance simply allows him to continue because she knows "exactly what evolutionary tree he was shimmying up" and she has long since decided that she "was put on this earth to raise the monsters" (8:6). Rather than teach Michael to be different, then, Constance simply accepts that he is a monster and does nothing to nurture the better part of his soul.

Ben Harmon, on the other hand, attempts to nurture Michael and lead him towards goodness after Michael finds Constance dead and, for the first and only time in the series, expresses regret and accepts that "it's all [his] fault" (8:6). Ben admits that Michael "wanted to be good, desperately," and together the two of them make progress toward that goal until Tate Langdon, Michael's biological father, rejects him by claiming "not even I could create something as monstrous, as evil, as you." After this rejection leads to Michael's murder and annihilation of the new residents, Ben turns his back on Michael, abandoning him: "I never could have helped you," he declares, despite the previous evidence to the contrary. "It was foolish to try" (8:6).

The Satanists Anton LaVey, Miriam Mead, and later Madelyn, of course, do nothing to curb Michael's tendencies since, as the son of Satan, Michael represents the best path to curry favor with his father. Similarly, Mutt and Jeff see Michael as the Antichrist and thus quickest and easiest way to "put an end to all this bullshit [and] burn this motherfucker to the ground" (8:9).

In short, each of Michael's elders seems to care only about his or her own self-interest: Constance wants peace, so she makes no attempt to change Michael. The Satanists want power, and Mutt and Jeff want destruction, and Michael's nature is the surest guarantee of those things. Even Ben, who is supposed to be a respected psychologist, declares Michael hopeless because what Ben really wanted out of his relationship with the boy was to fill the void in himself left by the stagnation of death:

> The more time I spent with him, the more I began to feel like a father to this boy [Ben explains]. Everything in this house was dead: my wife, my baby was never going to

grow up, Violet [Ben's daughter who killed herself in *Murder House*] was never going to get married, but Michael was alive, the only light to come out of all this. I wanted to give him everything [8:6].

All of this begs the question: Does Michael become the Antichrist because he is Satan's son or because those entrusted with his care expect him to be evil and thus do little or nothing to show him a better way?

That Michael is not inherently evil seems obvious. Constance recognized his love for her. Ben could read "in his eyes" how much Michael yearns to be good. Even after Michael's path seems set, after he has accepted his role as Antichrist and become determined to destroy the world, Cordelia recognizes the good in him: "There's humanity in you. I see it. If you come with me, maybe we can find it," she tells him as he mourns the death of Miriam Mead (8:8).

Later, as Michael waits for four days in the forest for Satan to instruct him, God twice sends emissaries to him. First a little girl offers him an apple (the biblical symbol of knowledge of good and evil), and when Michael tells her he must talk to his father, she replies, "You don't have to do anything. All are welcome. Come to the light." After Michael claims to have failed in his mission, God sends an angel to assure Michael that "God loves you" (8:8). If Michael were truly irredeemable, if his status as Antichrist were out of his control and an integral part of his nature, it seems unlikely that God would send emissaries to sway him to the light.

In fact, while Michael is clearly the son of Satan, it is not at all clear that he is the Antichrist. He only takes on the mantle because everyone around him, both the good and the bad, claim he is the Antichrist, and he is very seldom presented with evidence to the contrary. Matthew Boedy, in his book *Speaking of Evil: Rhetoric and the Responsibility to and for Language*, critiques humanity's habit of "overnaming." Where naming simply signifies an object or idea, overnaming solidifies the signified, preventing a concept from evolving and forcing it to adhere strictly to our own understanding of it in order to comprehend the totality of existence. Thus when we overname something evil, we then claim to have direct knowledge of its evil nature simply because it seems to fit our preconceived ideas about other evil things: "In other words, in overnaming, we claim a universal and timeless certainty to the divide of good and evil" (xiii). Thus, Michael is the Antichrist literally because everyone around him says he is. Despite the evidence of "humanity in [him]," as the child of Satan, the world expects him to be the Antichrist, and he is quite literally forced into the role.

Michael himself is clearly not the ultimate evil of *Apocalypse*. Indeed, once his backstory is told, Michael seems much more sympathetic than his appearance after the apocalypse would imply. He is a young man alone in the world looking for guidance. Sadly, even the witches Cordelia leads ultimately fail to recognize this. In order to prevent the apocalypse, Mallory, one of Cordelia's students and her heir apparent as Supreme, goes back in time to prevent Michael's rise. She arrives at an important turning point in Michael's life: shortly after his overnight aging when Constance discovers his murder of the priest and rejects him. Instead of using this as an opportunity to shepherd the confused young man to a better future, Mallory repeatedly runs him over with an SUV, killing him.

Perhaps what Michael's portrayal implies, then, is that the greatest evil facing society in this era is not the millennial, but humanity's habit of forcing the younger generations into preconceived categories and dismissing them as hopeless instead of listening to their concerns and helping them to reach their own potential.

Works Cited

"Antichrist." *Illustrated Dictionary & Concordance of the Bible*, Edited by Geoffrey Wigoder, et al., G.G. The Jerusalem Publishing House Ltd, 1986, p. 97.
Baigent, Michael, et al. *Holy Blood, Holy Grail*. Cape, 1982.
_____. *The Messianic Legacy*. Holt, 1987.
The Bible: New International Version, Hodder & Stoughton, 1989.
Blish, James. *The Devil's Day*. Baen, 1990.
Boedy, Matthew. *Speaking of Evil: Rhetoric and the Responsibility to and for Language*. Lexington Books, 2018.
Brown, Dan. *The Da Vinci Code: A Novel*. Doubleday, 2003.
Damien: The Omen II. Directed by Don Taylor, 20th Century Fox, 1978.
Dostoyevsky, Fyodor. *Brothers Karamazov*. Penguin Books Ltd, 2003.
Kampen, Robert Van. *The Fourth Reich*. Revell, 1997.
Lewis, C. S. *The Chronicles of Narnia*. HarperCollins USA, 2005.
The Omen. Directed by Richard Donner, 20th Century Fox, 1976.
The Omen III: The Final Conflict. Directed by Graham Baker, 20th Century Fox, 1981.
Russell, Jeffrey Burton. *The Devil: Perceptions of Evil from Antiquity to Primitive Christianity*. Cornell University Press, 1977.
_____. *Lucifer: The Devil in the Middle Ages*. Cornell University Press, 1984.
_____. *Mephistopheles: The Devil in the Modern World*. Cornell University Press, 1986.
_____. *The Prince of Darkness: Radical Evil and the Power of Good in History*. Cornell University Press, 1988.
_____. *Satan: The Early Christian Tradition*. Cornell University Press, 1981.
"The Secret of the Priory of Sion." *60 Minutes*, produced by Jeanne Langley, season 38, episode 31, CBS News, 30 Apr. 2006.
Vidal, Gore. *Messiah*. Dutton, 1954.

Part II
Space and Place

Derridean Hauntology as Cultural Praxis

The Strange Case of Murder House

Jonathan Greenaway

"*Time is Out of Joint.*"—*Jacques Derrida*

The aim of this essay will be to provide a reading of *American Horror Story: Murder House* by using the model of analysis Jacques Derrida proposed as "hauntology." The term is one that is not widely spread throughout Derrida's expansive oeuvre but comes from his work *Specters of Marx: The State of Debt, The Work of Mourning and the New International* from 1993, which forms one of the foundational political engagements within Derrida's wider, deconstructionist philosophical project. The meaning of hauntology is (somewhat unsurprisingly given Derrida's own deliberate attempts to destabilize too-fixed meanings) wide-ranging and flexible, and concerns the persistent presence of the ghosts of Marxism in a distinctly post–Communist world.[1] Given the terminological elasticity, "hauntology" has proven to be an extremely useful term in Gothic studies[2] for the examining of the complex interrelations of history, spectrality, and presence manifested throughout culture and literature. More generally, theorists and critics working in the early 2000s saw in the term something reflecting the wider cultural condition of the contemporary moment—at the end of history, we are all haunted by various cultural ghosts as capitalist hegemony strips away any possible conception of a radically different future.[3] The subject of this essay will be *Murder House*, the first season of the phenomenally popular FX show. At first glance, as with much of the recent TV New Gothic,[4] it would be simple and intuitively attractive to dismiss the show as an intoxicating mélange of recycled Gothic tropes, sex, and violence, yet this misses much of the show's depth. Over the course of this essay, *Murder House* will be shown to form a cultural rather than political model of hauntology. Furthermore, this essay will also seek to show how this praxis of cultural hauntology fits within the broader Derridean and deconstructionist search for a new articulation of cultural justice.

Firstly, then, it must be asked why a *cultural* analysis using hauntology. As Derrida explains, the concept is an analytical mode for mourning. In the wake of the end of history[5]—and living through an age of ever-increasing anxiety from terrorism, the ecological ravages of capitalism, and the precarity of employment—there is an increasing cultural awareness of the contingency of our collective cultural position. The middle-class bourgeois subject is revealed by the forces of neoliberal capitalism to be far from the universalized and secure subject it conceives itself to be. Here, then, we turn to the past and the search for the future that was promised, but ultimately seems to have been denied. As Fredric Jameson is so often quoted as saying, it is now "easier to imagine the end of the world, than the end of capitalism." Perhaps unsurprisingly, then, there has been a resurgence in a kind of nostalgic looking back, to a time where cultural certainties could be more forcefully held onto as the awareness that the future is not what we have been promised becomes more widely accepted.[6] In the light of these anxieties, the cultural work of placing the ghost, of articulating what and where and whom these ghosts are, becomes more urgent. As Derrida explains, hauntological analysis

> [c]onsists always in attempting to ontologize remains, to make them present, in the first place by identifying the bodily remains and by localizing the One to dead.... One has to know. One has to know it. One has to have knowledge [*En faut Ie* Now to *savoir*].... Now, to know is to know who and where, to know whose body it really is and what place it occupies, for it must stay in its place [9].

Here, then, an immediate connection emerges with *Murder House*; the house is an easily identifiable marker for a particular person, yet the same space can be occupied by countless others. The question of "whose house is this?" may initially seem obvious, yet the show goes out of its way to raise doubt on this point. The opening shot of the house in the pilot reveals it to be dilapidated and run-down, a site for the twins to run through with their baseball bats. Yet, as Addie so ominously warns them, the house most definitely belongs to someone else—a monstrous Other with the capacity to take life (in this case the horrific Infantata). The structure of the show further plays into this aspect, based as it is upon perhaps the most well established and culturally familiar Gothic trope, the haunted house; as Violet ironically remarks, "We're the Addams family now" (1:1). In this case, the haunted home is the site of decades of violence, medical experimentation, disfigurement, and murder, colloquially known as "the Murder House." The house is the remaining link to the physical, human world for dozens of ghosts who have passed away there, experienced life and often suffered violence there. To ontologize the remains of these ghosts is thus perhaps the philosophical preoccupation of *Murder House*, but the knowledge Derrida speaks of proves to be increasingly elusive thanks to the complex relationship the house shares with time, law, capital, and of course, its inhabitants.

Thus, the show becomes an attempt to grapple with the philosophical issues and problems caused by the constant capitalist recycling of a singular piece of housing. As anyone familiar with Marx's work will attest, the capitalist exchange is itself predicated upon the interaction of ghosts—the spectral form of pure capital and the almost theological fetishization of gold interacting with the free market.[7] The symbolic and simple economic exchange of selling and purchasing is thrown into sharp relief against the complexities and ambiguities of life, death, violence, and social extremity that makes up so much of personal subjective experience. To quote the character of Constance Langdon:

> But now there are no more virgin plots. We live on top of each other. That's California now ... and that's the world. There is no more space, and yet it's human nature to want to claim your own turf. So build away, we do. Every time you put up one of these ... monstrous temples to the gods of travertine, you're building on top of someone else's life [1:7].

Into this environment, the typically American family move—handsome and sensitive therapist Ben Harmon, wife and mother Vivian and the sullen, yet thoughtful teenage daughter, Violet. Strikingly, these characters are not the haunted tabula rasa of the stereotypical victim of ghosts, serving instead as a type of evidence of what Derrida terms the first time and repetitive nature of ghostly haunting. Moved across the country by Ben's infidelity and the stillbirth of their child, the family unit is moved into action by the consequences of that which is no longer present. The infidelity, now completely absent in any physical sense, is inescapable, a phantom or specter hanging over Ben and Vivian's conversation and interaction. The grief of losing their child affects their actions that bring them into the Murder House as concretely as if the child had been with them from the beginning. Haunting, then, is not necessarily merely a state one enters into by coming into a new geographically specific location. Rather, to be haunted is something that the Harmon family were always already experiencing. To offer the Shakespearean example that Derrida quotes, from the beginning of *Hamlet*, Marcellus' first question regarding the ghost is not if it has appeared but rather "What, has this thing appear'd again?" The ghost, then, is not a new, unique phenomenological idea but an immediately familiar figure, someone at once known and unknown simultaneously. Both politically and philosophically, we're aware of this phenomenon despite its relatively unacknowledged status. Francis Fukyama may have famously claimed that we reached the end of history, yet the claim is a philosophical echo of the claims of Heidegger, which is haunted by Nietzsche who is himself haunted by Marx. These claims of reaching the end of history, of ideology, or philosophy may break new ground but are once again specters that "have appear'd again." Thus, the introduction of the Harmons proves that we are always already carrying the ghosts or remnants of formative and traumatic events that have gone before.

From the second episode of the show we see this in practice; the analepsis that opens the episode is a dark and brutal murder scene of characters completely unfamiliar to us, yet taking place within an environment with which we, as viewers, are extremely familiar. The principle operates on a character level, too; Ben Harmon's affair rendered so abstract and absent in the season's opener suddenly becomes concretely present when it, quite literally, breaks in from the past and becomes present in "Home Invasion." Hayden is initially a strangely unsettling presence and an unfamiliar character, yet somehow familiar due to her "spectral presence" in the show's opening episode as the unspoken remains of Ben Harmon's infidelity. Ultimately, in Hayden's case, it seems that the weight of spectrality is unsustainable; she is a ghostly presence long before she is buried under the garden gazebo (1:3). Her human life simply cannot contain or bear her haunting presence and so she is forcibly removed from such an existence.

Likewise, the horror of "Home Invasion" is predicated upon this combination of both the immediately strange and familiar presented simultaneously. The character of Bianca breaks into the house with the help of two accomplices aiming to brutally murder all those inside, an act of moral and existential alienation recreating the murder of two student nurses from 1968. Violence is once again infinitely strange and consistently repeated, or as Derrida expresses it, "Repetition and first time: this is perhaps the question of the event as question of the ghost" (10). *Murder House*'s apex finishes with a family moving into a home whose inhabitants have recently died and begins with a family moving into a home whose inhabitants have recently died. The concerns from the past are necessarily concerns about what *will* happen—the future and the past are therefore reflected in the moment of the present. The ghost, freed from the constraints of linear chronology, highlights the almost insoluble tensions between the actual present perceived and the series of presents that make up our perception of time. In a very basic expression, the concern viewers might have for what will happen to the Harmon family is inextricably predicated upon a concern for what *has* happened in the house already, and the audience's knowledge of what has come before the Harmons' arrival contributes to the overall sense of danger within the Murder House.

To phrase this aspect of the hauntological process in a suitable piece of Derridean terminology, ghosts are subject to both a constant iterability as well as heterogeneity of subjective experience. To see this idea of repetition and unfamiliarity in a wider context, it's necessary to consider the role that time plays in our experiences. *Murder House*, much as with our experiences of life, is structured by chronology—an iterable process that influences all of the experiences that our lives contain. Yet *Murder House* is deeply subversive, featuring analepsis and prolepsis frequently whilst maintaining (or at the least, attempting to maintain) its narrative coherence. On a more subjective level, the characters of the ghosts themselves have no experience of the iterable process that so influences the Harmon family and the other characters existing within chronological time, despite their ability to influence and impact the current present moment. They are often trapped, unable to give themselves over to the movement of time. As Constance Langdon tells Moira, "Move on missy." But despite missing her mother and claiming that she wants to move on, ultimately, she finds that she "just can't" (1:3). To quote Derrida directly:

> What exactly is the difference from one century to the next? Is it the difference between a past world—for which the specter represented a coming threat—and a present world, today, where the specter would represent a threat that some would like to believe is past and whose return it would be necessary again, once again in the future, to conjure away? Why in both cases is the specter felt to be a threat? What is the time and what is the history of a specter? Is there a present of the specter? Are its comings and goings ordered according to the linear succession of a before and an after, between a present-past, a present-present, and a present-future, between a "real time" and a "deferred time"? [48].

Once again, to contextualize, we can point to *Murder House*'s characters. Particularly useful here are Chad and Patrick, the unhappy gay couple previously murdered in the home by the "Rubber Man." The two are effectively trapped—emotionally, chronologically, and geographically. Unable to leave the house, the two are isolated within a series of unhappy presents, neither completely separated from the chronology that affects the house but unable to escape the singular oft-repeated moments just before their untimely death. Time, then, is both deferred and endlessly present as the two pose both a threat to the present, yet are completely limited to their own past present.[8] Once more, to return to the example of *Hamlet*, "Time is out of joint." The two-part episode, "Halloween Part One" and "Halloween Part Two," in the midst of the season provides an in-depth break down of the ways in which the show treats the interaction of time and the ghost. Taking place over Halloween night, the ghosts are granted freedom to leave the house, yet the freedom of new experiences is once more deferred. Tate's victims, for example, can do nothing but endure their own death, taunting Tate for what he inflicted upon them yet unable to move beyond it; they become both a threat to the present and irrevocably stranded in "deferred time." Tate's actions have constantly deferred their own present, as new heterogeneous experiences are simply impossible. The same applies to Tate himself; in a quiet moment he gives a speech at the beach with Violet:

> I used to come here ... when the world closed in and got so small I couldn't breathe. I'd look out at the ocean, and I'd think "Yo, douchebag, high school counts for jack shit." Kurt Cobain, Quentin Tarantino, Brando, DeNiro, Pacino, all high school dropouts. I hated high school. So I come here and I look out at this vast limitless expanse and it's like that's your life man, you can do anything, you can be anything, screw high school that's just a blip in your timeline, don't get stuck there [1:4].

Ironically, this is precisely what happens to both Tate and his victims; he is unable to acknowledge the reality of what he has done and, despite his desperation to avoid it, has been stuck in high school for seventeen years. As Derrida puts it towards the beginning of *Specters of Marx*, haunting is historical, to be sure, but it is not dated, "it is never docilely given a date in the chain of presents, day after day" (3). Tate, like his victims, is removed from that chain, the forward motion of time; he and the lives he has taken are instead pinned into the past, anchored securely to a moment that they cannot move finally beyond.

This holds true even for the characters still existing within what we may term "chronological time." The character of Constance Langdon is a good example of how the subjective experiences of a singular subject can remove themselves from the flow of chronological time. Obsessed with the space that she used to own, embodying that question of "whose house" this is, Constance exists within her own "deferred time." Instead of new experiences or any sense of futurity, she consistently finds herself drawn to the house—and more specifically to the revenant of her son. Tate's own removal from the iterability of time in effect removes Constance from it, too. She is rarely seen outside of the Murder House and her actions throughout the first season are revealed to be entirely motivated by concern for her family. The ghosts of those that she loves, Tate especially, are now permanently isolated within their own non-contemporaneous time. Constance's choices become in effect the mitigation of new action as she is forced to remain even as Tate does. To quote a key line of dialogue from "Halloween Part Two":

> One of the comforts of having children is knowing one's youth has not fled, but merely been passed down to a new generation. They say when a parent dies, a child feels his own mortality. But when a child dies, it's immortality that a parent loses [1:5].

This separation and yet entanglement of haunting with temporality highlights the complexity of the relationship the specter has with everyday human chronological existence. Neither a direct threat nor completely

72   Part II—Space and Place

separated and safely isolated from chronological existence, the ghost is both at once accessible and quarantined, both constantly differing and deferred away from humanity. The non-contemporaneity of spectral experience of time with that of the Harmon family systematically destabilizes the opposition or dialectic between an actual effective presence and its other. The Murder House is populated by ghosts existing from a span across the whole twentieth century within one specific location. The present is shown as being entirely non-contemporaneous with itself; rather than a coherent, singular chronology the house is shown as a series of presents endued with various spectral presences.

From a structural point of view, the show systematically goes out of its way to disrupt the standard narrative progression that genre-savvy TV viewers might expect. Prominent analepsis and prolepsis ensure that a singular chronology can never be identified. The story of the Harmons begins with their moving into the Murder House in the present day, yet the opening episode is not necessarily "about" the Harmon family at all but is rather about the house and its inhabitants. Where does the chronology of the Murder House begin? With the death of the previous owners? With its construction? The pilot opens in 1978, with other episodes in the season moving from 1968, to 2010, to the present, to 1994, and to the Black Dahlia murder of the 1940s. Perhaps we might try and claim that things "begin" with the madness and grief of the first owners whose brutal murder/suicide first generated its reputation. The show stubbornly resists easy answers to these questions, presenting a show where narrative progression is episodic and non-linear, and the viewer must piece together narrative coherence (or in other words a kind of temporal progression) from the various singular presences that are presented. Form, then, feeds into the wider temporal disruption of the show, exacerbated still further by a television ecosystem of streaming, syndication, and endless late-night repeats. Once again, Derrida draws out the theoretical implications of the structural elements of the show's chronology, framing it as a

> [d]is-located time of the present, at the joining of a radically dis-jointed time, without certain conjunction. Not a time whose joinings are negated, broken, mistreated, dysfunctional, disadjusted, according to a *dys-* of negative opposition and dialectical disjunction, but a time without certain joining or determinable conjunction [20].

In short, the specters within the house obsessively re-enact various present moments; from Tate wishing to be free of the troubles of high school in the mid–1990s, to Chad and Patrick compulsively re-enacting the petty squabbles of the upper-middle class gay couple, time, throughout the Murder House, is *dis*-jointed (and as Derrida goes on to point out, this disjunction applies not only to the presentation of time, but history as well). Structurally and thematically, the temporality within *Murder House* is presented as disconnected from the notion of normative time—that linear movement from point A onto point B. Rather, there is the constant restaging of singular moments, or as Tate puts it, "blips on the timeline" (1:4), which are reworked repeatedly, manifested by the various spectral presences that are all condemned to live out their own present moments. One only need look at Nora's obsessions for a child or the vicious Chad who orders Vivian out of his house to see "this sort of non-contemporaneity of present time with itself" (Derrida 29). On a wider level, such a condemnation of the individual to exist within a minute "present moment" ties *Murder House* into a broader cultural and hauntological discourse. This understanding of the present as something we are condemned to live through repeatedly is symptomatic of the contemporary neo-liberal subject trying to navigate the political and economic climate today. The future has truly become *un*thinkable as life outside the structures of capitalism becomes ever more inconceivable. As a result, the show taps into a broader cultural nostalgia; mourning the utopia of a better future, television has increasingly returned to the Gothic past, staged in innovative ways in the contemporary present.

Here, then, the show's structure and plot suggest a new way of understanding the nature of time. It is the spectral presence, this disconnection between the perception of a singular forward flowing chronology and the reality that *Murder House* presents—of experience as non-linear, as perceived through the past and anticipation of the future. It is this recall of the past and the anticipation of the present that leads to the final aspect of hauntology to be examined here—the concept of justice. To paraphrase Derrida's opening remarks from *Specters of Marx*, what exists between the two conditions of living and death itself is the condition of justice where the subject can learn to live, finally:

> But to learn to live, to learn it from oneself and by oneself, all alone, to teach oneself to live ("I would like to learn to live finally"), is that not impossible for a living being? Is it not what logic itself forbids? To live, by definition, is not something one learns. Not from oneself, it is not learned from life, taught by life. Only from the other and by death. In any case from the other at the edge of life. At the internal border or the external border, it is a heterodidactics between life and death [xvii].

To leave out a discussion of justice from the nature of the cultural ghost is to ignore a crucial point that Derrida adroitly draws out. What kind of culture, what kind of ethics or politics, revolutionary or not, is possible, without in its principles the respect for those who are no longer present or those who are not yet. The depiction of the specter within the New Gothic is easily dismissible as nothing more than simulacra, a reworking of a generic trope for the purposes of simple entertainment, yet it is revelatory of the cultural ethics that we have inherited and created from those themselves who have come before us.

Without some sense of responsibility and a respect for justice, concerning those who are not yet there, who are not present and living, our questions of cultural ethics simply possess no sense. Whilst this high-minded idea of justice may seem appropriate in Derrida's political analysis, it yet may give some pause when approaching the intoxicating mix of sex, violence, and transgression that both *Murder House* and *AHS* offers. However, to dismiss the New Gothic and *AHS* as simple entertainment defeats the very object of any kind of cultural analysis, as well as ignoring the deeply ethical themes that the show explores through its use of violence and the horror aesthetic. Particularly pertinent to the discussion here is the treatment of the vulnerable, particularly women and children. Hayden comes to realize just how unjustly she has been treated by Ben, only after her death:

> I'm rotting from the inside out. What's happening to me? Oh, right. A gazebo, Ben? Not even a decent headstone? A gazebo? You thought I was gone, so you just thought you could throw me away like I didn't matter? Like I never even existed? Is that what you think of women, Ben? That they're just some disposable nothings that you can sit on top of as you casually drink iced tea? [1:5].

Hayden's speech, effectively delivered from beyond the grave, highlights the considerable misogyny latent in Ben Harmon's actions. Hidden behind the façade of being the dutiful family man, Ben instrumentalizes Hayden to sooth his grief over the loss of his child and then, literally and figuratively, buries her. The gazebo may disguise the site of her internment but, as with his phone records that Vivian later uses, it cannot keep her out of Ben's life with any degree of security. Ben's response, that demand for Hayden to "stop screwing with me," shows the extent to which the ethical demands of those who are no longer present are seen as nothing more than an inconvenience to be surmounted. Ben Harmon is, it seems, completely unaware of the impact of the specters until it is far too late, and his loaded demand that Hayden (and the rest) stop "screwing" with him shows the lack of engagement with the ghosts of his past that leads to disaster. Even so, the series' climax offers a compelling and fascinating example of justice in operation and the potential of the specter to function as a positive or negative figure for justice. The question of justice, in Derridean terms, arrives with relation to the future to come; in the case of this season, we see this future takes the form of a child—literally that which is not yet present in the world. At the conclusion of the first season, the story line revolves around Vivian's pregnancy, which divides the ghosts and revenants of the house into two separate camps. On the one hand there are those who wish to take the child away from the Harmons for various reasons, none of which could charitably be referred to as benign, from Hayden's desire for revenge to the obsessions of the bereft Nora to Chad and Patrick's desire for a child (1:11). In opposition are the ghosts who wish to spare the Harmon family any further pain, in the case of Dr. Montgomery even going so far as to help in the delivery of the twins despite being unable to save Vivian (1:11).

The story line shows the division and the potential in how haunted our sense of justice is. Typically, it seems that justice is restorative, and a form based upon vengeance. Hayden and the ghosts of the home invaders murder Ben Harmon for his role in Hayden's death. Chad and Patrick seek to abduct one of the babies in a (futile) attempt to give new meaning to their relationship, harnessing the child to try to repair the emotional and temporal closure within which the two have become trapped. The emerging and potential future that the unborn child represents is a vessel of punishment for wrongs received in the past. Thus, justice is in effect a function of *stasis*. Rather than any kind of positive potentiality, or even some sort of redemption, a justice dictated to, and haunted by, these wronged ghosts can only seek to induce vengeance for wrongs already suffered. This reaches the apocalyptic heights of the Son of the Devil being born upon the earth as a result of Tate raping Vivian. As Billie Dean tells Constance in the episode "Spooky Little Girl," "a child born of human and spirit will usher in the end of times, it is the essence of evil, a perversion of the immaculate conception" (1:9). Thus, vengeance is perpetuated upon the future as it emerges into the present. Vengeance as justice becomes simply a new endlessly repeated process, creating new wronged specters.

To return once more to Derrida, in the light of this idea, an important question emerges from his ethical and political engagement:

> If right or law stems from vengeance, as Hamlet seems to complain that it does—before Nietzsche, before Heidegger, before Benjamin—can one not yearn for a justice that one day, a day belonging no longer to history, a quasi-messianic day would finally be removed from the fatality of vengeance? Better than removed: infinitely foreign, heterogeneous at its source? [25]

The quasi-messianic day in question can come for the Harmons only once they have learned to live, in Derrida's memorable phrase, and moved into the state between life and death. Removed from the structures of vengeance the family find a new kind of familial unity. The old wrongs are not avenged but are forgiven as Ben confesses his flaws to his family and they seem to grow closer together. Vengeance becomes something "infinitely foreign" to the point of parody as the two brutally (re)enact violence on their bodies with no consequences or risks to themselves in the episode "Afterbirth" as Ben and Vivian stage their own grisly murder. The two use gore and horror to ensure that the next family that seeks to build a new present by moving into the Murder House is forcibly and rather graphically dissuaded. At the season's conclusion, it appears that this pattern of vengeance that

Derrida mentions can be negated through relationships that endure from one moment and state of existence to the next. However, at the same time, such a negation is impossible. After all, only when all of the Harmons have died does the show suggest that can there be a kind of new relationship between them. Here, then, Derrida's demand for justice can be seen as both ultimately necessary and impossible to fulfill, a demand that remains out of reach, but one that must always be aspired toward.

The specter is then revealed as both threat and benign, outside of time yet active within it, inescapably present yet as insubstantial as mist. They occupy the site of ambiguity and undecidability in our cultural midst, hovering half seen over the cultural landscape and influencing it and our participation within in it in ways we (like Ben Harmon) do not immediately recognize. All of this makes culture hauntologically unstable, and thus may give rise to a somewhat obvious question: Can the ghost be exorcised from our cultural expression? Perhaps the less obvious yet more important question should be addressed first: Should it be done? What possible effects might it have and what risks? The evidence from the show proposes two separate models of exorcism in the first season both worth noting. Firstly, from the episode "Birth" comes the repurposing of the "Croatoan" spell, which Violet uses to try and banish Chad and Patrick once she learns of their plan to steal Vivian's unborn twins. The section of the episode is given considerable weight, too; the historical myth of the lost settlement of 1590 is incorporated into the show's mythos (as well as being the entire focus of the show's sixth season) and the spell is presented as the only effective exorcism in the past five hundred years. However, the result is spectacularly ineffective as Chad merely laughs it off (1:11). The cultural rituals of society seem to lack power and efficacy (one can only presume that a more traditional Catholic exorcism would also lack the necessary power to truly be rid of a specter). Rituals and ceremonies are part of the cultural inheritance of the present, handed down from those who are no longer present within it. Thus, in a very concrete sense the ghost and specters of the present are the architects of the same cultural rituals and practices we seek to use to banish them. Seen this way, the complete failure of their effectiveness can hardly be seen as a surprise. Furthermore, this attempt to drive out the ghosts of culture using the same cultural rituals and rites that have been inherited shows a kind of naivety about the ways in which culture is constructed. In the case of *Murder House*, the spell that Violet uses is drawn from a period of American history where Indigenous culture was systematically and violently colonized. Modern American culture is thus built upon the bodies of the dead but depends upon an exorcising of the ghosts' presence from culture.

However, despite the failure of the formal spell, the show does give one way of banishing ghosts from the presence of an individual that proves to be successful. As Nora tells a terrified young Tate in "Birth," you just have to close your eyes and tell them to go away. Perhaps the most effective scene with this is towards the climax of the season after Violet has discovered the extent of what Tate has done—his violence, rape, and destruction of the family. Her banishment, her exorcism of him, is done both because and in spite of what he has inflicted upon her and because of and despite her own rather tenderly shown emotional attachment to him (1:12). Tate, already dead, is not destroyed by this exorcising but his death to Violet is made indelibly real. As Derrida puts it, "effective exorcism pretends to declare the death only in order to put to death. As a coroner might do, it certifies the death but here it is in order to inflict it" (59).

What is put to death in Violet's exorcism of Tate is not Tate himself, for as a non-corporeal being there is the acknowledgment that he cannot be truly destroyed. Rather what is finally "killed off" is their relationship—not just a relationship between two individuals but a communion of her present with his past. Tate himself recognizes that Violet has effectively severed the temporal connection between the two. He is, by the season's close, doubly trapped, by both his murderous actions and Violet's severing of the tie between them. His only recourse then is to "wait. Forever, if I have to" as he puts it (1:12). This is the danger of wishing to exorcise ourselves of the specters that exist and haunt the New Gothic. To do so may bring stability or even a new sense of moral respectability, yet it ends with a banishment of our collective pasts. There can be no hope for Tate, no way for him to change, and for those in the present there can be no way to learn from the darkness that he embodies. As Constance Langdon puts it, there is a duty to be caretakers of that which was here before us, that unlike the property developer Joe, who wishes to tear down the past, certain things demand our respect (1:7). The specters of the past are not limited to Marx, or indeed Derrida himself, but Radcliffe, Shelley, Matthew Lewis, Hitchcock, and Patrick Bateman all number amongst them. Despite the violence and the horrors of the past, we cannot ultimately rid ourselves of them. Culture cannot be completely sanitized, no matter how hard we may strive to do so. Every home is marked by the absence of those that have come before us, and even the land itself records the presence of specters, even if those who inhabit these homes and live on the land have seemingly forgotten them.

As David Punter so memorably concludes his *Texts of Terror*, no matter how passé, how outmoded or just plain distasteful we find the echoes of spectrality in our cultural expression, the haunting of *Murder House* is just the latest example of the near constant spectral returns. The Gothic has returned anew as culture has advanced past the eschaton of the millennium and even the apocalyptic fears of 2012. In an era coming to terms with the sense of the "end of history" and the cultural inertia and anxiety that brings with it, it seems we are distinctly preoccupied—haunted—by the past. As *Murder House* proves, exorcising our ghosts is as impossible as separating our present from our pasts. Despite the advances in technology, despite the ever-increasing sophistication of our lives under neo-liberal capitalism, it seems that we cannot expunge the contingency that the ghost brings to bear. The iterability of chronology and the subsequent inevitable tension with the plurality of unique subjective experiences creates a space that ghosts will always inhabit. Our choices are then to either sever the past away from ourselves, an act of ultimate abjection abandoning the positives of our past and hope for the future. The alternative is to keep on striving for that quasi-messianic day of justice for those not yet, and for those who are no longer.

To finish then, with a final question, what are we haunted by? What concerns and fears do the ghosts of *Murder House* represent? It seems that the show portrays fears deeply bound up to some of the foundational questions of what we think humanity is—the family, the home, the marriage, and connection to other people are shown to be all too easily fractured. The concerns of culture post-modernity seem to have remained as the grand narratives of the successful American or capitalist world are irrevocably haunted by failure. Marriage is susceptible to infidelity, property is a drain on finances, resources and even mental coherence and the hope endued in parenting leads to apathy so extreme the child itself can be unaware of its own mortality. Ben and Vivian are, in a sense, exemplars of the American Dream—prosperous, middle-class parents, with a distinct financial investment in the future. Yet, from the opening of the show, the past is a constant and intrusive present, and whilst the Harmons desperately seek to prevent the past coming back, it always threatens to re-emerge.

On a more structural level, the show highlights certain concerns that go beyond the economic, ideological, and emotional forces that surround the subject into the very body of the subject themselves. The repertory cast is a powerfully destabilizing tool here—Tate Langdon, the charismatic monster of *Murder House*, becomes the wrongly imprisoned hero protagonist of the next season, *Asylum*. Similarly, in the *Asylum* series, the tragic "nice-guy" Ben Harmon becomes the depraved psychopath killer. The coherent and cogent subject that persists through time becomes systematically problematized throughout the show, revealing that what haunts the post-modern cultural landscape is, in essence, the construction and contingency of ourselves. In the case of the Harmon family, initially presented as the perfect embodiment of American bourgeois ideology, the series functions to show both the inherent constructed-ness of such a family unit, and the deep fragility that resides just beneath the surface. Time, corporeality, our families, our homes, and indeed ourselves are riven with ambiguity where we believe only certainty resides.

As Derrida explores in *Specters of Marx,* there is a complex set of emotions and affects invested in the notions of the specter. In the case of communism, it remains as the ghost that, even today, haunts Europe, and perhaps, further afield, haunts that capitalist bastion that is the United States. Towards the close of *Specters of Marx,* he writes that "only mortals, only the living who are not living gods can bury the dead. Only mortals can watch over them, and can watch, period" (220). There is then, a duty that mortality carries with it—a requirement that we take note of, and learn from those who have gone before us, in order to move towards the messianic day of justice. At the same moment, the ghost that haunts our culture, and even the homes we live in, forms an uncanny reflection of ourselves. In short, the ghost forces us to expose the contradiction and frustrations hidden within the idea of psychological and subjective coherence—an uncomfortable process, yet as *Murder House* proves, it is one that is simply and ultimately inescapable.

Notes

1. The text was produced from the lectures that Derrida gave at the conference "Whither Marxism? Global Crises in International Perspective" April 22–24, 1993 and is intended to be read in conversation with the collected volume of the conference proceedings, *Whither Marxism? Global Crises in International Perspective.*

2. For example, see the discussions of contemporary Gothic writing put forward by Joanne Watkiss, titled *Gothic Contemporaries: The Haunted Text* (University of Wales Press, 2012).

3. See particularly the work of the late, great Mark Fisher, mostly known for his blog, k-punk (k-punk.abstractdynamics.org/) as well as *Capitalist Realism: Is there No Alternative?* (Zero Books, 2009) and *Ghosts of My Life: Writings on Depression, Hauntology and Lost Futures* (Zero Books, 2014).

4. Here I refer to a host of new shows that have emerged post–2000 which explicitly concern themselves with Gothic and horror themes. An exhaustive list is not possible in such a limited space, but key texts would certainly include *Dexter* (2006–2013), *True Blood* (2008–2014), *Bates Motel* (2013–), *The Walking Dead* (2010–) and *Hannibal* (2013–2015). For further academic work on defining and surveying the "New Gothic," see Helen Wheatley's *Gothic Television* (Manchester UP, 2006) and Lorna Jowett and Stacey Abbott's *TV Horror: Investigating the Darker Side of the Small Screen* (I.B Tauris, 2012).

5. See Francis Fukyama's *The End of History and the Last Man* (Penguin, 2012).

6. Perhaps nothing quite exemplifies this more clearly than the recent presidential campaign of Donald Trump and the incessant slogan of "Make America Great Again."

7. For a thorough exploration of this mix of Gothic metaphor and capitalism, see David McNally's *Monsters of the Market: Zombies, Vampires and Global Capitalism* (Haymarket Books, 2012).

8. The tragedy of Chad and Patrick goes some way to highlighting the extent to which an alternative future is something that haunts us. As José Esteban Muñoz argues, queerness is the illumination for a future horizon, yet the slow cancellation of the future in which *Murder House* and all its characters exist denies them this, adding a layer of pathos to their doomed attempts to always rebuild their ideal bourgeoise family unit. For more on this, see Muñoz's

Cruising Utopia: The Then and There of Queer of Futurity (NYU Press, 2009). A promising avenue for work on *AHS* would be an exploration of the ways in which queerness and futurity intersect, but time and space forbid it here.

Works Cited

Derrida, Jacques. *Specters of Marx: The State of the Debt, the Work of Mourning and the New International*. Translated by Peggy Kampf, Routledge, 1993.

Jameson, Fredric. "Future City." *New Left Review*, vol. 21, 2019, www.newleftreview.org/issues/II21/articles/fredric-jameson-future-city. Accessed 20 Feb. 2017.

Muñoz, José Esteban. *Cruising Utopia: The Then and There of Queer of Futurity*. NYU Press, 2009.

O'Hagan, Andrew. "Ghosting." *London Review of Books*, vol. 36, no. 5, 6 Mar. 2014, www.lrb.co.uk/v36/n05/andrew-ohagan/ghosting. Accessed 20 Feb. 2017.

Punter, David. *The Literature of Terror: A History of Gothic Fictions from 1765 to the Present Day, Vol. 2: The Modern Gothic*. Routledge, 1996.

The Psychiatric Clinic in Horror Cinema and TV

Asylum

Antonio Sanna

This essay inscribes *American Horror Story: Asylum* within the tradition of horror films and television through the genre's representation of madness and psychiatric clinics since the first decades of the twentieth century. In order to do this, it initially traces the representation of madness and asylums in Gothic literature and then in horror films and TV programs. Two different characterizations of the psychiatric clinic (the uncanny and frightening madhouse and the squalid and dirty clinic) are identified as the major models for its representation in horror films and television. This essay demonstrates how the frightening and uncanny representation of the madhouse is realized in *Asylum* through the use of thematic concerns such as violence and excessive emotions and through the mise-en-scène. Both aspects are instrumental in the creation of a message that criticizes the suffering of the abused patients (unjustly) confined within such a structure.

"Madness may be as old as mankind," Roy Porter affirms (10). In early religious myths and in the plays of Aeschylus, Sophocles, and Euripides, madness was treated as fate or punishment, whereas in Christian mythology the derangement of the individual soul was considered as schemed by Satan (10–14, 19). Madness is portrayed in the writings of Cervantes (*Don Quixote*), Shakespeare (*King Lear*, *Hamlet*, and *Macbeth*), Ariosto (*Orlando Furioso*) and in Lewis Carroll's *Alice in Wonderland*, but also in the *Batman* franchise as much as in the paintings of Hieronymus Bosch (*The Ship of Fools*) and of Hogarth (*The Rake's Progress* sequence), and in the philosophical insights of Erasmus and Friedrich Nietzsche. Formal segregation emerged around the end of the Middle Ages with the confinement of lunatics in towers or dungeons and was generally inspired by the Christian duty of charity (90). In London, the religious house of St. Mary of Bethlehem was founded in 1247 and began to cater for lunatics in the late fourteenth century, when it became known as Bethlem (or "Bedlam"). By the year 1800, around 5,000 people were held in both private and public asylums in England, a number that grew up to ten times by 1900 (112). In France, the Hopital Général was founded in Paris in 1656, whereas in German-speaking countries the houses of correction were created during the seventeenth century (the first madhouse opened in Hamburg in 1620). It was during the nineteenth century that insanity was turned into a pathology by contemporary scientists. Psychiatry as a practice was developed only subsequently for the diagnosis and treatment of the inmates of the asylums. As philosopher Michel Foucault specified, "medicine ... was regulated more in accordance with normality than with health" (35). Progressive therapeutic optimism was indeed often ushered under a pervasive paternalism: "the idea that social and professional elites had the right and responsibility to treat unfortunates" (Porter 122). This is especially the case of "hysterical" women, who came to be stigmatized as much as "witches" had been: "though they escaped legal penalties: misogyny remained, only the diagnosis changed" (Porter 28).

Madness and lunatic asylums have a marginal but appropriate role in Gothic literature, the fiction of horror and terror that developed in the United Kingdom during the second half of the eighteenth century and that counts Horace Walpole, Matthew Lewis, Ann Radcliffe, and Mary Shelley among the most illustrious representatives of its first generation. Gothic fiction often focuses on the places on the fringe, which are, according to Fred Botting, "antithetical locations in which selfish, criminal, and sexual passions are enacted" (260). Along with settings such as castles, ruins, and abbeys, the asylum contains those emotional excesses that are typically represented in Gothic fiction, especially those obsessive behaviors that characterize the villains of Gothic novels. Asylums can be considered as what Botting calls "heterotopias," places on the fringe, used for the containment and exclusion of the individuals who threaten the "established order" of society with their behavior (243). The first Gothic work that represents the lunatic asylum is Charles Maturin's novel *Melmoth the Wanderer* (1820), in which the character of Stanton is confined unjustly and treacherously to a madhouse. The narrator offers the following description of his experience:

> He was in complete darkness; the horror of his situation struck him at once. [...] His cries were in a moment echoed by a hundred voices. [...] The cries that he heard on every side seemed like a wild and infernal yell of joy, that their mansion had obtained another tenant. [...] He could not shut out these frightful cries nightly repeated, nor the frightful sound of the whip employed to still them. Hope began to fail him [48, 53].

This passage highlights some of the fundamental characteristics defining the fictional representation of the asylum, from the squalor of the setting and the abusive treatment of the inmates by the orderlies, to the residents' lack of privacy and the feeling of horror that they experience. The house of correction is represented as a Dantesque infernal circle, filled with suffering and desperate sinners that are subjected to cruel punishments and cannot escape from their own minds and pains, a place where hope is soon lost. Moreover, it is a site of contagion: the mentally stable Stanton slowly "assimilates" the frenzy of the surrounding inmates and descends into madness himself until he is saved by the diabolical Melmoth.

Negative emotions and feelings are associated with the lunatic asylum in Bram Stoker's *Dracula* as well. In this 1897 novel, the clinic of Carfax is one of the main settings of the narrative: the building itself is described by the character of Dr. Seward when returning from a visit to his sick beloved Lucy. The sad Seward reflects on "the grim sternness of my own cold stone building, with its wealth of breathing misery, and my own desolate heart to endure it" (142). His own depressive state is projected onto the madhouse and is mirrored by the sufferings of its patients. The same grim feeling is later shared by Mina Harker who, in Seward's words, "knew, of course, that the place was a lunatic asylum, but I could see that she was unable to repress a slight shudder when we entered" (262–63). Carfax is depicted in a negative light because it is not a healthy and safe environment where recovery could be achieved. Indeed, Seward's most important patient, Renfield, is killed inside of his cell because the doctor fails to realize that the nearby Carfax Abbey is the residence of Count Dracula and constitutes therefore a danger for his life. Furthermore, the doctor himself is often depicted as unprofessional and incompetent. On many occasions, Seward's actions betray his highly questionable ethics and his lack of experience in dealing with the inmates, as Clive Leatherdale has recognized (126). Although Seward expresses his intention to master Renfield's mind, to uncover the method of his madness in order to advance his branch of science (90), in his diary (which alternates his scientific observations with his personal notes on the woman he loves) he admits "in my manner of doing [with Renfield] there was, now I see, something of cruelty. I seemed to wish to keep him to the point of his madness" (78). The doctor is not interested in the patient's recovery, but he rather prioritizes his own medical research and achievements. Through the presentation of his character as incompetent and prejudiced, Stoker's novel thus casts a doubt on the efficacy of the treatment in lunatic asylums.

Melmoth the Wanderer and *Dracula* set the basis for the subsequent fictional representations of the asylum, especially in horror cinema and television. In this genre, the psychiatric clinic fulfills the same functions of all those dark, labyrinthine, and frightening locations where life and death often compete for the possession of the human body: the madhouse is a "heterotopia" where the people exiled from society are subjected to sufferings and where the supernatural intrudes to prey on the lives of the patients or of the main characters. There are mainly three models in the representation of the madhouse in horror cinema and television: the uncanny madhouse (a realistic environment made uncanny by the intervention of the supernatural or the appearance of a serial killer), the squalid and dirty clinic (where patients are severely mistreated), and, finally, the healthy madhouse (a positive environment where patients can actually recover from their illnesses and no horrific events occur). Common to the three models of the madhouse in horror cinema and TV are iron gratings, metallic platforms or stairs, bare walls, and long corridors. Insufficient or drab lighting, thrilling soundtracks, and eerie sound effects are instead characteristic of the first and second models of the fictional asylum and they contribute to the creation of a horrific atmosphere. These architectural, thematic, and visual characteristics, as well as the use of expedients such as darkness, directional lighting, and ominous soundtracks, are used in the representation of the madhouse in *Asylum* as well. *Asylum* applies the characteristics of both the first and second model of fictional madhouses in order to convey a representation of the environment as frightening and uncanny.[1]

The first model of representation of the asylum in horror films and television utilizes a realistic and luminous environment but transforms it into an uncanny and frightening location through the presence of a supernatural creature or of a villain. The first example of the uncanny madhouse is given in Robert Wiene's *The Cabinet of Dr. Caligari* (1920), one of the most popular films of the Weimar Republic, which focuses on madness, murderous actions and the alienation of the individual. The emblematic set of the madhouse, with its spirals painted on the pointy set designs, reflects the obsessive behavior of the titular doctor who hypnotizes a somnambulist patient of his to commit murders. Such a nightmarish representation of the clinic is subsequently reinforced in the frame narrative through the unexpected plot twist revealing that the alleged hero of the story is actually a patient of the asylum himself. The sense of oppression of the environment is rendered through the depiction of the evident psychotic behavior of the inmates and the delusions of the protagonist about the director's victimization of the other patients. The dismal and oppressive environment of the psychiatric clinic reproduces the scenarios of fear and addresses concerns such as "the helplessness of the individual in the face of power; the ubiquity of chaos and violence; the fascination with death and destruction" (Hake 223–24) that were typical of the films belonging to German expressionism. Such thematic concerns—along with the devices of chiaroscuro lighting and angled compositions—have been subsequently used in horror films and horror television and are central to the representation of the madhouse in *Asylum* as well.

Several contemporary horror films equally depicted the psychiatric asylum as an uncanny environment because of the presence of a supernatural creature or serial killer. In the case of Chuck Russell's *A Nightmare on Elm Street 3: Dream Warriors* (1987), Tony Randel's *Hellraiser 2* (1988), and the 1959 Hammer production of *The Mummy* directed by Terence Fisher, the asylum contains those characters who have experienced the supernatural as victims. Such patients have been excluded from society because their explanation of the illegal events in which they had been involved has not been considered as valid or sufficient, because the existence of the supernatural has not been accepted by the local authorities. The characters' madness is therefore the diagnosis established by the unbelieving representatives of the status quo as an alternative explanation for the presence of the supernatural. These clinics become horrific and uncanny places when the supernatural asserts its presence inside of them, that is, as soon as the testimony of the imprisoned characters becomes true (respectively with the apparitions of Freddy Kruger, the Cenobites, and the Egyptian mummy).[2] In Andrew Jones' *The Amityville Asylum* (2013), there is nothing frightening about High Hopes Hospital until the film's protagonist Lisa Templeton (Sophia Del Pizzo) begins experiencing hallucinations of the deceased patients wandering through the corridors. Similarly, the luminous and sterile environment of the psychiatric hospital in *Ginger Snaps Unleashed* (2003) is not portrayed as a frightening environment in itself, but its abandoned and decaying area functions as the clinic's dirty underside once it becomes the lair of the vicious werewolf that attacks the two protagonists.

Alternatively, in cinematic representations the asylum becomes an uncanny environment once a serial killer visits its premises. In Dario Argento's *Trauma* (1993), indeed, no supernatural events occur, but the choice of the serial killer's personal perspective transforms the clinic into a threatening environment where the menace gets closer and closer to the young protagonist, whose forced confinement is a source of suspense for the viewer. In *The Silence of the Lambs* (1991) by Jonathan Demme and its prequel *Red Dragon* (2002) by Brett Ratner, the characters of Clarice Starling (Jodie Foster) and William Graham (Edward Norton) have to pass through many metallic doors before reaching the dark corridor in the basement where Hannibal Lecter (Anthony Hopkins) is. Tension and an atmosphere of danger are established through the soundtrack and through the characters' (and the viewers') expectations on the forthcoming encounter with the villain, whose atrocities have been previously recounted by the director of the clinic in Demme's film or have been directly portrayed at the beginning of the story in Ratner's film. Another example of this model of madhouse is offered by the psychiatric care facility depicted in Rick Rosenthal's *Halloween: Resurrection* (2002), which becomes frightening only after the arrival of serial killer Michael Meyers, whose personal perspective (along with the ominous orchestral soundtrack and light designs verging on the blue and yellow) transforms the frames of the corridors, especially the smoky corridor of the basement, into a frightening environment. This occurs also in Rob Zombie's 2007 remake of *Halloween*, in which the asylum is a clean and neat environment in all of the scenes portraying Michael Meyers as a young boy being cured by the local doctors. The clinic becomes a disturbing place when Michael grows up and becomes a menacing man whose face is never revealed by the camera. An uncanny effect is achieved through the thrilling orchestral music intervening on each occasion in which Michael occupies at least a part of the frame and through the medium and large frames that cut the visual field in half.

TV horror mainly follows this model for the representation of the madhouse. On the one hand, indeed, the portrayal of the psychiatric clinic as an uncanny environment occurs in the 1968 episode "Dracula" (part of the TV series *Mystery and Imagination* [1966–70]), which begins in Whitby asylum, where Jonathan Harker (Corin Redgrave) is confined. The madhouse is here represented as a bare environment with uncomfortable rooms locked by robust, metallic doors, which is run by an incompetent staff (Harker easily escapes their custody twice) and becomes uncanny as soon as the vampire count visits its premises. Similarly, in the episode "Elegy" from the TV series *The X-Files* (1993–2002, 2016–18), Dana Skully (Gillian Anderson) witnesses the apparition of a ghost at the time of its body's death. The skeptic FBI agent is disturbed by the supernatural occurrence (a detail evidenced by the close-ups on her deeply distressed face alternating with the frames on the ghost), which transforms the bathroom of the clinic where it occurs into a haunted environment and further shakes Skully's belief in an exclusively rational and scientific interpretation of reality. In "The Pest House," from the series *Millennium* (1996–99), a series of murders is committed by a patient who absorbs the other inmates' evil and then shape-shifts into them. The eerie atmosphere is enhanced by the use of dim, blue lights, by the frames (often backlit) through the bars and those focusing on the characters walking through the clinic's corridors and the doors closing after them, as well as by the close-ups on the alleged murderers' body parts (a hook, a bleeding mouth) that might have committed the crimes. In the case of *Asylum*, the supernatural asserts its presence inside the clinic when the aliens steal some of the patients' bodies and appear in front of some terrorized characters, as well as when the young boy possessed by the devil frightens and threatens some of the narrative's main characters, transfers into the body of Sister Mary Eunice, the tame and naive nun working in the clinic, and brutally murders some of the inmates.

On the other hand, the madhouse is portrayed as an uncanny environment in horror TV series when a serial killer haunts its premises. Two episodes from the *Tales from the Crypt* (1989–96) depict it as the place where murderous actions are committed and evil is perpetrated. In the episode "Mute Witness to Murder," the clinic becomes a nightmarish location because of the unjust and forced confinement of the female protagonist by the actual villain who committed the crime that made her mute and unable to protest. The evidently disturbed doctor of the clinic repeatedly abuses the poor woman and even kills her suspicious boyfriend, but, at the end of the episode, the female protagonist recovers from her mutism and sadistically watches as her captor dies of a heart attack. In the 1991 episode "Top Billing," a desperate actor auditioning at a local theater finally discovers that the company is made of the criminally insane patients of a madhouse who have brutally slaughtered their guards and medical staff. When he accidentally enters the asylum through a backstage door, the camera reproduces his quick glances on the ravaged corpses scattered all over the rooms and corridors before depicting his brutal murder. *Asylum* equally transforms the madhouse into an uncanny and frightening environment through the depiction of the evil perpetrated inside the clinic by a serial killer, who haunts the premises some decades later, when Briarcliff has been abandoned.

The second model of lunatic asylum portrayed in horror films is the squalid and dirty clinic, where the inmates are subjected to mistreatment and torture by the members of the staff. The clinic itself is therefore a frightening environment, filled with sufferings and fear, where horrors are daily consumed. The occurrence of supernatural horror further adds to its frightening dimension by actualizing the threat of death for the characters. Terence Fisher's films *Frankenstein Must Be Destroyed* (1969) and *Frankenstein and the Monster from Hell* (1974), for example, focus on the chaotic aspect of the clinic through the representation of the noisy and confused male patients and the hysterical women screaming and easily falling into raptures. The inmates are the material bodies for the doctor's experiments: their lives are perennially at risk even before Frankenstein's creature escapes from the laboratory. In F.W. Murneau's *Nosferatu* (1922), viewers are briefly shown the interior of Knock's cell, a squalid place filled with signs on the walls and clearly distinguished from the tidy and clean office of the clinic's doctor. Similarly, in Werner Herzog's remake of *Nosferatu* (1979), Renfield's cell is presented as small, dark and furnished only with two heavy iron grates, a space certainly inappropriate for the detention of a human being.

In the case of Joe Johnston's remake of *The Wolfman* (2010), werewolf Lawrence Talbot (Benicio Del Toro) is arrested and sent to Lambeth Asylum in London, where he is subjected to a series of violent therapies such as electroshock and water cure that further devastate his already-tormented body and mind (he is traumatized by the death of his mother and his brother, who have been murdered by his father). In this film the madhouse is represented as decrepit: Lawrence's cell is wet, with crumbling walls filled with chains and it looks more like a stable than a person's private room. The horror of Lawrence's torture is then "avenged" through the massacre that the werewolf enacts over the doctors who believed him to be under the illusory conviction that he could actually transform into a vicious beast. The massacre thus becomes a sort of retribution for the sufferings that had been inflicted on the protagonist. John Badham's *Dracula* (1979) is mainly set in Seward's lunatic asylum, which is introduced during a storm as a dark and chaotic environment, filled with upset patients alternatively screaming, fighting against each other or chained to their beds. The climatic storm on the outside is thus matched by the storm of the inmates' deranged feelings inside the clinic, whose staff seems to have no control over them. The same occurs in Francis Ford Coppola's *Bram Stoker's Dracula* (1992), in which the orderlies wear metallic cages on their heads, a rather odd accessory designed by lamented Oscar-winner Eiko Ishioka that seems to represent the very closure of the staff's minds and their will to separate themselves from the surrounding "contaminated/contaminating" environment and its residents. *Asylum* equally represents the clinic as an unhealthy and squalid environment, as we shall see later in detail, where the safety of the patients and the recovery of their mental health are not considered as a priority by the members of the madhouse's staff. This is particularly evident in those sequences of the series' last episodes that are set in the near future, when the former inmates Lana and Kit (who were both internalized unjustly) return to the clinic and discover an overcrowded environment filled with dirty patients almost completely abandoned to themselves.

The TV series thus utilizes the horror genre's thematic concern with violence and excessive human emotions. The representation of the psychiatric clinic as an uncanny and horrific site is conveyed through the use of Gothic tropes such as illegal experimentation on human patients, demonic possession, sexual violation resulting in unwanted pregnancy, and the mortal threat by plural serial killers. Furthermore, the characterization of the settings as gloomy and claustrophobic is instrumental for the creation of a discomforting atmosphere. Briarcliff Manor is a Victorian structure filled with rooms vaulted by arcs and connected to each other by dark corridors. The doctor's office, one of the locations where the greatest atrocities are planned, is a claustrophobic environment because of its lower ceiling, a particular that is exacerbated by the fact that Dr. Arden (Briarcliff's physician, who is actually a Nazi war criminal) is a very tall figure that fills the space in an imposing way. Equally claustrophobic is the corridor located on the ground floor of Briarcliff, with its wagon used to carry the patients' corpses to the outside foggy woods.

As it occurs in what Lorna Jowett and Stacey Abbott call "horror TV" (20)—which includes recent programs such as *True Blood* (2008–14), *The Vampire Diaries* (2009–17) and *Hannibal* (2013–15)—*Asylum* exploits the spectacle of body horror for aesthetic purposes, as the camera lingers on graphic details such as bleeding wounds and mutilated body parts. The program presents a great variety of violent actions, insisting on their graphic details, as is the case of the girl run over by Sister Jude, the severe nun who oversees patients and staff at Briarcliff, whose sordid past is revealed in a series of flashback sequences (2:2). Other illustrative examples are the inert body of the boy who was previously possessed by the devil (and whose lifeless eyes are fixed on the roof) (2:2) and the Mexican lady whose throat is pierced by a pair of scissors and floods the bed with blood (2:3). Special attention is dedicated to the bodies of the patients on which Dr. Arden experiments. The stumps of Shelley's legs (amputated by the doctor in order to prevent her from escaping) are framed through several close-ups that depict the horrible scars. The close-up frames on the realistic wounds are then alternated to the terrorized faces of the victims or the metonymic close-ups on the tools of torture (2:3). Moreover, the creatures roaming the woods around Briarcliff possess monstrous bodies on whose bubonic limbs and deformed faces the camera lingers, especially during their cannibalistic and disgusting meals (2:3). Finally, the aliens, who appear frequently throughout *Asylum*, are depicted as equally frightening. Viewers are never shown the entirety of their bodies, but only close-up frames on their enormous heads (which have a vertical mouth) and their six two-fingered limbs.

Asylum also reprises the representation of the psychiatric clinic in horror films and Gothic TV series through its mise-en-scène as well. According to Helen Wheatley, Gothic television is indeed characterized by weird lighting, camera works, and sound recording that reproduce a subjective perspective, visually dark narratives, "a mise-en-scène dominated by drab and dismal colours, shadows and closed-in spaces" (3). Precisely as it occurs in programs such as *The X-Files*, *Buffy the Vampire Slayer* (1997–2003) or the more recent *Hemlock Grove* (2013–15), the light sources are very directional, enabling the general look to be dark, while allowing beams of light to illuminate necessary details (Johnson 102). This is particularly evident in those sequences set in the 1960s, in which the brief images interspersed among the various scenes portray the clinic's corridors as gloomy, with pale lights coming from the lamps and from the cells' interiors. This already occurs in the first episode, "Welcome to Braircliff," in which the character of Kit Walker (the innocent young man who has been accused of Bloody Face's murders) is beaten by the clinic's guards for a misunderstanding. The images that introduce him when he is in solitary confinement present one of Briarcliff's corridors from a high point of view, a perspective that emphasizes both the claustrophobic nature of the clinic and its bad illumination (the lights of the lamps are insufficient to illuminate the environment completely). The images portraying him lying on the cell's floor and wearing a straitjacket are alternated to a frame of the same corridor from the alleged perspective of an inmate, but the image is utterly out of focus and only the contours of the walls and iron doors in the background are distinguishable, while a red light at the end of the corridor illuminates a human figure closing (perhaps menacingly) to the camera. Some frames also depict the corridors while the lights are turned off one by one, from the farthest to the nearest, which results in a twitching effect of approaching darkness to the camera. Such a discomforting effect is emphasized in the episode "Tricks or Treats," in which a power failure occurs and intermittent red emergency lights are automatically activated. In this sequence Lana looks frighteningly at her cell's door (which is framed with a medium shot at the height of the grate that filters the light) and then leaves the cell after the door opens automatically. A scanning pan along the red-lit corridor portrays the inmates leaving their rooms and contributes to the presentation of the location as a horrific one, especially by means of the distant alarm signaling the approach of an imminent danger (2:2).

Directional lighting is used in all of the rooms of the asylum. Indeed, the common room possesses numerous large windows, but the light penetrating from the outside is unidirectional and it is never warm or comforting. When Dr. Arden looks for the aliens who stole the body of Grace in the corridor of the basement that leads to the woods, he is intermittently lit by the skylights present in the vaulted ceiling (2:8). The succession of light and darkness makes the scene all the more frightening and suspenseful, and the squalid corridor is transformed into an uncanny location for the character too, who does not understand what has occurred to him previously and behaves as if it were an unfamiliar place for him. The anxiety of the character is paralleled by the gloomy mise-en-scène therefore, as it occurs during the outburst of the storm when Sister Jude's office is lit mainly by the blue light filtering through the windows, which emphasizes the claustrophobic nature of the room (2:3). The lightning projects her shadow on the bare walls and the rage of the storm matches her tumult of emotions.

Furthermore, over the entire season a visual motif is established which associates a blinding white light with the intervention of the aliens, precisely as in many episodes of *The X-Files*. The arrival of the creatures is foretold by the sudden illumination appearing behind the doors of the asylum, but the sequences that depict the creatures on their spaceship use such a light also as the only referent for space. Indeed, directions are not clear in the shining whiteness of what should be their laboratory: there are not any walls, roof, machinery, or furniture. Both Alma (Kit's wife, secretly married to him because she is a woman of color) and Grace (the inmate who has been accused of murdering her own family and who later becomes Kit's lover) are subjected to an impregnation surgery by the aliens and their sufferings are emphasized by the perspective (which confounds the horizontal and vertical axis) as well as by their subjective point of view, focusing on some details of the menacing aliens whose outline appears out of the shining light (2:5).

Directional light sources are utilized also in those scenes that are set in contemporary times, when the building of Briarcliff Manor is abandoned and haunted by the serial killer Johnny Thredson (Bloody Face's son). A green filter is applied to the images and makes the scarce light penetrating from the windows all the more gloomy: spectators are allowed to see clearly only the backlit shape of the corridors at large or the details of the dirty floors framed by the visiting couple's torches. Johnny roams the ruins of the building, passing through many plastic cloths that block the complete vision of the environment, while torturing himself over the death of his father and the abandonment by his mother (2:13). Briarcliff is used by Johnny to reenact his own personal trauma of abandonment: his father and mother allegedly appear in front of him inside the abandoned building and remind him of Lana's decision to disown him as her own child. This scene occurs in the episode "Madness Ends" and explains the events set in contemporary times that precede the murder of the couple and the killer's copycats represented in the first three episodes of the series. The dirty and chaotic setting of Briarcliff thus coincides with the agitated thoughts of the character visiting the abandoned structure and when the couple mentions the name of "Bloody Face," actually the name of his own father, Johnny becomes furious and impersonates the role of serial killer by wearing his mask made of human tissue, cuts the man's arm, and then ferociously kills the copycats roaming the clinic (2:3). The creators, writers, and directors of the series thus establish an analogy between the deranged psyche of the characters and the labyrinthine structure of the asylum, its dark corridors, and claustrophobic cells. Space and identity are correlated.

The emphasis on concealment is nevertheless alternated to a voyeurism of the medical or merely curious gaze. On the one hand, in the sequences set in contemporary times, Bloody Face, Jr., and his copycats are hidden in the darkness and repeatedly appear out of it to follow their victims through the corridors of the abandoned clinic. The ambiguity on the number of the killers is played upon darkness and the labyrinthine structure of the place: what is hidden or obscured by the dark shadows is one of the major sources of suspense for the characters *and* the viewers. On the other hand, viewers are allowed to gaze inside of the patients' cells, to check on their actions, to attempt to analyze their behaviors and, through the use of close-ups, to share in their sufferings. The importance of the gaze reflects a typical politics of the asylum which was initiated at the end of the eighteenth century, when, as Foucault argues, "everything was organized so that the madman would recognize himself in a world of judgement that enveloped him on all sides; he must know that he is watched, judged, and condemned" (267). It was, Foucault suggests, a kind of clinic "where unreason would be entirely contained and offered as a spectacle" (206). In *Asylum*, the sense of imprisonment is conveyed through the use of many frames that focus on the faces of the patients behind the bars of their cells' doors. This is particularly evident during the conversation between Kit and Grace through the door's window in the episode "Welcome to Briarcliff." In this sequence the images alternate the reaction shots of the two characters but always show one of them behind the bars (2:1). Closure and the sense of entrapment are also emphasized by the external electric light filtering inside through the gratings, while shadows are excessively and unrealistically evidenced on the walls. Furthermore, Sister Jude's nocturnal rounds of inspection in the wards and her peering through the grates with a torch parallel the viewer's gaze on the inmates. In the first episodes of the season she is often framed while looking at the cells' interiors through the grated windows and checking on the patients. Foucault's words seem to resonate in these sequences: "here is madness elevated to spectacle. [...] It was madness itself, madness in flesh and blood, which was put on the show" (69)—a particularly true affirmation if we consider, for instance, that up to 1815 lunatics were exhibited for a penny, every Sunday, at the hospital of Bethlem (68).

Finally, horror is conveyed through an eerie non-diegetic soundtrack, which is mainly composed of metallic sounds and the cracking of electricity. This enhances the suspense created for the spectator, who cannot rely on common sounds and expects something horrible to happen every time the sound of electricity intervenes. On the other hand, the happy but obsessively repeated diegetic song "Dominique" (1963) endows the represented events with an inappropriate and uncanny musical background. According to Mark Blankenship,

> it's horrifying when something cheerful gets placed in a dark context, like when the masked thugs in *A Clockwork Orange* croon "Singin' in the Rain" while terrorizing a couple in their home. [...] This disconnect suggests that the emotional and moral order have dissolved, and as it distorts the intentions of something kind, it becomes an act of violence against our understanding of society.

In *Asylum*, each episode contains a couple of sequences that are set in the common room of Briarcliff, where the song "Dominique" is repeatedly played in order to calm down the inmates. The introduction of the room on the screen occurs simultaneously with the song, especially after those scenes in which a patient of the clinic has been tortured, either by Sister Jude or Dr. Arden. The song, with its allegro tone, should act as a relief of tension. However, its sharp contrast with the previous images of torture is discomforting and unsettling for the spectator. As Blankenship argues, "the distance between the implied emotion of the music and the actual experience of the violence is almost like a psychic break." Such a psychic break is exacerbated by the very lyrics of the song, which narrate about a poor and simple traveler who preaches about God throughout Europe, thus converting other travelers and convincing people to adopt a simple and jolly lifestyle. The song's positive message becomes inappropriate as the soundtrack of a place where religion is only a mask for the enactment of tortures and cruelties.

Indeed, in *Asylum* the *real* horror consists of the ill-treatment suffered by the patients on the hands of the clinic's staff. Strip searches, hot hydrotherapy, electroshock therapies, and lobotomies are practiced in the place of an actual form of (psychological or physiological) treatment. For example, Kit is severely beaten on several occasions even when he is not responsible for any kind of misbehavior: violence is portrayed as unmotivated and unnecessary on the part of orderlies. Similarly, Lana is electrocuted in order to silence her lucid reasoning and because she demonstrates a rebellious attitude. *Asylum* thus reinscribes the reality of eighteenth- and nineteenth-century clinics—where the use of whips, straitjackets, chains, drugs, and stock therapies such as bloodletting, purges, and vomits was a common practice against the violence of the insane and the explosion of their fury—into a modern context. In real asylums, invasive treatments such as immersion of maniacs into icy water or cold showers reflected the powerlessness of the tyrannized patients in the face of arrogant and reckless doctors. All of these practices masqueraded as therapeutic. Institutionalization thus reduced the mad to mere negation, an absence of humanity. This was due to the fact that "in no country before 1800 was medical supervision a legal requirement, nor did medical overlordship automatically ensure good care" (Porter 97). Similarly, in *Asylum* the inmates are not allowed any basic rights: they are at the mercy of the staff's whims and petty revenges which mask their practices as therapeutic, although there is no actual recovery for any patient.

Sister Jude represents a corruption of the idea of nuns as pious and chaste women dedicated to helping the people in need, particularly if we consider her previous history of promiscuity, alcoholism, and the brutal violence she (personally) inflicts on the patients and the other members of the staff. She is introduced in the first episode while shaving the head of young Shelley, who is merely guilty of being lustful, an unnecessary punishment that Sister Jude considers instead as fitting for the patient's sin. The Sister's brutality and her lack of compassion are evident in her tough posture, severe eyes, and contemptuous glances towards anyone. These are underlined by the many close-ups on her face, which are used frequently during the first episodes of the season, especially when she becomes angry or realizes that she is not being obeyed respectfully. Sister Jude does not regret her decision to confine the journalist Lana Winters to a cell without even informing her relatives because she is lesbian (1:1). Subsequently, she shows no hesitation in physically punishing Kit and Grace by beating their naked skins with canes (whose variegated collection in the nun's wardrobe is worthy of an experienced sadist) (2:2). Rather than demonstrating Christian piety, Sister Jude is ruthless in her attempts to redeem the patients' souls and in her treatment of madness. As the character of Lana affirms, "in spite of the religious icons everywhere, this is a godless place" (2:4)—a statement further confirmed by those scenes that depict Dr. Arden's and Sister Mary Eunice's blasphemous desecration of the icons.

Even more brutal is the behavior of Dr. Arden, who attempts to rape Shelley and then cuts her legs off. The doctor then practices lobotomy on the patient Charlotte in order to erase her deviant memories and subsequently plots the downfall of Sister Jude with Monsignor Howard, not hesitating to lock the nun in her office with a serial killer bent on avenging himself on her. As several episodes demonstrate, Arden has been experimenting on the clinic's patients, transforming them into the cannibalistic creatures (called "Raspers") that reside in the woods outside Briarcliff. His attempts to create (through injections of steroids and of the bacteria of syphilis and tuberculosis) a human being who could resist the blast of an atomic bomb—anxious fear of which was often experienced during the Cold War by both politicians and the general public—leads to disastrous results, especially when the creatures manage to penetrate the clinic and murder some members of the staff. Nevertheless, Arden's experiments allude also to the psychiatric politics endorsed by eugenism and degenerationism that emerged by 1900 and sustained the theory that the very lives of the mentally ill were not "worth living" (Porter 186). As Porter indicates, in the United States eugenism and degenerationism urged compulsory confinement and sterilization as well as the use of psychiatry in immigration control, whereas in Nazi Germany more than 70,000 mental patients were gassed (186). The very fact that Dr. Arden is a Nazi soldier who emigrated to the United States after the War with falsified documents confirms such an interpretation of his actions: according to the narrative he probably put eugenicist theories into practice even before working at Briarcliff and, as is the case of Dr. Seward in Stoker's *Dracula*, he prioritizes his own scientific achievements over the well-being of his patients, who are considered as expendable for the sake of science.

Finally, Monsignor Howard is represented as a corrupt character, whose ambition blinds him to the atrocities that occur under his administration of the asylum. He strangles the monstrous Shelley with his rosary after she escapes the clinic before a scandal could ruin his dream of becoming a cardinal first and later the pope (2:7). For the same reason, he first fires Sister Jude from the clinic and then imprisons her, lying shamelessly about her medical condition in order to silence her. The monsignor is not a man of faith: his personal interests overcome his religious mission and faith, and his suicide at the end of the season is dictated by cowardice rather than by an act of contrition. Science and religion, as represented respectively by Dr. Arden on the one hand and Sister Jude and Monsignor Howard on the other hand, both fail in their attempt to cure madness and rehabilitate the inmates of Briarcliff.

The brutality of the asylum's working staff is all the more evidenced by the contrast established by the program between them and the representation of death as a black angel who visits all the characters who want their sufferings to end. The angel has a calm attitude, serene face, compassionate expression and moves with elegance: her kisses grant peace to the asylum's victims, a liberation from the physical and mental pains they experience, as the case of Grace demonstrates when she receives the kiss and almost ecstatically affirms "I'm free" (2:7). This is a positive characterization of death, especially when compared to the murders committed by the monsignor, Dr. Arden, and the devil-possessed Sister Mary Eunice. On the other hand, the aliens as well are presented as a beneficial force compared to the clinic's staff, considering that they save both Alma's and Grace's children, protect Grace from the orderlies and the other patients and in the last episode of the season, they take a forty-year-old Kit away when he is terminally ill from cancer, probably to cure him since they have been always interested in his fate (2:13).

The horror of the clinic's inmates is expressed through the program's mise-en-scène. High and low angles as well as unconventional frames are frequently used in order to distort the proportions of the characters, a cinematic technique that evidences the latter's small proportions against a hostile environment. This is the case of Kit and Grace when they are forced to solitary confinement and are waiting for a sterilization procedure. Kit is framed from afar while leaning against the wall (lit with a chiaroscuro effect), a frame that seems to increase the dimension of the cell, but that actually emphasizes the character's loneliness. When he talks to Grace on the other side of the wall, his back (on which the shadow of the grate is reflected) is framed on the left side of the bare wall, which further evidences the emptiness of the cell and his discomfort. Grace is then framed from the other side of the cell while leaning against the grate: she is desperate and begs to be released. Her figure is rendered small because it is framed by a high angle, especially when she subsequently lies crying on the mattress and when she punches against the walls of the cell (2:5). Throughout the season the characters are also framed upside down or through blurred or out-of-focus frames. For example, after having imprisoned Lana in his basement, Dr. Thredson has breakfast with her on the bed. What would appear as a normal conversation in which intimacy is shared between the two characters is depicted as uncanny and disturbing through the use of a high frame shot that pans over Lana and Thredson along a bent axis (2:6).

Furthermore, priority is given to the use of subjective perspective in those sequences that portray some characters being victimized by the villain. This is the case of Thredson's torture of Lana in "Dark Cousin." The doctor, who has revealed his identity as the serial killer Bloody Face, stands over his victim on the bed while wearing his mask made of human skin and remains. Extreme close-ups of the mask are alternated to the close-ups of Lana's terrorized face. The idea of violence is then transmitted by means of the quick cuts between the various frames, which add to the discomfort, the confusion, and the sense of injustice stimulated by the images (2:7). The imprisonment of Kit, for example, is composed of almost thirty cuts within a space of twenty seconds. These medium frames and close-ups rapidly following each other are mainly focused on the orderlies' use of force in the application of the restraints, their injection of a tranquilizer in the patient's arm, and the compulsory shower administered with a high-pressure jet of water (2:1). Simultaneously, several images frame the body and face of Kit in pain for the treatment he is receiving. Similarly, when Lana is electrocuted, the sequence is punctuated by twenty-eight quick cuts between the frames of the machinery, Lana's expressions of pain and her own point of view of the chandelier hanging from the roof and of Sister Jude's serious expression of approval of the procedure (2:2). Such a perspective is rendered all the more realistic by the fact that Sister Jude is alternatively framed in and out of focus after the electric charge is activated. The actual sufferings of the patients are never hidden from the scrutinizing (and compassionate) gaze of the spectator. As is the case of Milos Forman's film *One Flew Over the Cuckoo's Nest* (1975)—which "mobilized opinion against gothic asylums and the policing and normalizing roles of psychiatry" (Porter 211)—*Asylum* thus questions the legitimacy of the internment and the disciplinary treatment of the patients.

The squalor of Briarcliff is presented through the characterization of its patients. They are often depicted in the repetitiveness of their gestures, in the lack of normativity that characterizes them and that is due to their perennial irrationality. One of the inmates dances continually, some play alone at board games compulsively, a woman cuddles a doll as if it were a live infant, a patient bangs uninterruptedly his head on the walls, and another one is a chronic masturbator. The representation of such a chaotic environment is exacerbated in those sequences set a few years after Lana's escape and Kit's release. As the episode "Continuum" demonstrates, in the intervening years the asylum has become overcrowded and there is not a sufficient amount of personnel to care for the inmates, who wander without any purpose or destination through the corridors and the common room. Patients are abandoned to themselves by the new management of the clinic: they are dirty, (half-)naked, and copulate with each other without any decency. What is horrific is the squalor and dirt of the clinic itself, a revelation that Lana's exposé report brings to the attention of the general public in the season's last episode (2:13). Her fictional journalistic piece is a fitting allegory for all the real-life telling chronicles that appeared during the 1970s and 1980s and that forced the closure of many asylums. In *Asylum* viewers are confronted with a fictional representation that recalls both the literary and cinematographic representations of the psychiatric clinic, but that actually reproduces faithfully the reality of many psychiatric clinics all over the world.

Precisely as is the case of TV series such as *Star Trek* (1966–68) and *Buffy the Vampire Slayer*, *Asylum* uses the fantastic to "invite the viewer to question, not the fantastic aspects themselves, but the normative conventions of the everyday" (Johnson 7), by both evoking and disturbing socio-cultural verisimilitude in order to offer new (and potentially subversive) perspectives on society. Literally, *Asylum* explores the uncanny and liminal world that exists between reason and unreason as well as the fictional representation of alien abduction, devil possession, and the creation of monsters through illegal experimentation. Simultaneously, it condemns the abuses perpetrated in the past against the people whom society first judged as "mentally unfit" and then marginalized. The TV program thus reminds us that not all of the inmates confined to madhouses were completely mad or incurable and that the application of violent therapies was useless for their recovery. As the cases of Lana and Sister Jude demonstrate, *Asylum* therefore does not represent merely the containment of unreason, but the segregation of individuals who do not fit within society's dominant rules and expectations and that are perceived as a threat or a disturbance to its morality. The visual cinematography of the TV program is very expressive of the horror of both the location and the discomfort of its residents. The use of specific frames and angles, distorted images, drab colors and directional lighting, as well as the insistence on the gory details and on the sense of entrapment experienced by the inmates, are specifically intended to characterize the asylum as an uncanny and frightening place. The depiction of the psychiatric clinic as a location of horror is then instrumental in the creation of a message that criticizes (and elicits the spectators' empathy and compassion for) the suffering of the abused patients confined within such a structure.

Notes

1. The third (and rarest) type of representation of the madhouse in cinema and on TV is realistic and positive: it shows the illness of the patients and their poor conditions, but offers a hopeful representation by depicting the asylum as a luminous place where the inmates are treated cordially by the caring members of the staff. This is the case of Tod Browning's *Dracula* (1931), for instance, which shows the madman Renfield only inside the doctor's office, an ordered environment where the patient is confronted by the calm control of the group of rational men forming "the Crew of Light." In the TV serial *Dracula* (broadcast for a single ten-episode season on NBC in 2013), Dr. Murray and his daughter Mina work in Bethlem. In this structure the patients (all dressed rigorously in white) are generally calm, they are continually attended by the medical staff, and a serene atmosphere reigns (as the episode "Goblin Merchant Men" demonstrates). The staff of the madhouse is sensitive towards the needs of its patients and affectionate towards them: Mina organizes a dance for the residents in order for them to experience a joyous moment, a recollection of their previous happiness, "a small reminder of the lives they left behind" (in the episode "Servant to Two Masters"). The corridors are well lit by large windows and only a single scene is played at night, when the rooms are nevertheless filled with the lights of tens of candles. Similarly, Alfred Hitchcock's *Spellbound* (1945) introduces the psychiatric clinic as an orderly place where, thanks to the application of psychoanalysis, "the devils of unreason are driven from the human soul." Even after the arrival of Dr. Anthony Edwardes (Gregory Peck), an impostor suffering from amnesia and allegedly a murderer, the madhouse is never portrayed as an uncanny or frightening environment. These three examples characterize the clinic as a healthy, clean, and comfortable environment; horror and fear take place outside of it and do not influence its inmates or staff. As the analysis of *Asylum* demonstrates, this model does not apply to the representation of the madhouse in the TV series.

2. Although it is not a horror film, some of the sequences of the Disney production *Return to Oz* (1985, by Walter Murch) actually offer a nightmarish vision of the psychiatric clinic. After the character of Dorothy Gale (Fairuza Balk) has been interviewed by Dr. Worley and has been assigned to electrical therapy, the corridors of the clinic are portrayed as narrow, dark, and unsettling. The lights go out intermittently while a furious storm rages on the outside, the noise of the stretchers' wheels make a sinister squeaking, and the severe Miss Wilson (Jean Marsh) becomes a severe Victorian-like figure of punishment. The inmates' screams during the blackout are anguishing for the young protagonist tightened to the stretcher. Such a terrifying environment is then translated into Dorothy's representation of the land of Oz, in which the actors and actresses interpreting the staff of the asylum are the same of the malevolent characters infesting the magical realm.

Works Cited

The Amityville Asylum. Directed by Andrew Jones, Independent Moving Pictures, 2013.
Blankenship, Mark. "The Crazy History of That 'American Horror Story' Song." *Logo*.

NewNowNext, 15 Oct. 2014, www.newnownext.com/american-horror-story-asylum-song-dominique/11/2012/. Accessed 22 Oct. 2014.
Botting, Fred. "Power in the Darkness: Heterotopias, Literature and Gothic Labyrinths." *Gothic: Critical Concepts in Literary and Cultural Studies*, edited by Fred Botting and Dale Townshend, Routledge, 2004, pp. 243–68.
Bram Stoker's Dracula. Directed by Francis Ford Coppola, Columbia, 1992.
The Cabinet of Dr. Caligari. Directed by Robert Wiene, Decla film, 1920.
Dracula. Directed by Tod Browning, Universal, 1931.
Dracula. Directed by John Badham, Universal, 1979.
"Dracula." *Mystery and Imagination*. Written by Charles Graham, directed by Patrick Dromgoole, ITV, 18 Nov. 1968.
"Elegy." *The X-Files*. Written by John Shiban, directed by James Charleston, Fox, 4 May 1997.
Foucault, Michel. *Madness & Civilization: A History of Insanity in the Age of Reason*. Translated by Richard Howard, Vintage Books, 1988.
Frankenstein and the Monster from Hell. Directed by Terence Fisher, Hammer, 1974.
Frankenstein Must Be Destroyed. Directed by Terence Fisher, Hammer, 1969.
Ginger Snaps Unleashed. Directed by Brett Sullivan, Lion Gates Films, 2003.
"Goblin Merchant Men." *Dracula*. Written by Harley Peyton, directed by Andy Goddard, Universal and Carnival, 8 Nov. 2013.
Hake, Sabine. "Transatlantic Careers: Ernst Lubitsch and Fritz Lang." *The German Cinema Book*, edited by Tim Bergfelder, Erica Carter and Deniz Göktürk, British Film Institute, 2002, pp. 217–26.
Halloween. Directed by Rob Zombie, Dimension Films, 2007.
Halloween: Resurrection. Directed by Rick Rosenthal, Dimension Films, 2002.
Hellbound: Hellraiser 2. Directed by Tony Randell, New World Pictures, 1988.
Johnson, Catherine. *Telefantasy*. British Film Institute, 2005.
Jowett, Lorna, and Stacey Abbott. *TV Horror: Investigating the Dark Side of the Small Screen*. I.B. Tauris, 2013.
Leatherdale, Clive. *Bram Stoker's Dracula Unearthed*. Desert Island Books, 1998.
Maturin, Charles. *Melmoth the Wanderer*. 1820. Oxford University Press, 1992.
The Mummy. Directed by Terence Fisher, Hammer, 1959.
"Mute Witness to Murder." *Tales from the Crypt*. Written by Steven Dodd, directed by Jim Simpson, HBO, 10 July 1990.
A Nightmare on Elm Street 3: Dream Warriors. Directed by Chuck Russell, New Line Cinema, 1987.
Nosferatu. Directed by F.W. Murnau, Film Arts Guild, 1922.
Nosferatu. Directed by Werner Herzog, Werner Herzog Film Produktion, 1979.
One Flew Over the Cuckoo's Nest. Directed by Milos Forman, Fantasy Films, 1975.
"The Pest House." *Millennium*. Written by Glen Morgan and James Wong, directed by Allen Coulter, Fox, 27 Feb. 1998.
Porter, Roy. *Madness: A Brief History*. Oxford UP, 2002.
Red Dragon. Directed by Brett Ratner, Universal, 2002.
Return to Oz. Directed by Walter Murch, Disney, 1985.
"Servant to Two Masters." *Dracula*. Written by Rebecca Kirsch, directed by Brian Tyler, Universal and Carnival, 3 Jan. 2014.
The Silence of the Lambs. Directed by Jonathan Demme, MGM, 1991.
Spellbound. Directed by Alfred Hitchcock, MGM, 1945.
Stoker, Bram. *Dracula*. 1897. Penguin, 1994.
"Top Billing." *Tales from the Crypt*. Written by Miles Berkowitz, directed by Todd Holland, HBO, 26 June 1991.
Trauma. Directed by Dario Argento, Penta Film, 1993.
Wheatley, Helen. *Gothic Television*. Manchester UP, 2006.
The Wolfman. Directed by Joe Johnston, Universal, 2010.

The Swampy Boundaries of "Otherness" in *Freak Show* and *Roanoke*

Cameron Williams Crawford

Much speculation surrounded the premiere of *American Horror Story*'s sixth season, *Roanoke*. Unlike the series' other cycles, the marketing strategies used to promote the season were designed to keep all details involving the cast and plot a secret; FX released teaser trailers that purposely misled audiences in regard to the season's theme, marking the first time in *AHS*' history that a season's subtitle was not released in advance of the first episode. Even after the first episode aired, audiences were still confused by the season's unusual metafictional structure. Whereas other iterations of *AHS* feature fairly linear storylines, *Roanoke* gives us a fictional show within a show. The first half of the season is presented as a documentary called *My Roanoke Nightmare* that reenacts the paranormal experiences of a married couple, Matt and Shelby Miller, after they move into an old mansion in North Carolina and are tormented by the ghosts of the Roanoke colonists; the second half takes the form of *Return to Roanoke*, a reality-type show that follows the cast of *My Roanoke Nightmare* as they spend three days in the mansion during the Blood Moon, a time when the ghosts are free to wreak murderous havoc on the living.

Given this atypical approach, audiences initially struggled to place *Roanoke* within the *AHS* universe, as previous seasons have featured overlapping characters, locations, or storylines indicating a connection between the series' cycles. Fans were therefore delighted when *Roanoke*'s fifth episode introduced the character Edward Phillipe Mott, the eccentric aristocrat who originally built the mansion sometime in the late eighteenth century. In a cameo on *My Roanoke Nightmare*, historian Doris Kearns

Goodwin explains that "Edward had what would probably be diagnosed now as severe social anxiety." Because Edward "hated being around people," he left behind his wife and child in Philadelphia and "found a plot of land deep in the North Carolina woods on Roanoke River's edge and bought it from the state." Following Edward's death, "the house remained in the Mott trust for over a century, but it was said that madness always ran in the family. The line ended in scandal when the last Mott died in South Florida in 1952" (6:5). Astute viewers were quick to identify this descendant of Edward's as Dandy Mott, the petulant, psychopathic mass murderer from *AHS*' fourth season, *Freak Show*.

In telling the history of the Mott family, *Roanoke* establishes an explicit connection to *Freak Show*. This connection is important, as I suggest, because it emphasizes an even more profound connection between the series' fourth and sixth seasons that can be found in their settings. *Freak Show* follows Fraulein Elsa and her "Cabinet of Curiosities," one of the last remaining freak shows in America in the early 1950s. Elsa's "freaks" are not welcomed by the other residents of Jupiter, Florida, and as such, they are spatially relegated to the fringes of town: the swamp. *Roanoke* is similarly placed in an isolated setting along North Carolina's Outer Banks; the mansion is evidently located somewhere "deep in the ... woods on Roanoke River's edge," an area replete with swampland. The space also serves as a refuge for marginalized or dangerous identities, including the homosexual Edward Mott, the ghosts of the Roanoke colonists, and the cannibalistic "hillbilly" Polk family. This overlap in setting is subtle, yet significant, especially when considering the symbolic resonance of the swamp. In *Shadow and Shelter: The Swamp in Southern Culture*, Anthony Wilson describes the swamp as a "uniquely" southern landscape, one that "occupies an intriguingly complex and liminal space in the Southern and national imaginations and signifies powerfully across discourses of race, cultural and literal contagion, ethnography, and ecology" (ix). *Freak Show* uses "freakishness" as an obvious metaphor for its exploration of "difference"—racial, class, sexual, ability. *Roanoke* similarly interrogates the othering of cultural outsiders in the way the season depicts "the forest beyond the settlement [as] the place where the representatives of 'civilization' are pitched against forces that embody 'savagery,' and order—moral, psychological, and geographical—is opposed to 'chaos'" (Fusco). As this essay argues, *Freak Show* and *Roanoke* draw on the complex and contradictory history of the swamp as a "subversive space" (Wilson, *Shadow and Shelter* x) that is intimately connected to the identity of its inhabitants; understanding how they evoke the cultural significance of the swamp illuminates the seasons' social commentary, particularly the ways they confront southern regional and national anxieties about difference.

The Swamp in Southern History and Culture

Swamps exist in various places around the world, but they are found in the highest concentration in the American South. In some ways, this makes the swamp an almost distinctly southern landscape. Swamps therefore hold a unique place in the nation's popular imaginary, particularly as they have a long history of being associated with discourses of "otherness." Rodney James Giblett explains that swamps "have often been seen as horrific places ... associated with death and disease, the monstrous and the melancholic, if not the downright mad. [Swamps] are 'black waters' ... seen as a threat to health and sanity, to the clean and proper body, and mind" (3). Much of this lore can be traced back to antebellum plantation culture, which regarded the swamp as both a literal and figurative obstacle, a space that stood as the antithesis of the agrarian, pastoral ideal that was such a part of the South's structuring mythology. Practically, swampland was difficult to cultivate; symbolically, as the plantation system was linked inseparably to "prevailing ideals of white Southern society" that insisted on upholding strict racial and class hierarchies, the swamp became even more distinctly "opposed" (Wilson, *Shadow and Shelter* xvii). As Wilson writes, the swamp was "a threat" to the social order of plantation society because it served as a sanctuary for society's outcasts and as a refuge for runaway slaves (xvii). That the swamp—although still considered a "place of fear and uncertainty"—was home to exiles, "the desperate and disenfranchised," and many a runaway slave gave its already "threatening significance for the white South a new and more profound dimension" (xvii-xviii). Because swamps remained formally uncolonized tracts of land, those that resided there were "rarely officially recorded"; and since most of the swamp's inhabitants were outcasts and fugitives who didn't submit to "the myth-making agenda of antebellum Southern society, this state of affairs was mutually beneficial to both Southern society and those who dwelt outside of it" (xvi). In the South, therefore, the swamp endures as a literal boundary "between the actual and the ideal" (xiii).

There is also notable ambiguity inherent in the definition of swamp. As Wilson writes, the swamp "defies easy categorization" (*Shadow and Shelter* xiii); as such, the true "horror" of swamps "lies in the fact that [they] are neither strictly land nor water" (Giblett 3). By definition, swamps are themselves an "other" landscape. With such characterization, compounded by centuries of lore and superstition, it is therefore understandable why the swamp holds such a central place in the Southern Gothic tradition, providing "classic locales for stories of ghosts, monsters, and devils, originating in antebellum oral and literary tradition and persisting ... even today" (Wilson, "Swamps" 152).

It was toward the turn of the twentieth century when the image of the swamp began to evolve. Increasing environmental awareness in the face of rising ecological exploitation and wetland loss encouraged a "new appreciation" for swamps, which is reflected in much of the southern literature of the time. Writers of the Southern Renascence eschewed "wistful evocations of romantic plantation life to render a more complex and multicultural South" (152). Black writers of the Harlem Renaissance also reexamined the importance of swamp spaces, particularly their history as a place of refuge for African Americans, thereby writing against traditional plantation narratives and depicting swamps not as obstacles, but "as pure, distinctive spaces, removed to some extent from the troubling legacies of Old South society" (152). While contemporary southern culture has a greater understanding of the environmental necessity of wetland conservation, the swamp's Gothic associations still linger, as *Freak Show* and *Roanoke* both make evident.

The Swamp in Freak Show

The swamp's association with the fear of "otherness," so much a part of the Southern Gothic tradition itself, plays directly into the narrative of the *AHS* franchise, which skillfully blends (and bends) the standard conventions of the horror genre with factual horrors taken straight out of the pages of American history. In *Freak Show*, Fraulein Elsa selects the swampland on the outskirts of Jupiter, Florida, as the ideal home for her Cabinet of Curiosities. When her traveling carnival is first introduced, the camera pans across a wide shot of the brightly colored circus tents erected in a vast, open field, surrounded on almost every side by water. The land is flat and marshy. Though shot on location in New Orleans—Ryan Murphy, in an interview with *Deadline*, says, "We really did take over acres and acres of farmland near the swamp" (Andreeva)—the landscape is a perfect substitute for any in Jupiter, Florida. Like Louisiana, Florida is hot, humid, and brimming with swamps, and Jupiter is located within the most famous swamp in America, the Everglades. It is significant that *Freak Show* uses the swamp as its setting; it is treated as a "subversive space" that is intimately connected to the identity of its inhabitants, and it accentuates the season's critical interrogation of otherness and difference.

In *Freak Show*, the swamp that Elsa makes home to her traveling carnival is primarily seen as a "horrific place"; there are several moments in the show that make conspicuous the ways that the swamp is associated with "death and disease, the monstrous and the melancholic, if not the downright mad" (Giblett 3). Elsa rents the tract of swampland for her freak show from an older couple, who after only two months into a year's lease decide they no longer want Elsa and her Cabinet as tenants. In the first episode, the landlord, Mr. Haddonfield, tells Elsa that he wants her and her "troupe" to vacate. He claims that there's a revival coming down from Georgia that wants to set up in the field, and apparently unlike Elsa, they pay upfront—in cash. After Elsa argues with him, Mr. Haddonfield steps closer to her and reluctantly admits the true reason that he wants Elsa and her troupe off his land: his wife doesn't like having the "freaks" staying in their field. "She's having nightmares," he tells her (4:1). Mrs. Haddonfield, it seems, regards the traveling carnival and Elsa's "monsters"—that Elsa insists wouldn't hurt a fly—with fear. That Mrs. Haddonfield wants the freaks off her land and is having nightmares about their presence suggests that she fears Elsa's traveling side show will corrupt or taint her land with their "monstrousness." In this same episode, Elsa recruits conjoined twins, Dot and Bette, to join her Cabinet and star as one of the show's main attractions. While Bette is excited to start a new life, Dot is not at all pleased with her new surroundings. She writes in her diary just after her arrival: "My soul plumbs new depths of despair. I long for the quiet of the farm, the warmth of my bed, the smell of flowers outside my window. I'm surrounded by a cesspool of activity. No words can do justice to the depravity that permeates the grounds … darkening further the edges of my nightmares" (4:1). Like Mrs. Haddonfield, Dot sees the freak show and the swamp wherein it resides as depraved and furthermore associates it—by calling it a cesspool—with disease and contagion. Dot also seems to see the space that "darkens the edges" of her nightmares as "evil."

In addition to being home for Fraulein Elsa's Cabinet of Curiosities, the swamp is home to the terrifying serial killer, Twisty the Clown. Through Twisty, *Freak Show* takes the swamp's association with "evil" to a grisly extreme. Twisty's appearance alone is horrifying. He wears a dirty, bloodstained clown outfit, the ruffled bib and oversized pom pom buttons no longer comical. On his head is what appears to be a very literal skin cap; the edges of this cap, which start at the top of his forehead, are dark with dried blood, indicating that it was likely fashioned out of someone's scalp. Adorning the top are three tufts of multicolored hair that stand on end. Most frightening, though, is Twisty's mask, a gruesome, black-lipped, toothy, Cheshire Cat–like grin that covers only the bottom half of his face. Twisty makes his disturbing, murderous intentions known from the moment he is first introduced when, on a bright afternoon at the secluded Lake Okeechobee, on the outskirts of Jupiter, Twisty attacks a young couple, Troy and Bonnie, that has just finished picnicking. After bludgeoning both in the head with a set of three bowling pins and knocking them unconscious, Twisty proceeds to mercilessly and repeatedly stab

Troy in the chest. Bonnie awakes to see this, and screams, jumps up, and tries desperately to run away, but Twisty captures her and takes her back to his "house" in the swamp where he locks her up in a cage (4:1). Twisty's "house" is an old school bus that's long been abandoned somewhere deep in the swamp—much deeper, notably, than Fraulein Elsa's traveling sideshow, suggesting that Twisty inhabits a level of "otherness" that far surpasses the Cabinet of Curiosities. The area is isolated and heavily wooded, the bus overgrown with thick vines. Locked in the cage along with Bonnie is a little boy named Corey (captured after Twisty brutally murders his parents). Corey and Bonnie are Twisty's captive audience; Twisty forces them to watch him do "clown stuff," like make balloon animals. But when the balloon pops and his audience screams in terror, Twisty gets angry and starts breaking things, throwing oversized bouncy balls around the bus and kicking and ominously rattling the cage. Twisty is indeed a horrifying figure and quite literal (murderous) threat to the outside world, and he embodies the swamp's historical association with "evil."

While Bonnie, Corey, and Mike—the third captive Twisty adds to the cage—are terrified of Twisty's bus in the swamp, Dandy Mott finds the space alluring. Dandy is the only son of Gloria, an obscenely wealthy single mother who dotes obsessively on Dandy and whose smothering has spoiled him rotten, pun definitely intended. Dandy *is* rotten to the core, a petulant grown adult with the arrested development of a child who throws tantrums anytime he doesn't get his way. Dandy also has a proclivity for killing animals and is thrilled by acts of violence. Imagine his excitement, then, when Gloria encounters Twisty while she's out driving and insists on taking him home to be a "friend" for Dandy. Dandy demands that the clown "amuse" him, but Twisty is not at home in Dandy's opulent mansion. Twisty knocks Dandy out with one of his bowling pins and flees back to the swamp. Dandy comes to just in time to follow Twisty and is delighted by what he discovers. Bonnie has managed to escape, and she runs into Dandy and begs him to help her. Instead, Dandy grabs her and drags her back toward the bus, calling, "Clown! Look what I have for you! You'll have to do a much better job of confinement," he tells Twisty, "if we're going to have any fun" (4:2). Dandy is so enthralled by Twisty's space in the swamp because he recognizes it as a place where he can get away with committing unspeakable acts that he can't safely commit while within the bounds of "normal" society. And in the first half of the series, Dandy does, in fact, return to the swamp multiple times. At one point, Dandy dons a clown costume and returns to Twisty's bus, taking with him a large knife with which he intends to torture and/or kill Twisty's prisoners (4:3). In a continuation of this scene, Dandy gets a chance to perform his grotesque desires in front of a live audience when—along with Twisty—he puts on a "magic" show for Twisty's captives wherein he attempts to saw Maggie/Esmerelda in half (4:4). Later, Dandy lures Andy, a man he "picks up" up at the local gay bar, back to Twisty's bus. There, he brutally stabs and kills him (4:5). Like Twisty, Dandy is able to satiate his depraved bloodlust most freely in the swamp.

Dot and the landlord's wife, Mrs. Haddonfield, associate the swamp—particularly on account of its inhabitants—with disease, depravity, and evil. Twisty and Dandy, two ruthless murderers, foster perceptions of the swamp as a horrific place. Elsa, however, sees the swamp as a safe space for her "monsters." She keeps them hidden there and strongly discourages them from ever venturing into town. For Elsa, the swamp provides a literal boundary that keeps her people in and keeps others out. When Jimmy—dubbed "Lobster Boy" because his fingers are fused together to resemble "pinchers"—flagrantly disregards that boundary, Elsa warns him that he's put himself in danger and has put the other "freaks" in danger as well, including his own mother, Ethel "the Bearded Lady." Elsa cautions Jimmy, "What happens when [they see] you? All of you? You know where you're going to end up. Where they send indigent freaks—the state mad house. And what about your mother? Huh? You want her to die drooling in some hideous asylum?" (4:1). For Elsa, and for the freaks themselves—Dot eventually included—the swamp offers a space where their "otherness" can thrive, no longer restrained by the rules of "normal" society. As Bette writes in her diary, now, at home in the carnival tents, she has finally been "freed from the shadows." While Dot initially longs to return to the farm where she and Bette once lived, Bette embraces her move into the swamp as an "escape from darkness" (4:1), darkness here signifying normalcy, the isolation she felt living among "normal" society.

If the swamp is a place where "otherness" thrives, it's also the site of uninhibited sexuality. In several episodes, *Freak Show* makes it clear that sexuality in the realm of "normal" Jupiter society must be contained. Jimmy's involvement with the Jupiter ladies' "Tupperware parties" perhaps best demonstrates this. During these parties, Jupiter's sexually-deprived housewives each secretly take turns in the bedroom with Jimmy, where he pleasures them with his "pinchers." Similarly, Stanley, the con artist who targets Elsa's show in the hopes of killing and selling one of (or part of) her freaks to the American Morbidity Museum, has hushed liaisons with male escorts in motel rooms. In the swamp, though, there's no need to hide; non-normative sexualities abound here. Penny, the candy striper Elsa meets while visiting Dot and Bette at the hospital, discovers she enjoyed being drugged and "ravaged" by an orgy of freaks, so much so that she returns in order to be with Paul, the Illustrated Seal Man (4:1). The show eventually becomes her permanent home when her father discovers what she's been up to and forcibly tattoos her with reptile scales, turning her into

Lizard Girl (4:6). In the swamp, the rules of ordinary society don't apply. It is a subversive space where "otherness" of all kinds can be expressed, unbound by any limitations.

In this way, then, the swamp furthermore serves as a site of resistance. This is best confirmed at the end of the season's first episode. After killing a policeman—a symbol of order, of convention—who comes out to the swamp to accuse the freaks as being responsible for the recent string of murders (actually committed by Twisty), Jimmy gathers the others around the cop's slain body and rallies them: "All we've ever wanted was a place where we could feel safe and be just the way we are," he tells them, "From this day on, if anyone tries to mess with us ... they're going to end up like this pig" (4:1). The others cheer in agreement and pull out their weapons, then—together—they proceed to ceremoniously hack up and dispose of the body of the cop. In this scene, Jimmy and the others quite literally destroy the rules of social order to claim the swamp as a free space, one that, like its inhabitants, can freely celebrate difference. The swamp as setting in this scene—indeed, throughout the season—adds another layer of dimension to this social commentary, reminding us that those boundaries that separate "normal" from "other" are themselves murky, swampy categories.

The Swamp in Roanoke

Ultimately, *Freak Show* uses the swamp as a vehicle for exploring southern regional and national anxieties about otherness and difference, suggesting, in the end, that those boundaries that separate "normal" from "other" are themselves "swampy." In *Roanoke*, the swamp is similarly represented as a liminal space, and a complex one, that indeed "signifies powerfully" across discourses of otherness. *Roanoke* builds on *Freak Show*'s central metaphor, and understanding the spatial politics of the swamp illuminates the season's examination of difference.

The swamp setting in *Roanoke* is arguably more subtle than in *Freak Show*. Nevertheless, the show makes the setting conspicuous by drawing on historical events surrounding the original Roanoke colony as well as through other context clues. Despite the season's title, *Roanoke* (and the titles of the shows within the show, *My Roanoke Nightmare* and *Return to Roanoke*), the mansion is not actually located on Roanoke Island proper, one of the islands along North Carolina's Outer Banks and part of the state's coastal plain region. Matt's sister, Lee, makes this apparent when the psychic medium Cricket arrives at the mansion to help locate her missing daughter, Flora. When Cricket tells the Millers that the only way to locate Flora "is to find out everything we can about *the enemy*"—Thomasin "the

Butcher" White and her band of Roanoke colonists—Lee is confused: "Roanoke has nothing to do with us," she says, "Everyone knows that Roanoke is nowhere even near here. There's a historical monument over an hour away" (6:3). In the season's fourth episode, a newspaper article and police report obtained by Dr. Elias Cunningham, the professor who stays in the mansion while researching his book, reveals that the mansion is situated somewhere in Martin County and therefore located on the state's coastal plain, a region notorious for its unique wetland habitats that include "high and low pocosin, bogs, fresh and brackish water marshes, hardwood swamps, and Atlantic white cedar swamps" ("Alligator River"). In fact, according to Bland Simpson, "Most of the largest remaining swamps (or 'dismals,' as early settlers called them) in the eastern United States are located in North Carolina's coastal plain." This includes the Great Dismal Swamp, one of the largest wetland areas on the Eastern seaboard. It is also the site of one of the prevailing theories regarding the disappearance of the Roanoke colonists, which suggests that the colonists integrated with a local tribe and moved north, eventually passing through the Great Dismal Swamp. *Roanoke* seemingly draws on this theory when Cricket reveals the backstory of the Butcher and the other colonists whose ghosts now terrorize the Millers. According to Cricket, when John White, the governor of the Roanoke colony, "was persuaded to travel back to England for more supplies," he left Thomasin, his wife, in charge until his return. The starving colonists begged Thomasin to move inland in search of food, and when she insisted on staying put as John instructed, they rebelled and banished her, locked in a scold's bridle, to the woods and left her to die. Thomasin was saved (so to speak) by the witch Scáthatch and returned to the colony, where she slaughtered those who rebelled against her. She moved with her remaining followers a hundred miles inland to the very land on which Edward Mott later builds his ill-fated mansion (6:3).

It is through the colonists that *Roanoke* most explicitly establishes the swamp as a horrific place associated with "death and disease, the monstrous and the melancholic, if not the downright mad" (Giblett 3). Thomasin is saved by Scáthatch, but at the cost of her soul. Scáthatch is depicted as a malevolent entity whose dark powers come from her devotion to ancient Pagan gods. In order to fulfill her pact with Scáthatch, Thomasin must commit atrocious acts such as ritually sacrificing children to "sanctify the land." Thomasin purposely ties the colonists' spirits to the land for eternity during her final blood sacrament, when she murders the remaining colonists during the Blood Moon and sacrifices herself to Scáthatch (6:3). Following this act, the land seemingly becomes a magnet for other evil, the best example of which can be seen in Miranda and Bridget Jane, the sisters who turn the mansion into an assisted living facility wherein they torture and murder their residents (6:2). The sisters move to the house in North Carolina when they're on the lam, wanted for murder in Rochester, New York. As in the case of *Freak Show*'s Twisty and Dandy, the swamp provides the sisters a space to most freely act out their nefarious fantasies that they cannot safely commit while within the bounds of "normal" society. Dr. Elias Cunningham surmises that the sisters were drawn by the "ominous history" of the mansion and the tract of land on which it sits (6:2). Notably, Elias manages to escape his stay without being killed by the Butcher or one of the mansion's other resident ghosts; however, his time there drives him to the brink of insanity, suggestive of the ways in which the swamp has historically been perceived as "a threat to health and sanity, to the clean and proper body, and mind" (Giblett 3). *Roanoke* depicts this space as sinister and cursed, and in this way builds on cultural assumptions that regard the swamp as a threatening place of evil.

This area of land is also home to the inbred, cannibalistic Polk family. Shelby identifies them as "swamp people," and they serve as another example of how *Roanoke* engages the swamp's association with that which is evil and "monstrous." Ishmael, Mama Polk, and their sons—Lot, Cain, and Jether—are the last descendants of a clan that has survived for generations by colluding with the Butcher and the colonists, providing them with victims for their ritual sacrifices. In addition, the Polks keep some victims for themselves to torture and turn into human jerky. Their taste for human flesh marks the Polks as especially depraved, as does their family's history of inbreeding. In the swamp, the Polks are uninhibited, free to openly flout the taboo behaviors that are restricted in "normal" society. The Polks furthermore live in abject squalor. As Katherine Fusco observes, "The scary-looking Polks wear trucker hats and have bad teeth and skin, those classic markers of class status"; what's more, "the barn where the family grows marijuana (the least of their crimes) features a Confederate flag as its most notable décor." Through the Polks, *Roanoke* therefore also confronts pernicious stereotypes about the rural white South, particularly those that "[locate] the culturally or politically disagreeable at the geographical as well as economic or cultural fringes of society" (Fusco). That the "monstrous" and culturally undesirable Polks are relegated to the swamp draws on the swamp's antebellum history as a space used to enforce strict racial and class hierarchies that view "otherness" as threatening.

At the same time, the Polks are also an example of how *Roanoke* problematizes those very hierarchies. Because swamps are neither strictly land nor strictly water, they resist "easy categorization," trouble boundaries. As is similarly true of *Freak Show*, *Roanoke* articulates a palpable tension between social classes that plays out in the conflict between the "other" antagonists—the Butcher and the colonists, but more specifically the Polks—and those representatives of "normal" society. While the Polks are some of "the more easily hateable ghouls roaming the landscape ... [the family] draws focus from the more banal sources of evil closer to home"; according to Fusco:

> To be fair, many truly disturbing horrors have marked America's rural landscapes, and these are on view in [*Roanoke*]: in the third episode, we learn the police are in cahoots with the Polk family; much use is made of mutilated pig corpses, recalling anti–Semitic and anti–Muslim hate crimes. Although the Polks won't turn out to be directly responsible, one black man meets an end that cannot recall anything but the United States' lynching history. It is, in short, a depiction of rural America as multi-cultural leftist nightmare, a leifmotif that the show repeats in a number of increasingly baroque and disturbing tableaus. Through such a rehearsal of the worst abuses of immigrants, gay people, and African-Americans, Murphy has readied his audience for vengeance against the Polk family. [...] The elites become as brutal as anyone, especially as the Polks come to fulfill the newcomers' initial suspicions about them. While early on the coastal elite characters use language like "inbred" and "swamp people" to describe the Polks, by episode eight, the series has so ratcheted up the Polks' abuses that the audience is rooting for the actress who bashes Mama Polk's head in with a hammer.

This reversal is careful on the part of *Roanoke*, as it purposely implicates us as an audience in further marginalizing the Polks. Yet this scene asks us, as does the scene in *Freak Show* when Jimmy and his friends murder the cop, who is truly the "other" in this moment? The cannibalistic Polks, or the now murderous "elites"?

Conclusion

The presence of Edward Mott in *Roanoke* directly links the season to *Freak Show* and its depraved villain, Dandy Mott, but the connection between these two seasons goes beyond the Mott family's history. It is certainly significant that the settings of both *Freak Show* and *Roanoke* include swamp spaces, and understanding how these seasons draw on the complex and contradictory cultural history of the swamp as a "subversive space" can only elucidate an analysis of their social commentary. In *Freak Show* and *Roanoke*, the southern swamp is a space that is intimately connected to the identity of its inhabitants. It is a liminal space, and a complex one, that indeed "signifies powerfully" across discourses of otherness. Ultimately, *Freak Show* and *Roanoke* use the swamp as a means by which to explore southern regional and national anxieties about otherness and difference, suggesting, in the end, that those boundaries that separate "normal" from "other" are themselves "swampy."

Works Cited

"Alligator River National Wildlife Refuge." *Roanoke Island Guide*, 2019, roanokeisland.net/alligatorriver.
Andreeva, Nellie. "Ryan Murphy on Jessica Lange's 'AHS' Exit & Possible Return, Building His 'Hotel' & Next 'American Crime Story'—Emmys." *Deadline*, 18 June 2015, deadline.com/2015/06/ryan-murphy-american-horror-story-hotel-jessica-lange-leaving-1201447985/.
Fusco, Katherine. "*AHS: My Roanoke Nightmare* and Our Incoherent Understanding of Trump Voters." *Dilettante Army*, 2017, www.dilettantearmy.com/articles/ahs-roanoke-trump-voters.
Giblett, Rodney James. *Postmodern Wetlands: Culture, History, Ecology*. Edinburgh UP, 1996.
Simpson, Bland. "Swamps." *NCPedia*, 2006, www.ncpedia.org/swamps.
Wilson, Anthony. *Shadow and Shelter: The Swamp in Southern Culture*. UP of Mississippi, 2006.
_____. "Swamps." *The New Encyclopedia of Southern Culture*, vol. 8, edited by Martin Melosi, UNC Press, 2007, pp. 150–53.

The Meta-Carnival

Monsters and Mothers in Freak Show

JENNIFER K. COX

The first episode of *American Horror Story*'s fourth season, *Freak Show*, drew a record 6.13 million viewers and still holds the title for the FX network's most-watched program (Kissell). In her review for *The New Yorker*, Emily Nussbaum applauds the choice to set "a show dedicated to spectacle" in a Florida freak show. "What could be more perfect?" she writes, "Brassy and divinely decadent, 'American Horror Story' ... is one of TV's truly experimental series—and, like many seedy carnivals, it's been subject to both nervous laughter and progressive criticism." Even two years after *Freak Show*'s success, carnivalesque overtones echo in comments on the show's reception. In a 2016 interview for *Entertainment Weekly*, Tim Stack notes series creator Ryan Murphy's genuine astonishment at its overall success when he remarks, "It went from being this thing that nobody believed in to something that's now an amusement park attraction" (23). The Emmy-winning horror anthology series incorporates a different theme and setting for each season, providing *Freak Show* with a wealth of material for nightmare fodder. This season pays homage to Tod Browning's 1932 horror film, *Freaks*, which became a cult classic known for its eerie refrain: "One of us! One of us!" Instead of relying on monsters or other supernatural elements to deliver scares, like the vengeful ghosts in *Murder House*, demon possession in *Asylum*, or witches in *Coven*, *Freak Show* focuses on the human capacity to commit monstrous acts as fuel for terror.

Although the freak performers may appear monstrous to "normal" townspeople, the real monsters in horror stories are never quite so obvious.[1] Subversive portrayals of motherhood evoke a deep sense of the uncanny for viewers who recognize characters that are supposed to be maternal figures, even as the story simultaneously defamiliarizes them. Added to the show's premise, the historical context of a small southern town in the 1950s further emphasizes pervasive social concerns about gender expectations and cultural identities. As Carol Margaret Davison writes, "The Gothic and television merged, appropriately and tellingly, in a disillusioned postwar America of the 1950s that was busy reestablishing its ideals" (491). Like so many other forms of mass entertainment in popular culture, television produces narratives that either reinforce or resist social norms. Davison points out how the American suburbs became symbolic of the American Dream as a kind of "bourgeois utopia [that] valorized the nuclear family, reified gender identities ... and served, through filmic and other discourses, to consolidate a mythic, collective middle-class identity involving shared goals and values" (491). Popular sitcoms like *Father Knows Best, Leave it to Beaver,* and *Ozzie and Harriet* illustrated a mythical suburban ideal for American audiences of the 1950s and 1960s; families that deviated from these popular scripts were considered abnormal.

Just as Browning scouted freak shows for performers to act in his infamous film,[2] *Freak Show* employs actors with physical disabilities to portray (some) freak performers. Such casting decisions highlight the constructed nature of individual identity labels based on physical appearances, like "disabled," "freak," or "monster." However, as Rachel Adams points out in *Sideshow U.S.A.*, "fictional representations of freaks cannot be crudely reduced to simple sociological or historical referents, [because] their meaning is equally diminished by reading them exclusively as archetypes for timeless human preoccupations" (8). While page limitations on this essay prohibit a thorough examination of the text via disability studies, the implications for such a reading remain ripe with interpretive possibilities. *Freak Show* resists portraying freaks as two-dimensional characters whose disabilities either define or allegorize them; audiences see physically disabled characters in everyday settings leading flawed human lives. Instead of imitating literary texts that "necessarily make disabled characters into freaks, stripped of normalizing contexts and engulfed by a single stigmatic trait" (Thomson 11), the show's three-dimensional portrayal neither lionizes nor demonizes characters with physical differences. In addition, the show highlights social constructions that define—and limit—families and other collective social units according to cultural norms.

Over the course of thirteen episodes, *Freak Show* endeavors to explore such individual and collective identities by questioning larger cultural ideas like family, the importance of home, and what it means to be a mother. Beyond identity politics, however, a fundamentally disturbing portrayal of motherhood undergirds the show's individual conflicts and mysteries. The concept of motherhood is foundational to understanding larger cultural ideas like family and home. As figures central to individual identity, and as cornerstones of domestic life and the moral authority it imparts, I suggest the show's portrayal of subversive mothers is what elicits true horror, particularly when set in a postwar America struggling to re-establish a sense of national identity. Non-traditional mothers—such as Elsa's role as devouring surrogate mother; Gloria's emotionally "dead" mother; and Ethel's masculinized Bearded Lady—reanimate deep-seated personal and national anxieties as horrific spectacles that we recognize as all too human.

Such spectacles are degraded forms of what Mikhail M. Bakhtin refers to as "the carnivalesque." In *Rabelais and His World*, Bakhtin describes medieval folk festivities as distinct from official (Church) rituals: "As opposed to the official feast, one might say that carnival celebrated temporary liberation from the prevailing truth and from the established order; it marked the suspension of all hierarchical rank, privileges, norms, and prohibitions" (10). Designed to invert social norms in a highly stratified society, carnival emphasizes laughter, grotesque imagery, and the use of everyday (and often obscene) language in parody and public spectacles. The universal participation in medieval folk festivals crossed class and status boundaries to celebrate a common humanity. This willing inversion of classes and castes resulted from "the peculiar logic of the 'inside out,' of the 'turnabout,' of a continual shifting ... of numerous parodies and travesties, humiliation, profanations, comic crownings and uncrownings. A second life, a second world of folk culture is thus constructed" (11). Bakhtin differentiates between the "official" medieval culture as defined by Church and governing authorities, and "folk culture" as a kind of unofficial or working-class version of medieval society. While social class and Church practices restricted participation in official medieval culture and rituals, unofficial folk culture embraced all members of society.

Similarly, the traveling company of Fraulein Elsa's Cabinet of Curiosities is set in a world that is both a part of and separate from mainstream U.S. culture: they make camp just outside the town limits, but never stay in one place long enough to become part of the larger community. As visibly Other, the freak show performers establish their own community of inverted norms: in the performers' camp, extraordinary and physically disabled bodies *are* the norm. If the primary function of carnival is to use a form of inside-out logic to invert established hierarchies, in Bakhtinian terms, *Freak Show* carnivalizes an already carnivalesque world by establishing the carnival performers as sympathetic focal characters and by normalizing the carnival setting as their home. Following this logic (if you will), *Freak Show* creates a kind of "meta-carnival" that extends and distorts the rules governing social norms. Against the backdrop of this designated carnival space, Murphy and co-creator Brad Falchuk stage events in a historically heteronormative America that idealized the nuclear family to further emphasize the inside-out logic of the freak show's carnivalesque social norms. Examining the basic elements of society within such a complex, self-aware text of popular culture offers scholars an entry into a critical discussion that is still only beginning.

Mothers, Monsters and Monstrosity: The Milkman Cometh

Aptly titled "Monsters Among Us," the first episode prolongs the audience's expectations by using flashback to introduce the story. Our first image is of Dot Tattler walking, while her disembodied voice promises a harrowing tale: "The shadows that had sheltered me were banished by the blinding light of scrutiny. I knew I was about to enter the gates of Hell. But like the inescapable pull of gravity, there was nothing I could do about it" (4:1). The scene cuts to black—prolonged just a bit to suggest a shift in the timeline—before opening on a farmhouse with a wide veranda; the sky is edged with pink as a rooster signals the early hour, and a chorus of birds and insects drowns out other sounds of civilization. From the driveway shrouded by moss-bedraped live oaks, a white truck emerges and rounds a gentle curve. The milkman exits and walks briskly up the porch stairs toward the front door. The scene's carefully crafted sense of mundane serenity starts to crack under the weight of audience expectations when the milkman tilts his head in wonder at three jars of milk, left untouched from the day before. He stares into the camera before another cut to black, this time with the time and setting in reverse type: Jupiter, Florida 1952.[3] Without knocking, milkman Bill Palmer enters the house to check on his customer, Mrs. Tattler. Receiving no response to his calls, he progresses down the hallway to discover her dead body in the kitchen and her daughters trembling in an upstairs closet.

Though it functions as a deliberate delay in revealing the show's eponymous performers, this careful depiction of a murdered mother in the season's opening episode suggests the maternal figure's integral role in generating horror for the rest of the season. In addition, an overview of maternal figures and imagery from these opening scenes foregrounds theoretical ideas and offers context for an analysis of the series' three central mother figures. Along with Elsa, Gloria Mott and Ethel Darling complete the trinity of maternal figures under examination; each one is a mother with a different appetite for consumption, and each falls well outside the boundaries of 1952 social norms. As Roger Salomon points out, "usually horror narrative makes explicit ... its dual environments and the problematic space between them" (11). These horror stories highlight anxieties triggered by the freak show's arrival on the outskirts of town, emphasizing how the physical boundary literalizes the metaphor of problematic liminal spaces.

Backed by colorful pennants and strings of lights, viewers only see Dot from the neck up as she walks during her voiceover. In the beginning, her destination is unclear; she is merely on her way, traversing a liminal space to arrive at a destination to be determined. Her profile occupies only the bottom right corner of the screen, using a technique Mary Anne Doane describes as "centring," whereby the unbalanced composition "[drains] the actual centre point of significance in order to deposit meaning on the margins" (141). Dot's flat tone communicates pessimism about her recent past as she relates her story, played out at the rural margins of small-town society. By the episode's end, framed by a mirror-image sequence during Bette's voiceover, viewers realize they have been walking into a larger-than-life carnival entrance shaped like the Devil's gaping mouth.

The opening scene's swift dissolution into tragedy sets up an underlying tension between public and domestic spaces that erupts in violent conflicts. The primary placement of Mrs. Tattler as the first murder victim emphasizes the foundational role of motherhood and of her character's influence in particular. Greeted by symbolically spoiled milk, Palmer enters the Tattler home, calling out in familiar tones. In the kitchen, the inner sanctum of domestic space, he sees flies hovering above an unfinished meal and Mrs. Tattler's body on the floor beyond the table. As his gaze sweeps up to find her face framed by a pool of blood, he drops the fresh bottles of milk, and they shatter just as the cuckoo clock explodes to announce the time. Suspicious noises prompt the milkman upstairs, armed with a rolling pin raised overhead. The camera assumes his perspective to build tension as he approaches white beadboard closet doors, slightly ajar, at the end of a dark hallway. Viewers never see the object of his gaze when the doors open, but his face reacts in a clear expression of terror, ending the scene before his scream begins.

Though details remain unclear, the milkman's entry into the sacred domestic space is what Barbara Creed describes as a representation of the primal scene, or a symbolic birth: "Although the 'mother' as a figure does not appear ... her presence forms a vast backdrop for the enactment of all events ... with its womb-like imagery, [and] the long, winding tunnels leading to inner chambers" (260). Spoiled milk, as negative maternal imagery, prompts the milkman to investigate the body of the house. The uneaten food, like the spoiled milk, indicates Mrs. Tattler's failure to feed her children; her parental failure and physical death thus figures the domestic space of the house as the archaic or generative mother. This aspect of motherhood, Creed clarifies, "constructed as a negative force—is represented in her phantasmagoric aspects ... as the voracious maw, the mysterious black hole which signifies female genitalia as a monstrous sign which threatens to give birth to equally horrific offspring as well as threatening to incorporate everything in its path" (261). By opening the doors of the closet, figured as the house's womb, the milkman's transgressive curiosity is rewarded by an (unseen) encounter with her "horrific offspring."

His discovery remains ambiguous until after viewers see a woman being rushed into an operating room. A nurse and a doctor exit immediately to vomit, suggesting all their surgical experience has not prepared them for this patient's shocking condition. The audience finally sees the patient as a doctor reads her X-ray results aloud from the screen and reveals her physical details in both excruciatingly intimate, yet coldly scientific terms: "One bladder, three kidneys ... four lungs, two hearts with a shared circulatory system." A newspaper article reveals the late Mrs. Tattler did not live alone, as neighbors had presumed, but with an "unfortunate creature" described as "monstrously deformed" (4:1). Conjoined at the pelvis, twin sisters Dorothy (Dot) and Bette Tattler arrive at the hospital with wounds of their own, not all of them visible. Their mother's death frees Dot and Bette from thirty years of suffocating maternal protection, but after her mysterious death, the physicians' unforgiving medical gaze imprisons them again. The police officer posted outside their hospital room reinforces the twins' medical deviance as social deviance as well. Though fleeting, Mrs. Tattler plays an important role in shaping the series' events, as her parental influence also shapes Dot and Bette profoundly. In addition, events surrounding her death spark the curiosity of Elsa Mars, the show's central mother figure, who eventually engineers a way to introduce herself to the twins, despite the layers of carceral systems that hide them from the world.

In seeming contrast to the Tattler home, the camera cuts to a well-attended Tupperware party set in a single-family suburban home. The scene ostensibly serves to illustrate acceptable social norms for 1950s middle-class families. The ladies sit in a family room that radiates nostalgia with its mid-century modern decor, and viewers see a screened-in pool through the wall of sliding-glass doors behind them. As the guests peruse their food-storage options, they also over-share details about their disappointing sex lives. Jimmy Darling, known as "Lobster Boy" at the freak show, offers his own brand of extra-curricular therapeutic "personal services" to relieve the sexual frustrations plaguing the disaffected housewives of Jupiter, clearly marking him as more man than boy.[4] A woman leaves the back bedroom and barely conceals a smile as she rejoins the party, and the camera follows the next customer down the hall. When she enters the bedroom, the camera zooms in on Jimmy's peculiar appendages, which look remarkably like marital aids, and he welcomes the young woman with a salacious Vulcan salute. The worried look as she reclines erupts in gasps of pleasure only seconds later, and viewers see Jimmy grin (4:1). Like the Tattler house, this domestic space also harbors a monster instead of domestic bliss, despite its outward appearance of normalcy. Even though the Tupperware party activities cause considerably less harm than murder, prostitution is still illegal in Florida, and readers can infer that such illicit acts could cause considerable harm by spreading sexually transmitted diseases.

The "Other Mothers" at the Tupperware party in *Freak Show* highlight the unreliability of the adjective "normal." From a structural perspective, the aberrant acts from the Tupperware party in "Monsters Among Us" turn into a horrific parody of domesticity in "Tupperware Party Massacre." Fatal stab wounds replace the consensual (if illegal) penetration, and the murderer dumps the women's bodies in the pool. An underwater image of the victims' bodies floating in the bloody water resembles a monstrous version of Jell-O salads prepared in Tupperware molds, ubiquitous in 1950s-era cookbooks and women's magazines: the middle-class consumers are themselves consumed. These "normal" mothers serve as foils for the individual transgressive mother figures to follow, as well as for the family of performers and the image of home.

While spatial configurations and setting often communicate elements of the archaic mother figure, particularly in the absence of actual female characters, the mother figures under examination correspond to three of the series' recurring performers. Their characters reflect different patterns of behavior that align them with some recognizable mythic or archetypal mothers, although the performances in *Freak Show* defy restriction to generalized types; the actors portray these mothers as complex individuals with more shades of nuance than parodic performances of mere type. However, this analysis highlights such recognizable characters as an entry point to larger critical discourses surrounding the *AHS* anthology. One of the common threads linking these maternal figures is the habit of consumption and the way the circulation of desire motivates their actions.

Medea: Parasitic Enchantress

The first image viewers see of Elsa Mars is the same gaping hellmouth image as the carnival entrance, wrought in needlepoint on the handbag she carries through the hospital corridors, en route to meet the Tattler twins. The camera follows her seamed stockings to a red dress, topped by a black and white fur stole worthy of Cruella DeVille. While the bold colors in her costuming communicate confidence, her willingness to wear fur at the end of a South Florida summer signals a singularly unwavering devotion to fashion. A German accent hints at her cosmopolitan background, and the image on her handbag signals her nonconformity but also functions as an advertisement for her venture in the entertainment business (4:1). Images of the Devil's open mouth as the opening to the carnival grounds recall the "voracious maw" Creed describes as a common image of horror. This could figure the background space as archaic mother, and while the Devil appears to consume carnival visitors, their transformation works through gestation rather than digestion. Thus, rather than implying that Elsa desires to eat her children, I suggest the infernal imagery signals her complicated mixture of maternal characteristics.

Euripides' tragic figure of Medea offers a complicated classical portrait of motherhood. Despite her immediate association with infanticide, her defining factors range well beyond her crime. I invoke her figure for her power as a sorceress, her outsider status as a barbarian among the Greeks, and her refusal to accept her femininity as a limitation. These qualities align Elsa closely with Medea, though by no means do they represent a full description. While Medea is a biological mother, Elsa is a surrogate mother, although not in any official sense. As proprietor, director, and producer, she acts as a mother to the "children" in her freak show performance troupe. In contrast to Medea's connubial connections with Jason and then Aegeus, Elsa avoids such commitments to any man until she finds one that suits her needs.

She wheedles her way into Dot and Bette's hospital room, first bribing a candy-striper for her costume with a cigarette and a free ticket to Fraulein Elsa's Cabinet of Curiosities. Clad in borrowed pink stripes, Elsa's masquerade charms nurses, doctors, and police before her meeting finally introduces viewers to the Tattler Twins (4:1). Until this point, the camera only offers fragmented glimpses of Dot and Bette; we see their feet on the gurney, the pathologized anatomy in the X-ray, and recognize the face from the opening shot as one of the twins. The nurses' gossip amplifies the local paper's details about their mother's death to scandalous heights. Elsa is the first to see the Tattler Twins in all their conjoined glory, and the first character to treat the girls like human beings rather than a two-headed monster, even if that's the kind of title she has planned for their act.

Elsa's initial reaction of open-mouthed, unchecked wonder expresses the importance she places on this meeting; her delight stems from the rarity of finding "real" conjoined twins. Her reaction also suggests that her own success is her primary motivation for making contact. Freak shows operate on an economy of spectacle: well outside the quotidian, performers deal mainly in the excessive aesthetic of the grotesque. Dot and Bette follow a tradition of classic conjoined freak show performers such as Chang and Eng, or Violet and Daisy Hilton, the latter having appeared in Browning's film. David Skal and Elias Savada point out that "by the turn of the century, the demand for sideshow attractions by traveling carnivals outstripped the supply of real human oddities, and 'gaffed,' or fraudulent, freaks ... became increasingly common" (23). Thus, historian Robert Bogdan notes, while "in its prime the freak show had been the main attraction of the midway, by 1940 it was losing its audience" (67). However, the Ringling Brothers had made Tampa their show's winter headquarters for years, and as Janet Davis reports, "Gibsonton, Florida, functioned as a home for sideshow performers since 1936" (236).[5] So, while most freak shows across the rest of the U.S. had been out of business for over a decade by the time the fictional events of *Freak Show* are set to take place in 1952, the series reflects a historically accurate anomaly: the freak show business was still alive and well in this little pocket of the tropics. Elsa Mars is in the right place at the right time. She just needs the right angle to convince Dot and Bette to run away and join *her* circus, even if that "angle" is blackmail.

During several visits to the hospital, Elsa brings them magazines, clothing, and a plan to escape, emphasizing that she's only trying to save them.[6] While plotting to help the girls avoid arrest for their mother's murder, Elsa defines her plan's success by whether or not the twins join her troupe, not simply by helping them escape (4:1). In other words, as Elsa declares herself their savior, she knows the twins will ultimately save her. Bette embraces the idea of finally living in freedom, but Elsa's kindness fuels Dot's suspicions. This catches viewers up to the episode's opening scenes: we understand that Dot's pessimistic voice narrates their arrival at the carnival.

Elsa promises "her monsters" that as the new headline act, Dot and Bette will save the struggling show. Although the episode's initial imagery paints Elsa in more infernal tones, members of her troupe see her as an Angel of Mercy[7] who saved each from their own personal hell so they could join her carnivalesque stage version of hell.[8] Though cautious at first, the twins become intimate members of the freak show family mothered by Miss Elsa, who regularly carries Ma Petite, an extraordinarily small female dwarf, on her hip like a surrogate infant. While she plays the role of central mother figure throughout the season, as the proprietor of the freak show, she also acts as Ringmaster, talent scout, and con artist, grasping at fame through a fog of schadenfreude. The name of her enterprise derives from a popular European trend: the *Wunderkammer*, or "Wonder Cabinet." Caroline Bynum explains the implications of this specific artifact:

> the early modern European impulse to collect and explore—displayed in such phenomena as the origins of the museum in the *Wunderkammer* ... has stressed the enthusiasm for wonders as expropriate and appropriative. The collections of narwhal horns and jewels, deformed fetuses and human captives, made by rulers, missionaries and naturalists have been understood as an early modern Orientalism—a projection of self or construction of "other" as self [40].

More than just a stage name for a freak show, "Fraulein Elsa's Cabinet of Curiosities" designates the individual freak performers she calls her "monsters" as objects she collects. The stain of Orientalism bleeds through most visibly in the case of Ma Petite, the "tiny miracle" from India whom Elsa ostensibly purchased from a Maharajah for three cases of Dr. Pepper (4:10). By curating their acts as an artist would arrange an assemblage, the manner in which she presents her collection projects her own identity through a kaleidoscopic lens ground from the fragments of others. She functions as a surrogate mother, but also channels Victor Frankenstein's blind ambition: her favorite "child" is her own artistic creation, which she realizes through other performers, but then abandons to pursue her own success. These actions also signal Elsa's connection to Medea, in her willingness to (metaphorically) sacrifice the children of her troupe in service of her individual fame. She uses them to feed her own artistic ambition, even though she genuinely nurtures many of her troupe members. For example, she teaches the microcephalic Pepper to read, rescues French-speaking strongman dwarf Toulouse from a chain gang, and bails Ethel out of a drunk tank (4:6), but she also complicates those maternal feelings by carrying on an Oedipal tryst with Paul, The Illustrated Seal. His disability (phocomelia) presents as stunted arms resembling a seal's flippers, which sprout from his shoulders: common to Thalidomide poisoning. Paul describes himself as handsome and explains he hadn't the heart to extend his tattoos to cover his pretty face (4:4). In addition to Elsa's volatile emotions, the unstable nature of show business itself contributes to abandonment anxieties among her "children," and these prove to be well-founded.

While Elsa clearly aligns with Medea as a devouring mother, she also makes similar moves against her situated gender norms. Brad Levett points out how Medea's mastery of language as a tool of persuasion, or "the ability to maintain control of one's own language … [is] understood as masculine" because Medea must overcome stereotypes about women and language (55). Elsa uses language, through a series of carefully orchestrated public and private performances, to queer heteronormative ideas of femininity. At other times she seems to reinforce expectations of femininity, such as when she chafes at the mention of Marlene Dietrich's name. Elsa bears more than a passing resemblance to her arch-nemesis, the woman who purportedly stole her career: both are German immigrants, with similar cabaret backgrounds from 1920s Weimar Berlin, and neither Elsa nor her silver screen doppelgänger is often without a cigarette. Allan Bell comments on Dietrich's role as an icon, and specifies that her

> persona is broadly that of the sultry/icy *femme fatale*. In Western culture, this persona is as old as Eve, and includes characteristics such as: mystery, unknowability, undefinability; otherness, marked through transgressing race boundaries (exotic, oriental,

European traits); and through transgressing gender boundaries—campness, androgyny, and bisexuality; powerful and bewitching sexuality, which is yoked with disdain, coldness, unattainability; leading to male servitude and domination; and on to darkness, chaos, and death [631–32].

Although she maintained her exotic sex symbol image, Dietrich was known for her menswear-inspired costumes and her husky voice, which Bell describes as "somewhere between a growl and a purr" (634). Elsa emulates these vocal and sartorial qualities that queer her performances in a heteronormative society and mark her as the freak in charge of the freak show. As Mary Ann Doane notes, "The transvestite wears clothes which signify a different sexuality, a sexuality which, for the woman, allows a mastery over the image" (138). Viewers learn of her physical deformity as the first episode closes and Elsa removes the wooden prostheses attached just above her knees. Fittingly, "Dietrich's legs were known before she was, through modeling for advertisements" (632). Like Dietrich, Elsa controls the images she wants to project, with clothing that allows her to "pass" as normal, as well as with the costumes that construct her performances—and everything is a performance. Whether dressed in masculine or feminine garb, Elsa's wardrobe deploys power in different registers. While masculine clothes offer women some access to the masculine position of power, feminine styles can assist women in leveraging the power of the gaze. Doane proposes the masquerade of femininity as a way to regain control of the spectator's (male) gaze when she writes, "The masquerade doubles representation; it is constituted by a hyperbolisation of the accoutrements of femininity.... This type of masquerade, an excess of femininity, is aligned with the femme fatale and ... is necessarily regarded by men as evil incarnate" (139). Elsa embodies this excess in "Edward Mordrake Part I," as she rehearses Lana Del Rey's "Gods and Monsters," squirming suggestively to the deliberately anachronistic Edenic lyrics while dressed in a deep green floor-length gown with matching opera-length satin gloves and haloed by a surround of marabou feathers. She performs for a "dark [male] stranger" she believes will launch her movie career and pulls out every weapon in her arsenal of feminine masquerade; but she is not the freak he seeks—this time (4:3). Her performance merges Eve and serpent, placing her squarely in Medea's neighborhood: the realm of gods and monsters—and the original mother.

Beyond physical difference, the word "freak" has been freighted with gender nonconformity and sexual deviance since at least the 1930s. As Adams notes, "freak describes the allegedly unnatural condition of homosexuality, an affliction that is immediately visible in the subject's appearance and personal demeanor" (93). Although many women performed in traveling shows, it would have been highly unusual to have a female proprietor, especially one of German origins in the Deep South after World War II. Susanna Federeici-Nebbiosi points out this cultural difference when she writes, "Medea is the mythical character that personifies narcissistic rage within the context of betrayal, and even more, within the context of cultural crash" (465). Elsa's distinctive Otherness—marked by her German accent, gender nonconformity, and bewitching sexuality—align her with both the femme fatale and Medea. Her narcissistic rage surfaces in times of betrayal, of which she accuses Paul, for having a "normal" lover (4:6), and cultural crash; while her German-ness is not often a cultural barrier, Elsa takes great offense at the demise of American culture as television increases in popularity. Her rage flares in moments when she is asked to compromise her Art or to cheapen her own sense of culture for performances supported by corporate advertisers. Her extreme reactions reinforce the notion of her own performance as the "child" of her own creativity; the whole is greater than its individual parts. This aberrant child also pre-figures her as an aberrant mother. Her tent, divided into thirds, drapes inhabitants in luxurious pink folds; perhaps this is an example of the setting performing the same hyper-feminine masquerade as Elsa. If her tent projects a sense of comfort or nurturing, perhaps the setting assists a character who entices those in need of "mothering," in order to consume their talent and absorb it into her own show.

Gertrude: Neglectful Absence

Socialite and frozen-food heiress Gloria Mott represents the "dead mother" figure that recurs in much American Gothic fiction. Viewers might also recognize the same traits in Shakespeare's Queen Gertrude, distant mother to moody Hamlet. In a theory proposed by Andre Green in 2001, the "dead mother" figure has gained traction in psychoanalytic discourses of literary and film criticism. Allan Lloyd Smith explains how problems might result from a "traumatic disruption" of maternal attachment when the mother is "emotionally dead rather than actually dead" (59). Psychoanalytic theory describes the early bond between mother and child as "primary narcissism." David Greven explains it as "a union of the child's and mother's bodies, the child experiencing its mother's body as continuous with its own. The separation that must occur between these bodies is traumatic for both. But when the mother becomes depressed or detached, an alien to the child, this separation becomes doubly traumatic, a double death" (171). While Shakespeare never really addresses Hamlet's early childhood development milestones, readers can assume that, as a member of the royal family, Gertrude had ample access to childcare and may not have been as directly involved to the degree Hamlet clearly needed. In *Freak Show*, Gloria raises her son Dandy as her parents raised her: under the constant supervision of household servants rather than in direct contact with his parents. This indicates a different standard of expectations for "normal" maternal behavior among wealthy American mothers, compared to the middle-class mothers at the Tupperware party who interact directly and constantly with their children. The "double death" rings true when Dandy claims Dot and Bette are the only ones he could ever truly love; only two women can compensate for his primary sense of loss.

Although much older than the children of the Tupperware moms— he's more likely to be the same age as their mothers, who appear to be in their early to mid-twenties—Dandy also lives at home with his mother, even if their home is more palatial in size. His bed occupies a literal "center stage" constructed in a bedroom that resembles a fantasy toyland, complete with life-size stuffed animals. As Greven suggests, "The dead mother allows the child to develop a way of both preserving and mourning the mysteriously vacant and attached—in a word, dead—mother who had once been affectionate and loving" (171). The puppet stage allows him to play out and preserve whatever he chooses. Though clearly an adult by external appearances, a childlike environment surrounds Dandy, extending a sense of childhood and insulating him from any demands for responsible behavior. Viewers learn from a conversation between Gloria and their housekeeper, Dora, that "more" animal remains have appeared in the garden, indicating Dandy's pattern of cruelty will likely continue unchecked (4:2).

Gloria overcompensates, either for her own emotional detachment or possibly for Dandy's absent father, and the spoiled man-child takes every advantage of her efforts. Near the end of "Monsters Among Us" she buys out the entire house at the carnival grounds when she brings Dandy to see the "Siamese Sisters" in their first performance. In the empty tent before the show starts she asks, "Do you like your seat, Dandy?" In a bored tone, he says, "They're ALL mine." Half a beat and half a glance later he adds, "I like the one you're in," and Gloria immediately scoots over so he can take her seat and she can pass his latest pop quiz for affection (4:1). Gloria embodies conspicuous consumerism, trying, too late, to buy her son's love.

She instructs Dora to prepare escargots because Dandy said he loved eating them in Paris, but he rejects them. This conversation seems stuck in a time loop from when Dandy was five, as many parents use the same pattern of logic to get children to eat unfamiliar food: "You like broccoli, don't you? Well, cauliflower is just like broccoli, but it's a different color." Perhaps Gloria defaults to the time she was finally able to re-connect emotionally as his mother, particularly if she suffered from postpartum depression. Her exchanges with her son are haunted by the years she lost, and she can only interact with him in condescending tones as the child she remembers. Even if he is insulted, Dandy's smart enough to know that when he withholds his affection, his mother goes to extravagant lengths to make him happy. She goes beyond consumerism and enters the realm of human trafficking when she tries to purchase Dot and Bette for her smitten son after their debut. When they decline, Dandy throws a depression tantrum.

Smith explains that some children react to early maternal alienation with a distinct lack of ability to express emotion or energy (60). Dandy overcorrects and heads back to the carnival grounds to declare his destiny lies with the theater, but his declaration falls on unsympathetic ears. In this instance, as Smith notes, some children "try to compensate for the fear of inner deadness 'through a hypersexuality or an addiction to thrills or induced crises'" (Modell qtd. in Smith 61). Unprepared for a rejection from his delusions of stardom, Dandy smacks his head against his steering wheel in frustration, leaving him dazed and empty-looking. As a surprise, Gloria hires Twisty the (murderous) Clown to cheer him up, crowing, "Look, darling! Your very own clown! You can do whatever you want with him!" (4:2). Although she pays Twisty, in Gloria's mind the exchange has reduced him to commodity status, and she presents him to Dandy as if he were another toy. Dandy and Twisty play out a tension-filled scene until Twisty escapes, knocking Dandy senseless; the twist at the end of the episode is a shot of Dandy's oxford in the pine scrub as he follows the clown to his lair and later tries to follow in his footsteps. Sufferers of the "dead mother" complex, as Greven points out, often report a recurring theme of "emptiness," an emptiness Green describes as a "blank mourning" that results from "some kind of deep, intense childhood experience with a depressed mother who withdrew emotionally" (171). Dandy's epiphany about his purpose in life, oddly reminiscent of Christian Bale's "Rocky montage" from *American Psycho*, comes with his narration: "This body IS America: strong, violent, and full of limitless potential" (4:5). His revelation follows a gruesome evening spent mimicking the killer clown, increasingly convinced of his chaotic role as a bringer of death.

As with many tales in the American Gothic tradition, Smith points out a pattern of discovering terrible family secrets. He notes that outside influences "can determine psychic development by linking certain states of mental disarray to the concealment of a secret rather than to that individual's unconscious as a repository of repressed wishes" (70). In this case, Dandy may be haunted both internally by his mother's distance and externally by family secrets. However, as family secrets go, it seems the only ones left are the ones Dandy keeps from Gloria, or the ones she refuses to acknowledge, if his claim—"Dora told me everything when I was five"—is true (4:8). Gloria recognizes her son's instability with her casual observation that "mental perversions are an affliction of the extremely affluent" and links her past husband's suicide to her son's actions upon learning he murdered their housekeeper Dora. She continues what sounds like a practiced rationalization: "Cousins marry cousins to protect the money, to keep the estate whole. Inbreeding. It becomes almost a rite of passage to have a psychotic or two in the bloodline" (4:5). Here, Gloria seems determined not to acknowledge the seriousness of the damage her emotional distance has caused. Her response not only rationalizes Dandy's actions, but also makes his violence a marker of racial and economic privilege. Furthermore, she positions herself as his co-conspirator, leaving precious little ground in which to cultivate a healthy relationship.

In "Blood Bath," Dora's daughter Regina calls for the first time to find out why her mother missed their weekly phone date, and Gloria asks if she remembers growing up as Dandy's friend. The word "friend" makes Regina visibly uncomfortable, but Gloria presses her with questions about her own role as Dandy's mother. Gloria seems to need to confess and tells Regina how, when Dandy was sick at a very young age, she left him in the care of a nurse instead of sitting up with him herself. Recognition flickers in her face when she recalls, "He never called for me again after that." Her material efforts can never make up for her emotional distance; she describes her son as a "foreigner" to her psychiatrist, "who could play the part, but didn't quite understand the language. Because words always had a different meaning for him. Especially the word 'No'" (4:8). After Gloria recounts a list of small animals and children Dandy has already harmed, her psychiatrist insists on seeing him, for his mother's safety.

The meeting with the doctor—under the false pretense of measuring Dandy's genius IQ—signals a sharp decline in his relationship with his mother. He confronts her lie but agrees to continue seeing the doctor on the condition that she kill Regina, who has arrived in person to find her mother. Having overheard part of Gloria's telephone conversation with the doctor, he finally confronts her about her own secrets and her feelings about him; Gloria's husband was also her second cousin, and Dandy believes he is born of deadly sin: "You knew what father had done to those little girls" (4:8). The audience learns nothing more but might infer that Dandy's father committed violent crimes against children, and those actions may or may not be connected to his suicide. As Greven comments, "Typically, it is the fatherly face of the patriarchal order that symbolizes the death drive" (172), a trend that Dandy seems to reflect as a family trait.

One of the things that makes Gloria and Dandy freaks is that they've both grown up under a different set of rules than those written for lower socioeconomic classes. Dandy denies his mother's plan to escape with him on a cruise, demanding, "How can I possibly be with a woman who hates me so much?" His ambiguous language does nothing to dispel the cloud of incest hanging over their conversation, and she responds in kind, claiming, "Your father wasn't the love of my life. You were. I loved all of you. Even the madness." During her pause, the audience sees a slow grin spread across Dandy's face until she continues, breaking the spell: "But you've tapped me out. I have no more love to give" (4:8). His sad smile, a shudder, and a small sob seem like mild reactions for someone who just shot his own mother in the head, but the fact that he reacts at all is an improvement for a burgeoning sociopath.

Although the audience sees less of Gloria's mothering than Ethel's and Elsa's, it is because there is less to see: Gloria's shocking lack of warmth produces the biggest villain of the entire *Freak Show* season. While Elsa aligns with Medea because of her willingness to kill her adopted children in a figurative sense, Dandy is indeed the bringer of death he claims to be, gunning down every freak he can find in the final episode. The son of the "dead mother" lacks empathy, save for Dot and Bette. The twins leverage what power they have: they agree to marry Dandy in a scheme that returns the wayward son to the womb/tomb he desperately craves. In a nod to Browning's *Freaks*, he wakes from the drugged wedding champagne to find himself in a glass tank used for Houdini's famous escape trick—minus the escape. As the lone survivors of the freak show massacre, Jimmy, Desiree, and Dot and Bette orchestrate the watery grave that serves as Dandy's carnival justice. Desi pronounces his sentence as the tank begins to fill: "That's where you think we belong: behind glass, a human car-crash to remind you how lucky you are?! You may look like a motion-picture dreamboat, but you are the biggest freak of them all!" (4:13). The surviving freaks watch from the house seats, calmly eating popcorn as the final act plays out.

St. Wilgefortis: Hermaphrodite Christ

The Bearded Beauty from Baltimore, Ethel Darling, may communicate pronounced masculine characteristics, but they do not detract from her maternal habits, and she takes on just as many parenting responsibilities for the troupe of performers as Elsa. While other bearded ladies of literature may be more well known, such as Tiresias[9] of Greek myth, or the Weird Sisters from Macbeth,[10] Ethel's character shares many striking similarities with the fifteenth century legend of St. Wilgefortis. As David Williams describes, "Her legend relates that she was the Christian daughter of a pagan king of Portugal who had betrothed her, despite her spiritual marriage to Jesus, to the pagan king of Sicily. In answer to her prayers to avoid the match, God allows her to grow a beard. Her enraged father has her crucified as a fitting consummation of the marriage with Christ, which she prefers" (173). This early bearded virgin martyr aligns with Ethel's character in that both women willingly sacrifice themselves for the ones they love; both St. Wilgefortis and Ethel represent hermaphroditic Christ-like figures.

This tradition of perceiving Christ as both Mother and Father is not new, as Julian of Norwich's fourteenth-century writings can attest. The bearded princess' story explains how, as Lewis Wallace writes, "she undergoes a gender crossing, transforming from a typical feminine virgin martyr into a virile woman who suffers like Christ on the cross" (63). Ethel's background mirrors the bearded saint's story in her transformation through suffering from innocent girl to strong, capable woman; however, while the miraculous beard saves the princess from unwanted marriage, Ethel's beard probably added to her attraction for Dell, a closeted homosexual.

Another interesting connection to Ethel's character is that in England, the saint goes by the name Uncumber, and for hundreds of years women have sought her "for assistance with getting rid of old, abusive, or impotent husbands, as well as being the saint invoked when a miscarriage is desired" (Wallace 173). Ethel loves her boy, Jimmy, who shows his father's recessive trait in his lobster-like hands. His father Dell left while the boy was still young, but as a gay man, Dell could only pretend with Ethel since she is still a woman. Dell meets his end when carnival justice demands his life for killing another troupe member (4:11). His widow, the treble-breasted hermaphrodite Desiree Dupree, becomes one of Ethel's closest friends.

Thus, Ethel acts as both mother and father to Jimmy; by extension, when paired with Elsa, the self-proclaimed mother of the freak show, Ethel embodies the masculine traits that figure her as Elsa's partner, the show's father. Together, they also animate a cultural fear that dare not speak its name; as Lauren Gutterman points out, "in the 1950s and early 1960s the lesbian wife became an object of pervasive fear and fascination within popular culture" (475). Driven by her love and faith in Elsa's vision, Ethel cooks dinner for her every night, queering her again from masculine father to feminine mother, but only because other characters frequently refer to her as "Betty Crocker"; although generally speaking, many men take pride in their culinary skills. Like Wilgefortis, who, as Williams notes was "above all the protectress of the deformed and the monstrous" (173), Ethel does more than simply prepare recipes. She provides nourishment for her family: her job is to make sure they eat and maintain the strength they need to survive.

Horrified by their introduction to the freak performers, Dot declares Ethel "the Sasquatch champion of law and order in this hellish sty. You heard me right, Diary: a lady. With a beard!" (4:1). While the Tattler twins take some time getting used to their new surroundings, Ethel makes their emotional investment her personal mission. She knows the box-office draw could save the company and scolds them for refusing to eat: "After all Elsa's done for you. She rescues the wretched and unloved and gives them a home. That's what she did for you—and for me. Now it's your turn. You're gonna be big stars!" (4:1). Ethel even enlists Jimmy to help Dot and Bette feel more welcome, trying to preserve their freak show family by simultaneously welcoming new members and easing his wanderlust. She warns him that leaving the troupe won't help: "There is no normal for us, Jimmy! This is as good as it gets. You want to help? Make those twins like it here, but NO flipper action." Her parenting skills are not without their flaws; she's not only aware of her son's side job at Tupperware parties, she expects him to collect the full amount he charges for his sexual services. Though not ideal, her advice is certainly practical in a time of economic uncertainty.

Elsa's opium-fueled confession to Ethel at the end of "Monsters Among Us" offers foreshadowing when she admits she lied about bringing Dot and Bette to the carnival grounds; instead of trying to save her whole freak show family, she brought them for her own selfish gain. She turns to Ethel with eyes brimming, and asks, "Is it too late for me to be a star?" Ethel answers immediately, "No, you're gonna be a household name," but as she speaks, her eyes are joyless (4:1). Her unflagging support slowly turns to doubt, and the final confrontation between her and Elsa carries strong undertones of a troubled marriage: she plans to shoot Elsa for betraying their family, then turn the gun on herself. "You were our mother! There's people around here who never even met theirs" (4:8). Ethel seeks an explanation, but realizes Elsa uses her maternal position as emotional leverage for her own gain. "You broke my heart in two," she accuses, positioning them as quarreling lovers. Elsa buys time by proposing they share a drink "for old times' sake" and asks about the fate of the rest of their children. Ethel's despondency, deepened by alcohol, ultimately prevents her from acting as a parent again, with or without Elsa. Her bullet hits Elsa's wooden leg, revealing her hidden deformity, and the shock creates a window of opportunity for Elsa to strike back. Her throwing-knife finds its target in Ethel's eye socket, killing her instantly, but Stanley helps cover Elsa's crime by staging an illusion of Ethel's death as a suicidal car crash that leaves only a decapitated body.

The family of performers surrounds the wreckage while Elsa mourns loudly for her "sweet sister"; Desi and Dell corroborate the suicide story, as Ethel had revealed earlier she was dying of cirrhosis and wanted them to look after Jimmy (4:3). The scene is laden with layers of maternal imagery. Greven comments on how "The car is a reification of the image of the mother as skull-faced corpse, a movement from the vestiges of a once-living woman to an apparatus that represents machine-tooled nonlife" (179–80). Though his analysis focuses on Hitchcock's *Psycho*, similar images appear in *Freak Show*: the car contains the body of a murdered woman, and while viewers do not see it removed from a feminized swamp, a long chain drags behind, like "a machine-age umbilical cord" (180). The manner of Ethel's death suggests Elsa punishes her for seeing through her "Angel of Mercy" act; the cover-up removes the other head of the freak show family, leaving Elsa a single mother. Her death may also be read as a warning: the whole freak show family will one day fall to new technologies, or machines, of entertainment. And yet, like the immortalized saint Wilgefortis, Ethel lives on, as Elsa claims, "because the show must go on."

Meta-Carnival Unmasking

Although historical studies on freak shows and circuses have commented on their decline in popularity, Adams' research led her to an opposing stance. She contends:

> Despite predictions of their impending demise, freak shows never really vanished. During the period of their decline, they maintained a hold on the imaginations of the many Americans who had visited them in better days. This Imaginative afterlife gave rise to a certain paradox: as actual freak shows were evicted from popular culture, their representational currency multiplied, granting them symbolic importance in inverse proportion to their declining status as a profitable mode of entertainment [2].

Freak Show is constantly aware of its cultural and cinematic antecedents, along with other aspects of popular culture (including other seasons of the same FX series). While some viewers may see the freaks themselves as scary, Salomon notes that the pattern of "the delineation of two apparently alternative spaces, the violation of boundaries between them, the overwhelming power of the more negative and deconstructive environment—is widely, almost universally shared by horror narratives" (10). Transgressing the boundaries between mother and child, domestic and public spaces, normal society and carnival space—and finding out which one is destructive—is often scarier than any figure readily identifiable as a "monster." What makes these transgressions so scary is that they threaten ideas fundamental to personal and collective identity. Presenting monstrous ideas of motherhood threatens the very idea of the Self.

Freak Show might align more closely with the medieval sense of "carnival" as a universal, immersive experience than with the transient sites erected by the modern American amusement industry. As Bakhtin points out, "Carnival is not a spectacle seen by the people; they live in it, and everyone participates because its very idea embraces all the people. While carnival lasts, there is no other life outside it. During carnival time life is subject only to its laws, that is, the laws of its own freedom" (7). As viewers, we participate in the freak show on the screen; the show itself is also a "freak" among shows, not only for its prodigious numbers of viewers, but because it plays with form to present a different kind of television series, and it draws attention to the peculiarly American proclivity to seek out new forms of spectacle. Watching *Freak Show* makes viewers recognize the freakish features in our own lives, and we are simultaneously repulsed and fascinated to find out what new truths that reveals about ourselves. When it comes down to it, we are all freaks—some of us have just known longer than others.

Notes

1. In *Sideshow U.S.A.*, Rachel Adams (among others) emphasizes that the word "freak" refers to a specific kind of performance, whereas a disabled actor or performer describes a more complex personhood.

2. Though many of the *Freak Show* cast members are actors with real physical disabilities, and not disabled people simply put "on display" for the public, I must point out that the actors with recurring roles in this anthology series used prosthetics and CGI effects to portray their freak personas. Page limit prohibits a full discussion of disability theory within this cultural text, but the implications have not escaped my attention.

3. The town of Jupiter, Florida, still thrives today (pop. circa 60,000 according to www.jupiter.fl.us/); however, *Freak Show* was filmed outside New Orleans, not in Florida. The small town of the small screen has become more well-known in recent history for its famous residents and their extravagant homes, including Jack Nicklaus, Michael Jackson, and Celine Dion. Filming Twisty the Clown's first scene, on the banks of Lake Okeechobee, would have been nearly impossible, as the lake is surrounded by the Hoover Dike. Constructed in the 1930s to prevent repeat flooding after two major hurricanes in 1926 and 1928, the Dike was expanded again in 1960.

4. Jimmy's character is based on the historical figure of Grady Stiles, Jr., one of the most famous performers to use the name "Lobster Boy." Though born too late (1937) to appear in Browning's film, his likeness appears in the opening credits for *Freak Show*.

5. Gibsonton, Florida is about 12 miles southeast of Tampa, on the west coast (Gulf side). Jupiter is further south on the opposite side of the state bordering the Atlantic Ocean.

6. To add urgency to the investigation of Mrs. Tattler's death, police learn of two missing children and discover three more murder victims, heaping suspicion on Dot and Bette. Viewers witness these crimes, carried out in silence by a disheveled clown with gruesome costuming. Although the incidents launch a major story arc featuring Twisty the Clown, the current scope of this paper does not allow me to explore it in detail here.

7. Recurring angel imagery could be an intertextual reference to Marlene Dietrich, who made at least two movies with "angel" in the title: she appeared as Lola-Lola in her first film, *The Blue Angel* (1930), and later appeared in a romantic comedy, *Angel* (1937).

8. Bakhtin describes hell's integral role in the medieval carnival traditions of diableries and mystery plays. Sets were designed to reflect the world's position, with a raised platform in front to symbolize earth, a background depicting paradise, and centered beneath the earthly platform at eye-level was "a large opening, indicating hell, covered by a broad curtain decorated with a huge mask of the devil (Harlequin). When the curtain was pulled back, the devils jumped out of Satan's gaping jaws, or sometimes out of his eyes" (384).

9. In Greek myth, he was a blind oracle who spent seven years as a woman.

10. Act I, Scene III, l. 46.

Works Cited

Adams, Rachel. *Sideshow U.S.A.: Freaks and the American Cultural Imagination*. U of Chicago P, 2001.

Bakhtin, Mikhail. *Rabelais and His World*. Translated by Hélène Iswolsky, Indiana UP, 1984.
Bell, Allan. "Falling in Love Again and Again: Marlene Dietrich and the Iconization of Non-native English." *Journal of Sociolinguistics*, vol. 15, no. 5, 2011, pp. 627–56.
Bogdan, Robert. *Freak Show: Presenting Human Oddities for Amusement and Profit*. U of Chicago P, 1990.
Bynum, Caroline Walker. *Metamorphosis and Identity*. Zone Books, 2001.
Cherlin, Andrew J. "The Deinstitutionalization of Marriage." *Journal of Marriage and Family*, vol. 66, no. 4, Nov. 2004, pp. 848–61.
Creed, Barbara. "Horror and the Monstrous-Feminine: An Imaginary Abjection." *Feminist Film Theory: A Reader*, edited by Sue Thornham, NYU Press, 1999, pp. 251–66.
Davis, Janet M. *The Circus Age: Culture and Society Under the American Big Top*. UNC Press, 2002.
Davison, Carol Margaret. "The American Dream/The American Nightmare: American Gothic on the Small Screen." *A Companion to American Gothic*, edited by Charles L. Crow, Wiley, 2014, pp. 488–502.
Doane, Mary Ann. "Film and the Masquerade: Theorising the Female Spectator." *Feminist Film Theory: A Reader*, edited by Sue Thornham, NYU Press, 1999, pp. 131–45.
Federici-Nebbiosi, Susanna. "'Earth, Speak to Me, Grass, Speak to Me!' Trauma, Tragedy, and the Crash Between Cultures in *Medea*." *Psychoanalytic Dialogues*, vol. 16, no. 4, 2006.
Greven, David. "The Death-Mother in *Psycho*: Hitchcock, Femininity, and Queer Desire." *Studies in Gender and Sexuality*, vol. 15, 2014, pp. 167–81.
Gutterman, Lauren Jae. "Another Enemy Within: Lesbian Wives, or the Hidden Threat to the Nuclear Family in Post-war America." *Gender & History*, vol. 24, no. 2, Aug. 2012, pp. 475–501.
Kissell, Rick. "'American Horror Story: Freak Show' Sets FX Ratings Record." *Variety*, 15 June 2015, variety.com/2015/tv/news/american-horror-story-freak-show-sets-fx-ratings-record-1201519900/.
Levett, Brad. "Verbal Autonomy and Verbal Self-Restraint in Euripides' *Medea*." *Classical Philology*, vol. 105, 2010, pp. 54–68.
Loyo, Hillaria. "Star and National Myths in Cold War Allegories: Marlene Dietrich's Star Persona and the Western in Fritz Lang's *Rancho Notorious* (1952)." *European Journal of American Studies*, vol. 5, no. 4, 2010, pp. 1–15.
Mitchell, David T., and Sharon L. Snyder. *Narrative Prosthesis: Disability and the Dependencies of Discourse*. Ann Arbor: U of Michigan P, 2000.
Nussbaum, Emily. "The New Abnormal: The Carnival Logic of *American Horror Story*." *The New Yorker*, 8 Dec. 2014. www.newyorker.com/magazine/2014/12/08/new-abnormal.
Salomon, Roger B. *Mazes of the Serpent: An Anatomy of Horror Narrative*. Cornell UP, 2002.
Skal, David J., and Elias Savada. *Dark Carnival: The Secret World of Tod Browning, Hollywood's Master of the Macabre*. Anchor Books, 1995.
Smith, Allan Lloyd. "Can Such Things Be? Ambrose Bierce, the 'Dead Mother,' and Other American Traumas." *Spectral America: Phantoms and the National Imagination*, edited by Jeffrey Andrew Weinstock, U of Wisconsin P, 2004, pp. 57–77.
Stack, Tim. "Maestro of the Universe." *Entertainment Weekly*, no. 1433, 30 Sep. 2016, pp. 20–25.
Thomson, Rosemarie Garland. *Extraordinary Bodies: Figuring Physical Disability in American Culture and Literature*. Columbia UP, 1997.
Wall, Kim, and Caterina Clerici. "Welcome to Gibtown, the Last 'Freakshow' Town in America." *The Guardian*, 26 Feb. 2015, www.theguardian.com/us-news/2015/feb/26/welcome-to-gibtown-the-last-freakshow-town-in-america.
Wallace, Lewis. "Bearded Woman, Female Christ: Gendered Transformations in the Legends and Cult of St. Wilgefortis." *Journal for Feminist Studies in Religion*, vol. 30, no. 1, 2014, pp. 43–63.
Williams, David. "Wilgefortis, Patron Saint of Monsters, and the Language of the Grotesque." *The Scope of the Fantastic—Culture, Biography, Themes, Children's Literature: Selected Essays from the First International Conference on the Fantastic in Literature and Film*, edited by Robert A. Collins and Howard D. Pearce, Greenwood Press, 1985, pp. 171–78.

Part III
Identity Politics

The Mother-Witch and Witch as Mother in *Coven*

SARAH FOUST VINSON

It is the age-old story—the daughter grows up to become her mother, taking her mother's place in the world, and, in the transition, mother and daughter must work through the issues of their tumultuous past. So ends *American Horror Story: Coven*, the third installment of Ryan Murphy's FX television show. This season is about witches and mothers, highlighting the "one incontestably monstrous role in the horror [genre] that belongs to woman—that of the witch" (Creed 73). In one of the final scenes of the third season, Fiona, who has been a notoriously bad mother, dies in her daughter's arms after a heartfelt exchange. Cordelia, the daughter, has become the new Supreme, the witch who has the most powers and who is now to lead the coven, usurping this role from her mother. In their final exchange in "The Seven Wonders," Cordelia asks her mother if it made it harder, knowing the one who would take her power was her own daughter, and Fiona responds, "Not really." Instead, Fiona admits, "You took my power the minute I gave birth to you." She continues, "A woman becomes a mother. She can't help but see her mortality in that cherubic face. Every time I looked at you, I saw my own death." But then she continues, "I loved you plenty, though. In just my own way, which I'll admit had its limitations. Your fault was you were always looking for another version of motherhood" (3:13). It is this final line that is most interesting, as it suggests that the show is very aware of how it is representing what it means to be a mother, and it is challenging us to ask if Fiona's version of mothering, as bad as it is, is providing a new model for our understanding of motherhood and mothering.

Choosing to focus the third season of *AHS* on witches and witchcraft is not surprising, for it allows the show's creators to delve deeply into questions of female power and relationships while critiquing America's treatment of those who are seen as other or different. Depicting images of both the power and persecution of witches and images tied to America's history of racism, the show challenges viewers to scrutinize the horrors of America's racist past, and it also plays into our history of seeing powerful (magical) women who challenge traditional expectations "regarded as evil or dangerous" (Fischer 44). To best understand how *Coven* engages questions of motherhood, it is first useful to explore how concepts of mothering have previously been combined with images of the witch. As Lucy Fischer explains, witch characters are often "cast as a figure of great perversity" and are "clearly a figure of great terror" (44). Fisher goes on to suggest that, historically, witchcraft was associated with women's power and sexuality and notes that many midwives were accused of being witches, linking "female magic" to mothering and motherhood (44). She explains that midwives were often accused of using magic to impact fertility and that they were, in turn, blamed when a delivery did not go as planned. She continues, "Even when the birth was successful, midwives might still be charged with selling an infant's soul to the devil" (80). While much work has been done to challenge "liturgical discourse, reclaiming the figure of the midwife/witch" (80), there are clear connections between motherhood and the history of witchcraft. Barbara Creed's analysis of the witch in film further connects the notion of the witch to motherhood. She explains, "During her periods of pregnancy, woman was seen as the source of a particularly powerful form of magic." Thus, she clarifies, "the earliest known witches were feared not as agents of the devil—as the Christian church later argued—but because they were thought to possess magical, terrifying powers" (74). These links between witchcraft and motherhood come from a long history of equating the threat of women's power with the maternal figure.

One of the ways this connection between motherhood and the witch manifests is through what E. Ann Kaplan identifies in her analysis of mothers and melodrama as a "'Master' Motherhood Discourse" (8), or a set of ideologies about mothering which are particularly evident in nineteenth- and early twentieth-century representations of mothers. In this historical period, Kaplan locates two "prevailing cultural discourse[s]" or myths surrounding the image of the mother figure—the mother is either "the Ideal 'angel' Mother" or "her evil 'witch' opposite" (9). Even as Kaplan does identify some representations of motherhood that "resist" this binary, she notes the "persistence" of these myths in our cultural representations of mothers, and she highlights this pattern of angel "pitted against" witch again and again in numerous examples (15, 9). Indeed, she suggests, "No matter how hard we try, [representations] seem to insist on these polarities" of the "idealized and monstrous mothers" (42).

Kaplan's reading of these mother myths stems from psychoanalytic theory in which she sees "the evil 'phallic' or witch mother [as] the underside of the self-sacrificing ideal mother" (18). The "Ideal mother" stems from the Angel of the House notion of women as "pious, pure, domestic, and submissive" (24). Her angelic, ideal nature comes from the assumption that she is utterly self-sacrificing for the sake of her husband and children. Heather Addison, Mary Kate Goodwin-Kelly, and Elaine Roth build on this concept: "The ideal of good motherhood (white, middle-class, devoted, selfless, and so on) becomes the yardstick by which women are judged; deviation from this pattern is justification for disparagement—or at least suspicion" (6). On the other hand, the opposite of the ideal mother, the witch mother, is either over-indulgent so as to satisfy her own needs or the "evil, possessive and destructive all-devouring" mother (Kaplan 48). This witch mother "satisfies needs for power that her ideal function prohibits" (47). Kaplan suggests these "dominant motherhood paradigms threaten to collapse into one another, for both arise from similar castration fears expressed in opposite ways" (124). While I don't intend to explore the psychoanalytic theory driving Kaplan's argument, what I do find useful is her observation that both of these "master-mother discourses" perpetuate a traditional, patriarchal image of mothering—she is either positioned as a signifier of "lack, absence ... passivity," making her "blameless and heroic," or she is morally condemned for being possessive because she is a "threat to the male unconscious" (124).

After identifying these patterns, Kaplan's work attempts to locate texts that resist such limiting depictions of motherhood, and while she notes the struggle between old and new discourses is "often bitter, hostile, and violent," she suggests that by the 1970s, the "angel/witch mother dichotomy" only appears occasionally (14, 182). Still, it seems that such representations continue to be found in today's cinema. According to Suzanna Dunata Walters and Laura Harrison, "For much of the history of the representation of motherhood, though, mothers have been depicted along the binary lines of saintly sacrifices ... giving all for their progeny's upward mobility and emotional sustenance, or viperous spiders weaving webs of neurosis and deceit that endlessly entrap hubby and kids in a mire of unrequited love and emotional bankruptcy" (39). They suggest that such "dire and depressingly familiar" depictions of motherhood are still persistent (39), even as they attempt to locate examples that resist these traditional forms. Moreover, Addison, Goodwin-Kelly, and Roth highlight the "striking consistency of Hollywood's constructions of motherhood," noting that mothers in film "reproduce dominant ideology ... yet also become ready targets if they fail to uphold prevailing notions of 'good' motherhood" (4). These patterns, therefore, remain pervasive, even today.

Still, in looking at contemporary television shows like *Weeds* and *Mad Men*, Walters and Harrison have recognized mothers who are "behaving badly, really badly" on television, but who avoid the "celluloid slapdown" or other punishments that are the typical reward of "bad" mothering (41), and they suggest that a new type of mother has emerged in recent television who comes from but complicates the angel/witch dichotomy. This mother is "Neither monster nor angel. She is not quite a twenty-first century feminist heroine but she does upend more traditional depictions of maternal identity. [She is] unabashedly sexual, idiosyncratic to a fault, and seriously deleterious in her caretaking skills" (40). What Walters and Harrison have identified in these more recent mother-depictions is that even as these new moms do still feel the "sting of contrition and external judgment," unlike the deviant mothers who are punished "to serve as reminders of the power of normative familialism and rigid gender ideologies," for these new mothers, the "judgment is assuredly more nuanced and ambivalent than in the past" (48). Moreover, these "bad" mothers don't fit into either the over-indulgent or all-devouring modes of mothering that Kaplan identifies. Instead, for these mothers, motherhood is "narratively secondary. In other words, her identity as a *woman*—and as a character—is not wholly determined by her behavior as a mother." Instead, "the more general aberrant practices (drug dealing, drug taking, neurotic unhappiness, multiple personalities) both precede and trump maternal identity" (48). Walters and Harrison see these new figurations of bad mothers as "strangely hopeful," as they create new possibilities outside of the simple angel/witch binary (51).

It is with this context that I turn to *Coven*, a show that, as one *Jezebel* reviewer notes, has "major mommy issues" (Davies). Showrunner Ryan Murphy has claimed that this season is "a meditation on race relations in this country," but it is also "about female power" (qtd. in Doyle). Moreover, the show depicts literal witch mothers, consciously playing with the notion of mother as witch. It seems the show's writers are quite aware of the master discourses surrounding motherhood. For instance, when we first see Fiona Goode with her daughter, Cordelia, in "Bitchcraft," Fiona quips, "I was just on this wonderful spiritual retreat with Shirley MacLaine in Sedona. It was all about forgiveness" (3:1). Here, Fiona mocks the often-analyzed mother/daughter relationship presented in *Terms of Endearment* and suggests the show will push the boundaries of our understanding of mother/daughter relationships. Her ironic tone also suggests that the relationship between Cordelia and Fiona will not mirror that of the mother-daughter relationship in *Terms*, but instead is going to be something new and different. Likewise, the show seems poised to challenge such discourses, since "the witch is defined as an abject figure in that she is represented within patriarchal discourse as an implacable enemy of the symbolic order" (Creed 76). Witch characters, then, should be poised to break down traditional patriarchal conceptions of motherhood.

The show does begin with the premise that mothers are their children's bedrocks, and we expect this, especially from the non-witch mothers. We assume that if the witches are what will make *AHS* horrifying, the non-witch mothers will fulfill the image of the good, virtuous, angelic mother. In "Boy Parts," after Kyle has been killed and then reanimated, Zoe takes him to his mother, telling him, "She's the one person in the world you'll remember. Everything will make sense when you see her" (3:2). Of course, it quickly becomes evident that Kyle's mother is sexually abusive towards her son, and soon after, we meet another non-witch mother, the devout Christian, Joan Ramsey, who, in believing her son Luke to be unclean, forces him to have an Ajax enema (3:8). Later, in the same episode, Luke stands up to her and she threatens, "I'm your mother. I made you, and I can unmake you" (3:8), which acts as foreshadowing for the fact that she ultimately kills him, smothering him with a pillow in the next episode. There is no doubt, as Rachel Shukert notes, that all kinds of mothers in the show, "biological mothers, surrogate mothers, symbolic goddess-worshiping mothers ... are, essentially, totally insane monsters."

This examination of bad mothers is heightened in the character of Madame Delphine LaLaurie, a wealthy New Orleans socialite who sadistically tortured and killed numerous slaves in her attic in the 1800s. Though the show delves into the horrific racism and terror she represents, it also remains focused on her role as a mother. In fact, the show opens as she introduces her daughters to potential suitors in 1834 New Orleans, and immediately depicts a strain in her mother/daughter relationship when her daughter challenges her: "You can't control me, mother" (3:1). By the fifth episode, "Burn, Witch. Burn!" we see Madame LaLaurie dragging her daughters up to her attic torture chamber and locking them in cages to assert her power over them. She remains a horrible person and mother—a serial killer, a racist—and yet she is not a "witch," which calls us to ask how the show is attempting to challenge or rewrite the mothering dialectic.

When put next to these non-witch, evil mothers, Fiona Goode, at least initially, seems to be almost angelic. She is the reigning Supreme of the coven, and at the beginning of the show she has returned to help protect the witches at Miss Robichaux's Academy for Exceptional Young Ladies, a school for young witches where her daughter is headmistress. It is clear that the relationship between Cordelia and her mother is strained—early on Cordelia says to her, "When are you going to die and stop ruining my life?" (3:1)—but Fiona comes, at least initially, with the intent to protect both her real and her surrogate daughters, the girls at the school. Fiona's presence at the school does depict her in the role of protector and matriarch. She protects Zoe and Madison from the police after they have flipped the bus in "Boy Parts" (3:2), she helps to heal Queenie after she is attacked by the Minotaur in "Fearful Pranks Ensue" (3:4), and she, more generally, helps the girls foster their magic and understand their history.

Moreover, it is suggested that the girls do need her. After Zoe unintentionally kills a young man during her first sexual encounter, her mother tells her, "There is something I should have told you a long time ago. I prayed it would skip your generation. Your great-grandmother had the same genetic affliction" (3:1). Zoe's "genetic affliction" leads her to her realization, "So, apparently, I'm a witch." This is something that her own mother is unequipped to handle. She tells Zoe, "I'm sorry, we can't keep you here anymore. It's not safe" (3:1). Then, she stands by, helpless, as Zoe is dragged from the house pleading for her mother. Thus, Zoe is in need of a new mother figure as she begins her time at Miss Robichaux's Academy. Indeed, it is clear we are meant to think of the elders at the school as substitute mother figures, for when Myrtle, acting as a representative of the school, comes to pick up Zoe, Myrtle tells Zoe's mother, "She's our daughter now, Nora. You've done all you can" (3:1). The other girls are also parentless. In "The Replacements," Madison describes her mother as horrible, telling Fiona, "The last time I saw her, she snorted half my coke and then let the cops bust me for it. She's a selfish bitch" (3:3). Queenie was brought up in foster care, and there is no mention of Nan's parents, or Misty's for that matter.[1] Even Cordelia suggests that to be sent off to the school is to be left motherless. As an adult, she still harbors resentment for being sent there: "You dumped me here." However, when headmistress Cordelia does tell her mother to leave, Fiona explains that she is "here to help." She argues, "It is Salem all over again; there is a storm coming" (3:1). Fiona's approach to facing such threats from the outside world run counter to her daughter's approach. Fiona criticizes Cordelia's teaching style: "You teach them to cower and to hide in the shadows. Well there are no shadows, not any more. You really think with Twitter and Facebook if a witch does anything at all she won't be videotaped and turned into some viral freak show like a dog who says I love you?" (3:1). Thus, she declares she is there to stay in order to teach and mother these otherwise motherless girls.

Still, we know from Fiona's first scene in the show that she is struggling with aging and the threat of her own mortality. It is even possible that her return to her daughter's life is tied to wanting to make amends as she is facing her own demise, since she looks hurt when Cordelia asks her when she will die and leave her alone. Still, Fiona is not giving in to aging without a fight. When we first meet her, she is yelling at a doctor: "What I need is an infusion of vitality, of youth"; she later visits a plastic surgeon who tells her he cannot help her, and we see her struggling over her loss of desirability and sexuality as she observes some men at a bar looking past her to a group of younger women (3:1). Moreover, what would likely be typical aging and loss in the real world becomes tied up in the fact that she is the Supreme. There is one Supreme in each generation, and as one Supreme ages, her figurative "daughter" grows up to take her place. In this transformation, the old Supreme's life force, power, and vitality pour into the body of the new Supreme. Fiona's struggle in the show, then, becomes a literal struggle between her desire for self-preservation, something she tells us is "the most primal instinct of the human psyche" (3:3), versus her need to protect and mother both her real daughter and her figurative daughters in the coven.

Fiona is not alone in her fear of aging, nor in highlighting the notion that as the daughter ages, so too, does the mother. Immediately after the initial scene of the show depicting Madame LaLaurie's daughter challenging her mother as she is being introduced to potential suitors in a clear coming-of-age moment, we see Madame LaLaurie painting her face with a bloody poultice made of a human pancreas. As she paints, she scrutinizes her aging face, complaining "Just look at this wattle" (3:1). Her blood-mask is even more clearly linked to her anti-aging process (and becomes all the more horrific) in a later episode, "The Dead," when she tells the young slave girl that the blood of her newborn son, fathered by Madame LaLaurie's husband, is the secret ingredient in her concoction. Her words, "youth begets youth," are chilling (3:7). The lengths she will go to be cruel are juxtaposed with her desire to mask her aging, and these acts parallel Fiona's own meetings with doctors at the beginning of the show where she first demands untested treatments to extend her life, and later, sucks the life out of the doctor who refuses her, which visibly diminishes the signs of aging momentarily before quickly reverting back to a face creased by a lifetime of experience. Unlike Madame LaLaurie and Fiona, Marie Laveau, the Vodou Queen, has a different experience, for magic has made her immortal. Interestingly, she owns and operates a beauty parlor, linking her perpetual youth with the desire for youth in others. Moreover, towards the end of the series, we see that her longevity and vitality are actually linked to perpetual sacrifice of innocent life, which began by her giving up her own child to gain immortality. Each year she must steal another baby to present to Papa Legba, a Vodou god. This annual act remains a reminder of what she has given up, for as she holds the baby in her arms, she explains, "I barely remember my baby's face, so when I look at this child I feel like she's mine. But Papa's coming" (3:10). For these three characters, their children become mirrors of their own aging (or lack of it, in the case of Marie Laveau). Moreover, in all three cases, they are willing to sacrifice their children to maintain their own vitality.

Even though Fiona would sacrifice almost anything to maintain her vitality and power, she is somewhat aware of the mothering choices she has made, making her similar to the bad mothers explored by Walters and

Harrison. In their reading of Nancy, the mother in *Weeds,* Walters and Harrison suggest that she does become aware "of her maternal failures" and such failures seem "to register but she inevitably manages to sweep them under the rug and redeem herself with a showy display of motherly devotion" (41). Like Nancy, Fiona does seem aware of her failures, but this awareness does not seem to impact many of her decisions. In the first episode, she tells Cordelia, "One of my greatest disappointments in life is that you never fully realized the extent of your power" (3:1). While this could be read as an admission that she has failed in her role as mother, it could also be seen as a critique of Cordelia's abilities. Indeed, there are times that she does articulate her own failures, though not to Cordelia until their very last moments. In "The Replacements," she tells Madison, "I was a horrible mother and I regret it," but she feels it is too late to change (3:3). Later, when Cordelia is in the hospital, she admits to Hank, Cordelia's husband, "I may have not been the mother she needed me to be," but she goes on to critique him, suggesting that he is much worse than she has ever been (3:5). She is honestly upset when someone throws acid at Cordelia, and in what seems an act of contrition that she was unable to protect her child, she brings another mother's stillborn daughter back to life after telling that mother, "You have to keep them close so they feel safe." She then makes the mother promise, "I'll never leave you. I'll be your mother until you die" (3:5). However, this act also parallels Walters and Harrison's suggestion that "these aberrant mothers are often explicitly vengeful when they perceive a threat or even a minor slight to their children" (41). In other words, she responds only when there is an outside threat to her child. She later uses Cordelia's blinding as a way to frame Myrtle Snow and, in turn, protect herself from the authority of the coven elders. Thus, while she does recognize that she has not been an ideal mother, she rejects the notion that this is a significant problem.

There is also a moment where she decides to kill herself so that a new Supreme can take over, explaining, "I'm trying to do something decent, something noble for the coven" (3:8). Before she swallows a handful of pills, she tells Myrtle, "Look after my beautiful Delia, would you? My most terrible failure. It will torment me to eternity I imagine" (3:8). Indeed, there are moments where we see her grappling with her failure to meet society's standards when it comes to mothering, and those failures come with a sense of regret. Fischer explains that it is common to find maternal melodrama that "wallows in guilt and redemption" (12). Still, Fiona does not die for the sake of the coven, nor does she wallow for long. Spalding, the butler, actually confronts her, calling her act "horseshit" and telling her that she has only done this to make a martyr of herself (3:8). In turn, she reasserts her position as the Supreme, while also being proud of Cordelia for orchestrating the situation. She tells her, "I am so proud; you really are my daughter," and Cordelia jokes back, "I would have made an attempt on your life years ago if it were that easy to win approval" (3:8). Instead of filling the expected role of utterly self-sacrificing mother, then, Fiona rejects this position as a limiting and limited role and comes out of the experience all the more determined to survive at whatever cost.

The same could be said for Marie Laveau. In describing the deal that she made with Papa Legba centuries before, she explains, "I had just come into my prime, and my magic was strong, shockingly strong." She was pregnant at the time, linking power, magic, and motherhood, and she felt "invincible" (3:10). Like Fiona, she is willing to do whatever it takes to maintain that "prime" and thus sells her soul to the Vodou god, expecting that her yearly "dues" for eternal life would be "some sort of sexual favors." Unfortunately, after he tells her "Motherhood looks good on you," he exacts his price—her infant and an additional innocent soul each year. When she begs him to "Take the spell back," it is too late. Still, while it is clear that this sacrifice was traumatic at the time, centuries of procuring innocent babies seem to have distanced Marie Laveau from a connection to motherhood. When the police stop her after she steals the baby from the hospital, she tells them, "Don't mess with me. I need this baby." She then tells the crying baby to "Shut up," adding "I'll give you something to cry about" (3:10). She sees the infant as a payment she must make for eternal youth, and no more. Even her later comment to Fiona that sounds remorseful—"[W]hen I look at this child I feel like she's mine"—ends with "But Papa's coming," suggesting that she has come to terms with the fact that for her to maintain her youth, she must continue to sacrifice her child (3:10). Interestingly, Fiona helps her avoid sacrificing this particular baby, killing Nan and offering her to Papa Legba instead. Though this could be seen as the women protecting the perpetually sacrificed infant, and thus reclaiming their position as caring mothers, this baby ends up with Spalding, the (now ghost) butler, which may not be a much better fate. Like Fiona, then, Marie Laveau may regret some of her mothering choices, but she also sees herself as having only limited power to change her circumstances, and she adjusts to the notion that for her to continue to flourish, she must continue to symbolically sacrifice her child.

Madame LaLaurie's experience also moves her to question her mothering choices, though she does seem to be more regretful when it comes to how she treated her children than Fiona. Mirroring Fiona's language in the last episode, she tells Fiona, "I loved my girls in my own way. Even the ugly one. From the moment she came out of my belly, she was a shame to me. She had the face of a damned hippo, but I loved her just the same" (3:2). While her words here are hypocritical and hurtful, just like so many other elements that shape Madame LaLaurie's character, it is clear she is haunted by what she has done to her daughters. Upon being dug up after being buried alive for 180 years, she tells Fiona, "Hell is real. I've seen it down in that box. Time disappears. The only thing that's left is what's in your mind's eye. All I saw in mine was the faces of my girls" (3:2). Those faces later become reanimated as her daughters return to haunt her as zombies in "Burn, Witch. Burn!" It is when she comes face to face with her zombie-daughter that she begins to express her own complicity in the damage done to her daughters: "Borquita, my daughter, my child. What has she done to you? No, what have I done to you? There must still be something inside you that knows the mother who bore you. Come back to me child, I will make amends." She later explains, "They deserved a better mother than I ever could hope to be" (3:5). While there are many horrific events for which Madame Delphine LaLaurie should feel regret, and she is not ever redeemed within the show, it is clear that what haunts her most is her horrific mothering. She, like Marie Laveau and Fiona, must live with those choices.

Ultimately, for Fiona, her love for Cordelia is secondary to her role as Supreme—a role she is determined to maintain. As viewers are shown Fiona's past, it is of no surprise that she feels the extreme threat of a new Supreme taking power, for we see how she came to power herself. As a young woman, feeling her own strength growing, she slit the throat of Anna Lee Leighton, the reigning Supreme, after telling her, "They say when a new Supreme starts to flower, the old Supreme begins to fade" (3:2). She clearly believes that the role of the daughter is to kill off the mother figure to take her power. Years later, when she believes her own power is being threatened by Madison, a young witch that likely reminds her of herself at that age, we see her struggle between her role as mother/protector and her desire for continued power. She tells Madison, "My life force is literally pouring out of my body and into yours," and she fights with Madison, ultimately telling Madison just to kill her (3:3). From her past experience, this is what she would see as the natural order of things. Still, in a split-second turn of events, Fiona slits Madison's throat, later joking, "The coven doesn't need a new Supreme. It needs a new rug" (3:3). As time goes on, she becomes willing to do anything to halt her aging and maintain her power and vitality. She even tries to make a deal with Papa Legba, who can grant immortality in exchange for one's soul. He asks her, "Would you cripple your daughter?" She responds, "Today, absolutely." He continues, "Murder someone you love?" She counters, "Whatever it takes" (3:10). Ultimately, he tells her she has no soul to sell, and her response is that if she has no soul, she might as well just kill everyone in her way to maintain her power.

As viewers, we are disturbed and thrilled by Fiona's badness. She is so bad that she's fun to watch, which parallels what Walters and Harrison suggest of their new mothers: "Watching these aberrant mothers thus induces some serious head spinning and, we would venture, some deep ambivalence. We are simultaneously thrilled at their absolute refusal to follow the rule book, their 'me-first' narcissism that has long been assayed as the bête noire of good mothering" (50). Fiona is an awful mother figure, but in so many ways that is beside the point of her character—she is about maintaining power at whatever cost—and we cheer even as we are horrified. Moreover, her struggle between her own power and her desire to protect her daughter helps her to remain sympathetic enough that we do not hate her; instead, we see her as deeply flawed. Indeed, as she admits to Cordelia in their final exchange in "The Seven Wonders," "Every time I looked at you I saw my own death. You were a constant reminder of my worst fears," but, at the same time, she also recognizes that for Cordelia to live, she must die: "I have to die for you to truly live" (3:13). This is even truer when we consider that Cordelia is revealed to be the next Supreme. Fiona has been right all along; her daughter is the one who will ultimately take her power. A now more wise and powerful Cordelia ultimately tells Fiona, "No one can help you mother. You have to do this alone, and the only way out is through, so feel the fear and the pain. Let it all in and then let it all up." Then, as Cordelia takes her mother in her arms and comments, "I don't think we ever hugged," Fiona dies (3:13). This ending could be read as a redemptive moment for Fiona. She looks broken down, and missing her wig, she has lost all of her glamor and poise as she slumps in her chair, aged and decrepit. She has lost all, and her last moments are spent embracing her daughter. However, this is not the last we see of her.

Indeed, the show does not just leave us with the truly "evil" non-witch mothers or Fiona's boundary-pushing but still evil witch-mother, and this is where the show, in trying to revise the notion of the witch-mother, falls back into Kaplan's master-witch/angel dichotomy. While there are only a few images of the angel mother-type in the show, they exist, and not only do they exist, but they are held up as the ideal. Myrtle Snow acts as Cordelia's surrogate mother in the show. After Cordelia is blinded, Myrtle tells her, "If I could pluck my own eyes out of my head and give them to you, I would." She would fulfill this act of self-sacrifice, for she explains, "I've always loved you like a daughter." This statement of love is not surprising when we see a flashback scene: when Cordelia first comes to Miss Robichaux's school as a student, she asks Myrtle, "Will you be my mother now?" (3:9). In the finale, Myrtle tells Cordelia that Cordelia must burn her at the stake to confirm Delia's leadership role. Cordelia tells her, "You were my mother, my true mother, just as you promised you would be." As Myrtle is tied to the stake to be burned for a second time, she says, "Delia, my sweet daughter, I've never been more proud" (3:13). To be a good mother, then, is to sacrifice oneself fully for the success of the child, a theme depicted repeatedly in television and filmic depictions of mothering. As Molly Haskell explains, in Hollywood depictions of mothering, "The sacrifice of and for children—two sides of the same coin—is a disease passing for a national virtue, and a constant theme in films that preach one thing, and for anyone who is listening, say another" (169). This motif of motherly sacrifice can also be seen in the coven's story of Prudence Mather, the Supreme who took her own life to save the lives of those in the coven (3:8). Again, to be a good mother/Supreme is to sacrifice for the good of the coven. This is, of course, in contrast to Fiona who refuses to do the same. They are ideal—she is not.

Cordelia is also depicted as the angel-mother. At the beginning of the show, Cordelia wants to get pregnant, and she and Hank have been trying to conceive for a year. At the doctor's office she quips, "How's the oven? Ready for a bun?" Later she expresses her frustration at her inability to get pregnant without the use of magic: "I should be able to have a baby, just like any other woman" (3:2). Still, when she still finds herself unable to conceive, and she attempts her own magic, her power is too weak. Likewise, when she visits Marie Laveau for a fertility spell, she is refused. While she is unable to bear her own child, it is clear that she becomes the true mother of the coven. When she is first blinded, she gains second sight, something she loses when Myrtle gives her new eyes. When she realizes that she needs the second sight to save the coven, she pierces her own newly seeing eyes. In "Protect the Coven," Myrtle explains to Fiona and viewers that this act was an act of self-sacrifice for the sake of the coven: "Because your daughter has something you will never understand, Fiona. She's a hero. The girl has ripped her own eyes out of her skull for one reason. To protect the coven" (3:11). We also see that it is her motherly grief over the loss of Misty Day that finally prompts her to attempt the Seven Wonders; it is almost as if she must accept her role as mother of the coven to be shown her own power. In other words, her power comes from her acceptance of her role as mother. Thus, as we see her fulfill the role of Supreme in the final episode, she has gone public, calling all of the young witches who may find themselves isolated and alone, that they should call or come to New Orleans for there is "a home and a family waiting for you" (3:13). It is worth noting that once she is Supreme, her position on how to teach has shifted from guiding her students to hide their power to recognizing those powers publicly. As the line of young witches seeking that family stretches around the block and then comes into the foyer, we also see Cordelia named the Supreme publicly, fully enacting the role of the mother figure/mother-superior. In the world of the show, she is the true angelic witch-mother.

Not only does the show finish by upholding the angel-mother image, it also fully punishes its evil witch-like mothers. In "Go to Hell," a laughing Papa Legba says, "Eventually everybody pays" (3:12). It is true. Kyle's mother is beaten to death by Kyle, himself; Luke's mother is forced to drink bleach; Madame LaLaurie finds herself in her personal hell, trapped in a cage next to her daughter, unable to protect the daughter and constantly reminded of her failures as a mother: "There is no greater pain than being this close and not being able to reach you, to comfort you. I am consumed with regret" (3:12). However, it is Fiona's end that is most interesting. Walters and Harrison suggest that part of our pleasure in watching these new "bad" mothers "is watching them resist male control—of their sexuality, their work, their parenting" (51). These mothers resist patriarchal notions of mothering and the self. However, in Fiona's final scene, she wakes in her personal hell—a farm cottage where she will perpetually play the loyal housewife for all eternity. It is true that the show could be problematizing traditional patriarchy by suggesting this is "hell," but still, there is no question that for her refusal to "play by the rules" of good mothering and good womanhood, she must be punished. Moreover, we hear her pleading, "I want Delia, I want my daughter." Like Madame LaLaurie, she will be constantly reminded of her mothering faults.

So even as Fiona's lines quoted at the beginning—"Your fault was you were always looking for another version of motherhood"—suggest that her character represents some new, interesting version of motherhood, her trajectory still finds itself embedded in the witch/angel dichotomy, and the other characters also fall neatly into these traditional roles. Indeed, it is a dichotomy that remains persistent even today and continues to haunt representations of motherhood even as we try to escape it. While *Coven's* version of mothering thrills and horrifies viewers, pushing them towards a new and different understanding of mother figures, the show remains stuck within this limiting ideological framework. At best, the mothers in *Coven* illustrate the persistence and problems with the witch/angel dichotomy. At worst, it perpetuates the dichotomy which continues to shape our perceptions and expectations for motherhood not only on television, but in the world. In either case, we are left still "looking for another version of motherhood."

Notes

1. It is not clear if Misty's family is present when she reanimates the bird, nor if they are involved when she is burned at the stake, though it remains a chilling possibility that her parents were among those standing in shadow during the attempted execution (3:1).

Works Cited

Addison, Heather, et al., editors. *Motherhood Misconceived: Representing the Maternal in U.S. Films*. State U of New York P, 2009.
Creed, Barbara. *The Monstrous-Feminine: Film, Feminism, Psychoanalysis*. Routledge, 1993.
Davies, Madeline. "*American Horror Story* Baddest Witch: All of These Moms Are Terrible." *Jezebel*, 5 Jan. 2013, jezebel.com/american-horror-story-baddest-witch-all-of-these-moms-1477492109. Accessed 23 Feb. 2017.
Doyle, Sady. "Double, Double, Race and Gender Trouble." *In These Times: With Liberty and Justice for All*, 13 Dec. 2013, inthesetimes.com/article/15992/american_horror_story_coven. Accessed 24 Feb. 2017.
Fisher, Lucy. *Cinematernity: Film, Motherhood, Genre*. Princeton UP, 1996.
Haskell, Molly. *From Reverence to Rape: The Treatment of Women in the Movies*. Holt, Rinehart and Winston, 1973.
Kaplan, E. Ann. *Motherhood and Representation: The Mother in Popular Culture and Melodrama*. Routledge, 1992.
Shukert, Rachel. "*American Horror Story: Coven* Will Make You Feel Better About Your Mother." *Tablet Magazine*, 3 Jan. 2014, www.tabletmag.com/jewish-arts-and-culture/157982/american-horror-story. Accessed 23 Feb. 2017.
Walters, Suzanna Daunata, and Laura Harrison. "Not Ready to Make Nice: Aberrant Mothers in Contemporary Culture." *Feminist Media Studies*, vol. 14, no. 1, 2014, pp. 38–55.

Wear Something Black

Fashion and Fierce Femininity in the Witch Drag of Coven

Michelle L. Pribbernow

The figure of the witch in Euro-American popular media has long been associated with deviant women. Often, she is a conservative figure, reinforcing essentialist notions of womanhood and the inevitable punishment for knowing, active, or sexual women. The costumes in *American Horror Story: Coven* reference diverse pop culture images of American witches, from the Puritans to Stevie Nicks and the occult-inspired fashion of the early 1970s to the goth-clad witches of the 1990s. *Coven,* first broadcast in 2013–2014, appeared alongside a revival of interest in the occult and the emergence of witch-influenced fashion in areas as varied as couture collections (Saint Laurent, Alexander McQueen), Instagram artists (@_spirits, @bloodmilk), and popular musicians (Beyoncé, The Black Belles, Florence Welch). Additionally, the woman-dominated show is self-consciously in dialogue with contemporary high fashion, embracing and celebrating a stereotypically feminine act. Here, I explore what these "witch wear" references suggest about the version of female power portrayed in the show and its potential for a subversive version of femininity. Based on the narrative, as well as the costuming, the show suggests that women's collective power need not be marginal and trapped in the past, but rather, that a long line of fringe females have been and are still moving into the mainstream, bringing with them disruptive depictions of what power and solidarity look like. The standard realist narrative function of costuming in television programs is both disrupted and enhanced in *Coven* as extra-textual references broaden the semiotic language of clothing used in the show. Drawing on theories of the performativity of gender, camp, and drag, the costuming in *Coven* may be read as "witch drag," a playful, sexualized, space for the representation of a subversive but socially integrated and distinctively feminine power. In this essay, I advance the literature on film and televisual costuming by demonstrating the feminist potential of a decidedly femininely gendered mise-en-scène and story. Building on previous scholarship, I argue that *Coven* uses the spectacular potential of both a nearly all-female cast and dramatically non-normative clothing to subvert dominant notions of female sexuality and power in a narrative that presents empowered women as agents joining together to face the future, while drawing from a long female legacy of resistance.

Extensive academic exploration of fashion as an important medium of visual culture has only substantially emerged in the last twenty years (Bruzzi and Gibson 7). The amount of literature focused on apparel design in film remains limited, and there is even less critical work on the role of costuming and fashion in television shows. However, earlier work on fashion and taste in general may be applied to the field and in general forms the groundwork for current scholarship. Most notably, Roland Barthes' work on symbolic interactionism informs critical understandings of fashion by recognizing the importance of socially comprehensible symbols to convey mutual legible meaning. Fashion creates a cultural network of meaning. Costume designers communicate in the semiotic system of fashion to quickly communicate to an audience key aspects of characterization and/or narrative. Orthodox use of the non-verbal discourse of fashion is a key component of realist film and television. Pierre Bourdieu's notion that fashion can "extend the boundaries of the object to which it refers" allows the costume designer to communicate visually to the audience and incorporate intertextual meaning to the narrative (Finkelstein 27). Onscreen fashion may be understood as a semiotic language, conveying meaning from both in and outside the diegetic context (Warner, *Fashion on Television* 2). Mutual understanding of that language between audience and producers is necessary to understand the cues a costume designer utilizes:

> Because of socially-shared cognitions it is possible for a costume designer to convey information about a particular character visually such that the information is widely understood by audiences. In the context of visual information, socially-shared cognition occurs when a group of people recognizes and understands the meaning of a visual cultural icon (e.g., Santa Claus).... Theater costume designers identify the primary function of stage costume to be the enhancement of characterization [Johnson and Lennon 106].

Common in the literature on film and televisual costuming is the assumption that visually stunning costumes may interrupt the narrative. Rather than blending into the mise-en-scène, costume may function "as a spectacular intervention" (Gilligan 149). In most studies of costume design, "fashion is either expressive (of narrative and characterisation) or excessive (working against narrative flow)" (Warner, "Style" 183). This is typically viewed as disruptive to realist media. Stella Bruzi argues instead that clothing, especially disruptive clothing, contributes to characterization and works to construct narrative via character. Helen Warner also contests this assumption and argues that spectacular fashion may serve as a metaphor for the narrative, rather than an interruption of it ("Style" 182; *Fashion* 6). Warner's research on television shows *Sex and the City* (1998–2004), *Ugly Betty* (2006–2010), and *Gossip Girl* (2007–2012) demonstrates the potential of what is commonly referred to as "quality television" to use fashion as spectacle as a narrative, rather than distracting, tool.

Peter McNeil finds that "film audiences read these costumes avidly, their indicator and signs offering a visual subtext to the main plot" (5). He finds it true as well in novels, like Flaubert's *Madame Bovary*, which explicitly describe "the power of fashionable fictions, that apart from characterization, fashion in the novel frequently propels the plot and therefore reinscribes fashion's association with change" (3). Both Warner and McNeil argue for a shift in understanding the role of spectacular fashion in media and recognizing the driving effect it can produce.

Jane Gaines notes in "Costume and Narrative" that costume must remain subservient to the narrative, standing out enough only "to punctuate the actor against the backdrop," and the failure to do so results in audience distraction, breaking the spell of realism (193). Gaines bases her work on Laura Mulvey's theory of the (heterosexual) male gaze as the default and omnipresent lens through which cinema is viewed and created. For Mulvey, anytime a woman is on screen, she creates a freeze in the flow of action as she is, being an object to be consumed visually, always a spectacle. Warner notes that following this logic, Gaines' notion of narrative distraction is necessarily gendered and posits the question, "is the notion that females are inherently distracting to be read positively as subversive, or is this simply rendering women as objects of the male gaze?" ("Style" 183). A reasonable answer to this query is yes; both are possible and the result is dependent on the narrative context of the display.

Depictions of the Witch in Mass Media and on the Runway

That the witch may be used as a feminist symbol is contested and its feminist merits will be considered further below. The prominence of witches and occult imagery from 2013 to the present is more unambiguous. After popular culture peaks in the late 1960s to early 1970s and again after the success of the teen witch film *The Craft* (1996), the witch has returned to the cinematic, televisual, and sartorial scenes. Recent films like *Oz: The*

Great and Powerful (2013), *Beautiful Creatures* (2013), and *Hansel & Gretel: Witch Hunters* (2013) have featured beautiful, glamorous witches. Following in the footsteps of *Bewitched* (1964–1972) and later *Charmed* (1998–2006) and *Buffy the Vampire Slayer* (1997–2003), witches have returned to the small screen in *Salem* (2014–), *Secret Circle* (2011–2012), *Witches of East End* (2013–2014), and *True Blood* (2008–2014) in addition to *Coven*. As Stevie Nicks did previously, popular musicians are again calling to mind the image of the witch in their stylizations, purposefully invoking an otherworldly, strong femininity. Users curate galleries of glamorous witchy fashion on sites like Tumblr, Pinterest, and Imgur; the latter includes several galleries in the category of "Witchwear." Molly Mulshine has coined the term "Instagram Witches" to refer to various women, like user _spirits, who have highly popular Instagram accounts focusing on artsy occult images they stage and capture. As Emma Rault notes, "The image of the witch runs deep in feminist and female-centered art," and this is clearly a tradition that continues to the present, across a variety of artistic and technological platforms.

Those who collect images of witchy fashion from the runway have had no shortage of images to choose from. While dark and Gothic influences on runway fashion appear periodically and as early as Elsa Schiaparelli's 1938 Circus Collection (Pass), fashion news media outlets reported general peaks in Autumn/Winter 2008 and the 2013–2014 collections (Anderson; Spooner, "Dark Looks" 143; La Ferla). While there are many examples of witch-inspired wear to choose from, collections that stand out as being dominated by the trend in 2013 include Saint Laurent spring 2013 and Thom Browne fall 2013. The occult zeitgeist carried into other designers' works as well. Fashion magazines also chose to style these and other fashions in distinctly witchy ways, with somber groups of women in large hats or individually in natural settings.

As mass media and high fashion mutually influence each other, it is not surprising that peaks in films about witches coincide with witchy looks in haute couture. The late 1990s occult boom that was kicked off by *The Craft* and continued with *Charmed* is well-represented in the dark, dramatic runway fashion of the decade. Similarly, the influx of recent witches on both the big and small screens coincides with runway trends for fall 2016 described as "gothic glam" by *Vogue*, while *Harper's Bazaar* named the number one trend for the season "Black Magic" (Satenstein; Hillman). As "Gothic: Dark Glamour" exhibit curator Valerie Steele observes why Gothic keeps coming back into fashion, "people respond emotionally to that whole vocabulary of images and stories that have been built up over the years about the Gothic and people respond to feelings of monstrosity, the respond to the eroticism … that visual iconography keeps being added to" (qtd. in Spooner, "Dark Looks" 159). A design from Alexander McQueen of a bejeweled and moon-covered gown, worn by Nicole Kidman in early May of 2016 at a gala for a new costume exhibit at the Metropolitan Museum of Art in New York, is a perfect example of the glamorous update to the runway witch from the late 1990s to the present.

The Glamourous Witches of Coven

Coven is the most self-consciously fashionable of all of the recent television offerings focusing on witches. Having recently ended its ninth season, *AHS* has a different story arc, characters, and settings for each season of 9–13 episodes. Most of the main actors reappear from season to season but as completely different characters. The show centers on familiar tropes from American horror: a haunted house, an evil asylum, witches and Vodou practitioners in New Orleans, a carnival freak show, and a sinister hotel. References to horror archetypes like mad scientists, psychotic killers, vampires, and demon children abound and visual intertextual references are frequent. Thus, the show is rich with meaning for those with a knowledge of the semiotic language of horror. It is postmodern horror, *par excellence*.

AHS was co-created by Ryan Murphy and stands as an example of the tensions between feminism and misogyny, LGBTQ+ activism and anti-queer ideology often found in Murphy's work. Murphy's corpus frequently includes or centers on empowered women characters who are especially varied in age, ability, and sexuality, but also frequently depicts the brutalization of female bodies for shock value. Rape has been used as a plot driver in nearly every season, including *Coven*, in which two of the main adolescent characters are raped. While queer sexualities and genders are both normalized and celebrated in *The Politician* (2019–), *Glee* (2009–2015), and in some episodes of *AHS*, negative stereotypical depictions of queer characters are found in *Nip/Tuck* (2003–2010) and both *Murder House* and *Hotel*, which feature the gruesome deaths of men via anal rape. Murphy's work has certainly challenged television depictions of diverse genders and sexualities, and these representations are varied in their progressive political utility, and this is certainly the case throughout the *AHS* series.

Coven focuses on a dwindling coven of witches masquerading as a boarding school for girls. The coven faces threats from the outside in the form of a threatened and uneasy truce with local Vodou priestess, Marie Laveau, and a group of all-male witch hunters who refer to themselves as the "Corporation." The coven is also being threatened from within as the Supreme, the most powerful witch and their leader, Fiona Goode, attempts to discover and murder her successor so she can remain in power. Fiona's daughter, Cordelia, is the head of the school and guides the teenage pupils—Misty, Nan, Queenie, Madison, and Zoe—with guidance from Myrtle Snow, a contemporary of Fiona and a surrogate mother to Cordelia. There are only a few men in the house and they are decidedly peripheral: Spalding, a mute manservant who has long been in love with Fiona and spends his free time in the attic, playing with dolls; Kyle, Zoe's boyfriend that she and Madison constructed by piecing together parts from dead fraternity boys; and Hank, Cordelia's husband, who is actually a member of the Corporation, spying on the coven. By eventually working together, the surviving witches overcome all threats and prepare to welcome dozens of new students.

Flippant comments referencing designers abound in the show, demonstrating a knowledge of both desirable fashion labels and the history of fashion. Additionally, designer Lou Eyrich won an Emmy Award in 2014, with Elizabeth Macey and Ken Van Duyne, for her costumes for the show. The expert fashion knowledge conveyed by the characters and the remarkable costumes they wear position the show as a fashion authority. *Vogue* writer Nick Remsen describes the show as "an unexpected fashion hit" and the *Huffington Post* has collated some of the show's fashion-centric dialogue highlights, as well as a how-to for the look (HuffPost TV; Heyward). *NY Magazine* featured Myrtle Snow's personal greatest moments (Shepherd). Eyrich costumed Myrtle according to show creator Ryan Murphy's specifications that she "be a cross between [iconic fashion editors] Diana Vreeland and Grace Coddington" (Scharf). Myrtle delivers some of the show's best tidbits of fashion history: great lines include "You're just like Halston when he sold his brand to J.C. Penney. You've forsaken your destiny" (3:12); "I had a love like that once. Egon Von Furstenberg. He dumped me, but everything worked out all right in the end. You know why? Because he went on to marry the divine Diane. And without Egon's support, Diane Von Furstenberg never would have created the greatest invention of the century, the wrap dress!" (3:11); and her last words before being burned at the stake, "Balenciaga!" (3:13).

Myrtle is by no means the only fashionable witch in the coven. Fiona is nearly always clad in little black dresses and wears clothing by designers like Givenchy, Saint Laurent, Ralph Lauren, and Gucci, paired with Lanvin shoes or Prada boots (Scharf). Describing her personal approach to being the Supreme, she says, "All that power ... I just took it, poured it back into myself, and dressed it up in Chanel" (3:3). Misty Day dresses like her idol Stevie Nicks, sporting flowing skirts and fringed shawls in flowing layers. Cordelia is always clad in tasteful, stylish outfits in shades of cream, tan, and black.

Some of the most interesting costuming, however, is reserved for the young witches in training at the school. Reflecting their status as students and young women, their fashion identity as witches is not yet fully formed. Their default clothing is fairly typical for their demographic: jeans, shorts, or leggings paired with slogan or patterned t-shirts. When they first meet Fiona, she is appalled and has them change clothes before taking them out on a field trip, instructing them to "Wear something black" (3:1). She is instructing them that, as witches, they are to be visible and to be a spectacle. Visually marked otherness is expected and sets them apart from non-witches; norm violation is a requirement. With glamorous, Gothic, and historical referents incorporated in their garb, I label their style as "witch drag" and explore its subversive potential below.

Witch Drag in Coven

Gabrielle Finnane references Roberts' 1994 work *Civilization without Sexes* notes that after World War I, the visual became intertwined with behavior. In other words, style began to imply certain activities. This is certainly a central element of witch style and is utilized in *Coven*. When the girls are on trips away from the house with Fiona or are practicing their craft within it, they are dressed to the nines in striking black ensembles. When they are eating breakfast or talking in their bedrooms, they dress much like other teenagers. Spectacular clothing is a marker of impending spectacular activities. Additionally, the adoption of witchy clothing by the girls denotes their close relationship with each other and the older witches. It is, in a sense, a uniform they don to mark membership in the long lineage of American witches, from the puritans to the present coven. As Michel Foucault notes, uniforms also discipline and control the body. The young witches learn both to control their powers and to be controlled by their elders, and this is visually represented by their adoption of the witch uniform.

The witch uniform comprises black clothing, black hats, distinctive footwear, and includes nods to early colonial American fashion. All of these act as both tie-signs, showing the connection between the women, and as intertextual cues, which deepen the narrative by connecting it to other witches in popular culture and history. That each of these aspects is non-normative is not coincidental. Witch fashion is dysfunctional in that it is deviant behavior: "It threatens the social order by making social life difficult and unpredictable. It causes uncertainty about society's norms and values. It undermines trust in the idea that people will behave according to certain rules of conduct" (Workman and Freeburg 104). Witches dress to unsettle.

Wearing black is the first and most obvious marker of outsider status in witch clothing. Black clothing has been associated with dangerous outsiders from Lord Byron to twentieth-century Gothic subculture. Vicki Karaminas cites Anne Hollander's 1993 work, "Seeing through Clothes," saying that the "Romantic man wore black to establish remoteness. It was a style with strong literary connections, which marked him as a 'fatal man.' For Hollander the fatal man was 'specifically connected with spiritual unrest and personal solitude [and in league with] ... a dark power that exempted him from the responsibilities of common feeling and experience'" (53). These are certainly all characteristics of the witch in popular culture, and the characters in *Coven* are, as stated above, intentionally set apart by the injunction to "Wear something black."

Hats are also a key marker of the witch character. Now uncommon in everyday street wear, hats were *de rigueur* until relatively recently and their appearance in the series is intentionally anachronistic, disrupting visual realism. The ubiquity of the hat, especially wide-brimmed hats, in *Coven* and runway witch glam calls to mind the storybook image of the witch, with her tall, pointed hat, itself derived from Puritan dress. All of the girls wear hats on their initial outing with Fiona and appear in new headwear often. Where these hats, or the stylish ensembles they top, come from is never disclosed. Their sudden appearance, free of any extended transformation or shopping sequence, is part of their spectacular nature.

Aspects of the stereotypical witch ensemble are also visually isolated or dramatically emphasized, like fetish objects, in both the anthropological and counter-cultural uses of the term. This especially applies to footwear, another notable aspect of witch garb. There are two directions the costumers favor when it comes to shoes in *Coven*: sleek, stiletto heels and chunky oxfords or boots. Even before the show first aired, dramatic stilettos were used in promotional materials. Televised teasers and still advertisements for print media often featured models in spike-heeled, patent booties. The show's credit sequence is an amalgamation of occult, bestial, horrific, Vodou, and high-fashion imagery, including a fragmented catwalk strut by a model wearing literally spiked heels. These are in no way shoes meant for street wear but instead belong to the fetish fashion world. As such, they call to mind the female dominatrix and her shoes as weapons: "Fetishistic pornography often describes how the male is scratched, stabbed, and penetrated by the woman's high heels" (Steele 101). These shoes evoke a very specific, complex, gendered power dynamic, very much in alignment with the subversive agency of appealing, yet dangerous, witches.

Fiona's shoes are the first things the audience sees of her, an extreme close-up shot repeated several times thereafter, and their stylishness and extreme height convey her glamour and sophistication (3:1). In her study of goth culture, Dunja Brill notes that "[e]xtreme stilettos, [Wright] argues, represented an excess of sexualised femininity in style which went beyond the bounds of what was socially acceptable for women in that era, thus becoming capable of symbolising power and a rejection of convention" (66). Taken in conjunction with the miniskirts that also appear in these images, subversive femininity is suggested in extremes:

> McDowell makes a similar point in relation to the changes which the miniskirt underwent over the decades. He argues that the shorter and hence sexier the miniskirt got, the stronger, more aggressive and menacing was the image of femininity conveyed. This line of argument points towards the empowering potential of taking femininity and sexiness to extremes in female style [Brill 66].

On the other end of the footwear spectrum are the chunky lace-up or buckled shoes often worn by the teenage witches. These suggest historical footwear, especially the Victorian "granny" style boots favored by goths and buckled pilgrims' shoes. In combination with their hats and wide, white collars or blouse tops, their looks often reference Puritan clothing, which calls to mind the Salem witch trials and the beginning of witchcraft history in white, European-America.

It should be noted that Queenie, the sole black witch, is sometimes exempt from this ensemble. Her membership to the coven is questioned as Marie Laveau attempts to draw her to the Vodou practitioners' side and, like her costuming, she is torn between both groups. The show depicts a strict racial divide between the two groups of witches, who are sworn enemies, until they must join together to fight their mutual, patriarchal enemy. While being a witch is genetic in the show's mythology, the white witches are descended from Salem witches who learned/appropriated their craft from Tituba, a black, Vodou practicing slave. The black witches are led by Laveau and function as a closely knit religious and familial group, in opposition to the white witches' hierarchal, intrigue-filled, competitive, school. Queenie's position in the school as partial outsider and infinitely penetrable "human voodoo doll" are one piece of the show's troubled depictions of race, as separately investigated by LeKeisha Hughes and Antoinette Winstead.

Besides referring to Salem implicitly, the show also refers to it in several scenes shot to resemble silent film but set during the 1600s, showing the testing and persecution of their predecessors. The sense of history is important when considering the figure of the witch, especially as a potentially subversive, feminist archetype. The sense of time passing, being repeated and being oppressive in the space of the school is itself important in calling to mind the chaos and darkness of the witch. As Chris Baldrick notes, one major aspect of the Gothic is "a fearful sense of inheritance in time with a claustrophobic sense of enclosure in space, these two dimensions reinforcing each other to produce an impression of sickening descent into disintegration" (89). Like many ancient houses in Gothic literature, Miss Robichaux's Academy for Exceptional Young Ladies seems to be on the verge of falling apart, literally and figuratively, and that decay threatens its inhabitants.

Camp, Drag and Gender

In "Notes on 'Camp,'" which was the first to address the subject in a critical academic context, Susan Sontag observed that "Camp is a certain mode of aestheticism" and that "[a]ll Camp objects, and persons, contain a large element of artifice" (54, 55). The aesthetic of camp embraces not only artifice but also the extraordinary; "Camp is the attempt to do something extraordinary. But extraordinary in the sense, often, of being special, glamourous ... the glamor, the theatricality—that marks off certain extravagances as Camp" (60). As previously described, the multiple visual markers of the witches on *Coven* revel in artifice, glamour, and extravagance. By referencing the past through nods to both historical fashion and witch persecution, it is clear that these markers are deliberately selected and exaggerated. The main interior set of the show is the New Orleans mansion, which houses the academy. Its walls and much of the furniture are stark white, a dramatic stage that serves to highlight the women and their costumes. It is a reverse of the traditional costuming theories discussed above and keeps distractions to a minimum. Viewers enjoy an unobstructed view of camp, witchy fashion.

Pamela Robertson Wojcik argues for the tradition of feminist camp, which may or may not be performed by heterosexual women but is decidedly queer and enacts "oppositional modes of performance and reception" (9). Rooted in masquerade and burlesque, this form of gender parody is a political negotiation of the subject position performed by women, challenging the situation of woman as object in the performing arts. The witches of *Coven* are certainly empowered subjects, and their visual excess does not reduce them to object status, but rather calls attention to their transgressive autonomy.

While the term drag is most commonly used to describe individuals, usually men, dressing as an extreme version of the opposite gender, it can also be used in the postmodern context to discuss camp same-sex/gender activities. Drag, as opposed to cross-dressing, is not intended to "fool" onlookers as the biological sex of the individual. "Passing" would ruin the joke and, like camp, drag requires obvious artifice. It is specifically engaged in for theatrical performances and is typically relegated to an official stage or stage-like space. As repeatedly noted by Esther Newton in her 1972 study of Chicago cross-dressers and drag performers, exaggeration and the extraordinary are required to differentiate drag from cross-dressing.

The subversive potential of drag, as most famously discussed by Judith Butler, is that it makes explicit the performative, constructed nature of gender and disrupts hegemonic notions of gender as biologically determined. Same-sex drag operates similarly but takes this to the level of metacommentary as performers, like faux-queens or bio-queens, dress as the gender assigned to their biological sex but in an exaggerated, hyper-sexualized fashion. The knowing wink created by their performance again calls to mind the concept of camp. Audience and actor share and enjoy levels of meaning provoked by the performance and grounded in shared cultural knowledge. Humor is crafted through surprise, and possible discomfort, as boundaries are knowingly challenged and violated: "Subversive potential is thus located in appropriating dominant discourse, in resignifying hegemonic definitions through their repetition—i.e., their citation—in contexts not intended by the law" (Brill 19). Hegemonic definitions of femininity include sexiness and objectification of the female body. Drag (mis)places visual cues that do just that to subversive effect.

Defining Witch Drag

"Fashion, like femininity, is marked as the context of the other. Masculinity (especially hegemonic masculinity), by way of contrast, is more serious, changes in slower and more subtle ways, and eschews ornamentation" (Kaiser 125). Witches may well be added to the short list, which opens Kaiser's statement. Thus, highly fashionable, provocatively feminine witches—campy, rather than serious, changing in spectacular ways, and highly ornamented—are the other *par excellence*. The witches of *Coven* are deliberately set outside the pale and become spectacular interruptions to narrative, as well as the drivers of action, resulting in a provocative, "in your face" alternative femininity, highlighted by alternative televisual stylings. Hyperfemininity, as discussed above, is crucial to drag performance and, as a deliberate performance, creates a distance between subject and viewer. For women who wish to appear feminine and sexy, but not be harassed by men, an aggressive, alternative femininity can create safety: "As proposed by academic theories of feminine masquerade, Goth women—even without establishing a conscious ironic distance between themselves and their hyperfeminine image—seem to take control of their own image precisely by projecting an excessive femininity and sexiness which invites the male gaze only to confound it and keep it at a distance" (Brill 65).

Campy humor runs throughout *Coven*. In the first episode, Fiona threatens Cordelia, "Don't make me drop a house on you," and later dresses as a witch, complete with tall, pointed hat, for Halloween (3:1; 3:4). As mentioned above, the various pre-release teasers were dependent on insider cultural knowledge of both witch and high fashion imagery. Items of costuming, like Zoe's outfit in the episode "Burn, Witch, Burn!," are themselves camp, referencing witch trials at a modern day burning of a witch, tied to a stake. Combining the notion of camp as an integral aspect of drag, as well as exaggerated dress and mannerisms, the costuming in *Coven* may be described as "witch drag." From the scene in the first episode where the young witches follow Fiona's command to wear black and appear arrayed, from closets unknown, in chic, tongue-in-cheek ensembles, to the final episode when they descend the mansion stairs for their final supper before their trials, each with a shawl and dressed in black evening dresses, when it is time for serious witch-business, it is time for stunning witch fashion.

Conclusion

From the Satanic feminism of *Fin de Siècle* Paris (Le Despenser) to the 1968–1969 activist group W.I.T.C.H. (Women's International Terrorist Conspiracy from Hell) to the narrative of the "Burning Times" as a persecution of spiritual women by the patriarchy (Orion), the witch has often been used to represent strong, dangerous women. This can, of course, be problematic. It places women outside of social power structures and essentializes the concept of woman to be firmly other: of nature, irrational, mythic, mystic, etc. Furthermore, if the witch is seen only as a rebellious individual with no agency within the social system, she is at best neo-feminist, rather than advancing second-wave feminist projects of social reform or third-wave identity politics (Radner and Smith). However, a rejection of all things feminine and adoption of the masculine as a source of power only serves to reinforce existing hegemonic gendered hierarchies by privileging all things coded male.

The witch drag of *Coven* presents a powerful feminine but also socially embedded possibility for female viewers to identify with. In past narratives of the witch, she typically ended her story by hiding away or, more often, by being killed. In *Coven*, Cordelia rises as the new Supreme of the coven, and her first action is to announce to the press that witches exist and that she is opening the school publicly to any young women who think they might be witches. As Catherine Spooner notes, the potential for fashion to be subversive has to do with the story being told around it, the context ("Dark Looks" 156). If the coven remained hidden and separate from mainstream social structures, the witch figure they present would not ultimately be subversive. That this new witch, clearly identifying as a witch connected to a long lineage of dangerous women, steps into the spotlight and embraces both her biological power (magical abilities in this narrative are inherited) and her femininity and claims these things to be valuable and powerful within the world dramatically shifts the narrative from past tales.

One of the most interesting things about this new witch is her relationship to the male gaze and male desire. She is not sexless by any means but is also not defined by her relationship to men. The witch drag presented by this new character is sometimes sexy, and sometimes it is not. As *Fashionista* style blog senior editor Hayley Phelan notes of runway witch wear, "Maxi dresses and capes are not really revealing a lot of skin ... they're celebrating a kind of beauty that maybe appeals more to other women than to men" (La Ferla). Possibly usurping the 1990s trend for vampire film and television, the witch presents a more complicated, agentic figure:

> Unlike the female leads in most vampire stories, women in witchcraft stories are typically depicted as strong, capable characters. They might not always be noble, but they're certainly not weak or passive characters who sit on the sidelines while the men take charge. Fictional witches are well-rounded characters with rich interior lives, while the females in vampire stories are the supernatural equivalent of the Manic Pixie Dream Girl.... Witches discuss themselves, their powers, nature, oppression and, yes, sometimes men. But finding a scene where two female characters discuss something other than a man is laughably easy in a show about witches. In a vampire story, much less so [Gibson].

Helen Berger and Douglas Ezzy found that mass media depictions of witches do influence young, self-identified witches: "Whatever their evaluations of the movies and television shows, they are almost always aware of them, and these mass media representations of Witches have become a cultural resource integrated into the reflexive project of the self" (511). Young women who do not practice witchcraft but do consume the styles, whether on their bodies or their social media feeds, are also influenced. Representation does matter and multiple, complex and subversive depictions of feminine power give media consumers options to, if nothing else, complicate outdated, essentialist notions of womanhood. Brill notes that "[t]reating gender as a contested discourse enables the researcher to ask what part representations of femininity and masculinity in the media—and in cultural signifying practices generally—play in the ongoing construction and negotiation of gender" (19). Images like witch drag allow not only the researcher but also the consumer to query the performance of gender and assumptions of biological determinism.

Both witches and young women must do as Sofia Coppola's *Marie Antoinette* (2006) did: "a young ... vulnerable woman, a subject *other*, as we would say today, who, in a hostile environment, builds a defensive strategy to strengthen her own individuality" before they can be secure enough to enact social reform (Flores 621). Threatened by late capitalist patriarchy, represented by the all-male, witch-hunting Corporation in *Coven*, that would co-opt their bodies and (reproductive/magical) powers for its own pleasure and productive use, the witches subversively resist through humor, excess, and a new version of the deviant female. They must distance, protect, and empower both themselves and each other to not only survive, but thrive within society, rather than in its shadows. They must also unite as a new sisterhood, visible to the world, opening to newcomers and focused on nurturing, rather than competing with, each other. As Fiona says, "When witches don't fight, we burn."

Works Cited

Andersen, Kristin. "20 of the Best Gothic Runway Looks of All Time." *Vogue*, 31 Oct. 2015, www.vogue.com/article/gothic-style-runway-fashion-halloween. Accessed 6 Oct. 2017.
Baldick, Chris. *The Oxford Book of Gothic Tales*. Oxford UP, 2001.
Berger, Helen A., and Douglas Ezzy. "Mass Media and Religious Identity: A Case Study of Young Witches." *Journal for the Scientific Study of Religion*, vol. 48, no. 3, 2009, pp. 501–14.
Brill, Dunja. *Goth Culture: Gender, Sexuality and Style*. Berg Publishers, 2008.
Bruzzi, Stella. *Undressing Cinema: Clothing and Identity in the Movies*. Psychology Press, 1997.
Bruzzi, Stella, and Pamela C. Gibson. *Fashion Cultures Revisited: Theories, Explorations and Analysis*. Routledge, 2013.
Butler, Judith. *Bodies That Matter: On the Discursive Limits of Sex*. Routledge, 1993.
_____. *Gender Trouble: Feminism and the Subversion of Gender*. Routledge, 1990.
Finkelstein, Joanne. *Fashion: An Introduction*. NYU Press, 1996.
Finnane, Gabrielle. "Holly Golightly and the Fashioning of the Waif." *Fashion in Fiction: Text and Clothing in Literature, Film and Television*, edited by Peter McNeil, Vicki Karaminas, and Catherine Cole, Berg, 2009, pp. 137–48.
Fleming, Andrew, director. *The Craft*. Columbia Pictures Corporation, 1996.
Flores, Pamela. "Fashion and Otherness: The Passionate Journey of Coppola's Marie Antoinette from a Semiotic Perspective." *Fashion Theory*, vol. 17, no. 5, 2013, pp. 605–22.
Foucault, Michel. *Discipline and Punish: The Birth of the Prison*. Vintage, 1977.
Gaines, Jane. "Costume and Narrative: How Dress Tells the Woman's Story." *Fabrications: Costume and the Female Body*. Routledge, 1990.
Gaines, Jane, and Charlotte Herzog, editors. *Fabrications Costume and the Female Body*. Routledge, 1990.
Gibson, Megan. "Witches Are the New Vampires—and That's a Good Thing." *Time*, 11 Nov. 2013, entertainment.time.com/2013/11/11/witches-are-the-new-vampires-andthats-a-good-thing/. Accessed 6 Oct. 2017.
Gilligan, Sarah. "Becoming Neo: Costume and Transforming Masculinity in the Matrix Films." *Fashion in Fiction: Text and Clothing in Literature, Film and Television*. Berg, 2009, pp. 149–59.
Heyward, Bianca. "Witch Is the New Black: How to Dress Like Your Favorite Sorceress." *HuffPost*, 28 Dec. 2014, www.huffpost.com/entry/witch-is-the-black-howto_b_6058444. Accessed 6 Oct. 2017.
Hillman, Joanna. "New York Fashion Week Fall 2016 Trend Report." *Harper's Bazaar*, 23 Feb. 2016, www.harpersbazaar.com/fashion/fashionweek/g6878/new-york-fashion-week-fall-2016-trend-report/. Accessed 6 Oct. 2017.

HuffPost TV. "15 Ways *American Horror Story: Coven* Kills It with Fashion." *HuffPost*, 30 Jan. 2014, www.huffpost.com/entry/american-horror-story-coven-fashion_n_4697327. Accessed 6 Oct. 2017.
Hughes, LeKeisha. "Horrible Imaginings: The Monstrosities of Memory in Kara Walker's 'Slavery! Slavery!' and 'American Horror Story.'" 37th Annual SWPACA Conference, 11 Feb. 2016, Hyatt Regency Hotel and Conference Center, Albuquerque, NM.
Johnson, Kim K., and Sharron J. Lennon. *Appearance and Power*. Bloomsbury Academic, 1999.
Kaiser, Susan B. *Fashion and Cultural Studies*. A&C Black, 2012.
Karaminas, Vicki. "Australian Gothic: Black Light Angels, Appearance and Subcultural Style." *Fashion in Popular Culture: Literature, Media and Contemporary Studies*. Intellect Books, 2013, pp. 49–65.
La Ferla, Ruth. "Witches Lose the Warts." *New York Times*, 6 Mar. 2013, www.nytimes.com/2013/03/07/fashion/witches-have-a-fashion-moment.html. Accessed 6 Oct. 2017.
LaGravanese, Richard, director. *Beautiful Creatures*, Alcon Entertainment, 2013.
Le Despencer, Madeleine. "The Flowers of Evil: Satanic Feminists of Bohemian Paris." *Madeleine Le Despencer: Artist, Author, Demimondaine*, 2 July 2019, www.ledespencer.com/2019/07/the-flower-ofevil-berthe-de-courriere-satanic-woman-of-bohemian-paris/. Accessed 6 Oct. 2017.
McNeil, Peter, et al. *Fashion in Fiction: Text and Clothing in Literature, Film and Television*. Berg, 2009.
Mulshine, Molly. "These Instagram Witches Will Turn Your Feed Into a Chic Digital Seance." *Observer*, 25 July 2014, observer.com/2014/07/these-instagram-witches-will-turn-yourfeed-into-a-chic-digital-seance/. Accessed 6 Oct. 2017.
Mulvey, Laura. "Visual Pleasure and Narrative Cinema." *Media and Cultural Studies*, Blackwell Publishing, 2006, pp. 342–52.
Newton, Esther. *Mother Camp: Female Impersonators in America*. U of Chicago P, 1972.
Orion, Loretta. *Never Again the Burning Times: Paganism Revived*. Waveland Press Inc., 1995.
Pass, Victoria R. "Schiaparelli's Dark Circus." *Fashion, Style & Popular Culture*, vol. 1, no. 1, 2013, pp. 29–43.
Radner, Hilary. "Fashionable Dunedin and 'Rooted Cosmopolitanism' in the Twenty-First Century: NOM* D and Company of Strangers." *Journal of Asia-Pacific Pop Culture*, vol. 1, no. 1, 2016, pp. 57–78.
Raimi, Sam, director. *Oz: The Great and Powerful*, produced by Walt Disney Pictures, 2013.
Rault, Emma. "The Witchy Feminism of Modern Music Videos." *BitchMedia*, 14 Mar. 2016, www.bitchmedia.org/article/witchy-feminism-modern-music-videos. Accessed 6 Oct. 2017.
Remsen, Nick. "*American Horror Story: Coven* an Unexpected Fashion Hit." *Vogue*, 29 Jan. 2014, www.vogue.com/article/emamerican-horror-story-covenemanunexpected-fashion-hit. Accessed 6 Oct. 2017.
Satenstein, Liana. "How to Get That Glam Goth Look That's All Over the Runways." *Vogue*, 24 Feb. 2016, www.vogue.com/article/gothic-glam-trend-fall-2016. Accessed 6 Oct. 2017.
Scharf, Lindzi. "'American Horror Story' Costume Designer on 'Coven' and Working on Ryan Murphy's New Series." *Entertainment Weekly*, 30 Jan.2014, ew.com/article/2014/01/30/american-horror-story-costume-designer-on-coven-and-workingon-ryan-murphys-new-series/. Accessed 6 Oct. 2017.
Shepherd, Julianne E. "Myrtle Snows Best Fashion Moments from *American Horror Story: Coven*." *The Cut*, 31 Jan. 2014, www.thecut.com/2014/01/myrtlesbest-looks-on-american-horror-story.html. Accessed 6 Oct. 2017.
Sontag, Susan. "Notes on Camp." *Camp: Queer Aesthetics and the Performing Subject: A Reader*. U of Michigan P, 1999, pp. 53–65.
Spooner, Catherine. "Dark Looks: An Interview with Valerie Steele." *Horror Studies*, vol. 1, no. 1, 2010, pp. 143–60.
_____. *Fashioning Gothic Bodies*. Manchester UP, 2004.
Steele, Valerie. *Fetish: Fashion, Sex and Power*. Oxford UP, 1996.
Warner, Helen. *Fashion on Television: Identity and Celebrity Culture*. A&C Black, 2014.

———. "Style Over Substance?: Fashion, Spectacle and Narrative in Contemporary US Television." *Journal of Popular Narrative Media*, vol. 2, no. 2, 2009, pp. 181–93.
———. "Tracing Patterns: Critical Approaches to On-Screen Fashion." *Film, Fashion & Consumption*, vol. 1, no. 1, 2011, pp. 121–32.
Winstead, Antoinette. "The Expendables: How Horror Television and Film Desensitizes Audiences to Violence Against Black Bodies." 37th Annual SWPACA Conference, 11 February 2016, Hyatt Regency Hotel and Conference Center, Albuquerque, NM.
Wirkola, Tommy, director. *Hansel & Gretel: Witch Hunters*, Paramount Pictures, 2013.
Wojick, Pamela Robertson. *Guilty Pleasures: Feminist Camp from Mae West to Madonna*. Duke UP, 1996.
Workman, Jane E., and Beth W. Freeburg. *Dress and Society*. Fairchild New York, 2009.

Destructive Leadership in *Coven, Freak Show* and *Cult*

Corrine E. Hinton

Two seasons of the acclaimed *American Horror Story* anthology series, *Coven* and *Freak Show*, are unique in that both focus on the collective survival of a group bound by a shared existence. *Coven* follows a group of young, rebellious witches in New Orleans under the charge of aging Supreme Fiona Goode. *Freak Show* recounts the struggles of one of the last surviving freak shows in Jupiter, Florida, guided by the conflicted and calculating Elsa Mars. Other seasons of the show have followed the fate of a single family (*Murder House* and *Roanoke*) or the intertwining lives of many individuals who, unlike the witches and freaks, do not share equal concern over the fates of those with whom they share space (*Asylum, Hotel,* and *1984*). Thus, the community orientation of *Coven* and *Freak Show* allows us to examine the characters, environment, conflicts, and resolutions from a distinct perspective not afforded to us by the other seasons.

Organizational studies offers us an opportunity to navigate *Coven* and *Freak Show* in ways that evoke questions about each of the communities' histories and cultures as well as the members' individual and collective motivations, goals, and behaviors. As the designated leaders, Fiona and Elsa are particularly interesting characters to observe because their words, behaviors, and decisions have direct influence on the followers within their communities and on the health of their communities as a whole. However, in both seasons, Fiona and Elsa face competition in maintaining their leadership positions; Fiona contends with her own daughter, Cordelia, for control over the coven while Elsa struggles to maintain the respect and trust of her troupe amidst much internal and external opposition. By dissecting the leadership strategies and discourses these women employ, we can identify how they position themselves as leaders, influence their followers, and unify or divide the communities they serve.

This essay begins with a brief review of *AHS* scholarship, highlighting previous work and noting how social institutions affect character behaviors in *Asylum*. Between institutions and individuals are the characters who emerge as leaders, presenting opportunities for viewers to follow, and then question, their actions, motivations, and moral codes as they align with or diverge from the institution. Critical findings from research in leadership and management reveal the difficulty in separating destructive leaders from destructive leadership while providing some common ground in leader dispositions and motivations. Ultimately, the organizational environment, followers, and leadership demonstrated in both *Coven* and *Freak Show* exemplify what Art Padilla, Robert Hogan, and Robert Kaiser call "the toxic triangle": a perfect storm allowing destructive leaders like Fiona Goode and Elsa Mars to rule, and then nearly destroy, the organizations in their charge (176). Finally, we will look at *Cult* and how Kai Anderson contributes to and complicates fictionalized leaders as we witness the formation, rise, and downfall of his community.

AHS and American Social Imprisonment

Since the show's premier season in 2011, critical attention toward the *AHS* franchise has both grown and evolved steadily. As additional seasons have led viewers on new adventures and introduced them to frightening characters, they likewise have presented scholars with tantalizing and complex entanglements of gender, race, history, disability, and queerness for them to explore in both the show's content and form. Perhaps unsurprisingly, and yet still importantly, is the securing of the series' place within contemporary televisual Gothic provided by Dawn Keetley. Keetley's analysis is perhaps the first piece of scholarship on the series and notably calls attention to some of the show's approach in its uptake of Gothic motifs. In particular, Keetley identifies the central setting of *Murder House* as not only reminiscent and emblematic of the haunted Gothic mansion but also a "space of primitive entropy" where characters, like the American public after the economic turmoil perpetuated by the housing market crash, suffer from prolonged anxieties and succumb to the inescapability of history (102). As the series' subsequent seasons demonstrate, both history and imprisonment play important roles in the show's signature brand of television Gothic.

One constant in the *AHS* franchise formula is its peppering of real people, events, and places throughout each season's fictitious central narratives. As such, it invites the audience to reexamine and reexperience history by anchoring the imaginary in reality. In their introduction to a special issue of the *European Journal of American Culture* dedicated to the series, Harriett Earle and Jessica Clark explain, "The type of historiography that *AHS* employs creates a gruesome patchwork of the most interesting and degenerate parts of American public history, the parts of American life that horrify and titillate. The narrative of America that is created takes its cues from a cultural obsession with crime and depravity" (7).

Imprisonment, a seminal Gothic convention, operates within *AHS* spatially to amplify melodramatic suspense and socially to magnify the realistic terror associated with groupthink. Characters face imprisonment in the labyrinthian histories and iconic spaces of American horror culture: the haunted house (*Murder House*), the insane asylum (*Asylum*), the hotel (*Hotel*), the abandoned house in the woods (*Roanoke*), and the summer camp (*1984*). Layered atop spatial, corporeal imprisonment is social imprisonment, as characters work to influence and oppress each other. Previous *AHS* scholarship has accounted for some of the systems that allow such influence to occur. Jocelyn Sakal-Froese and Christina Fawcett analyze *Asylum* to examine how three institutional systems (medicine, religion, and journalism) compete for control over the season's central setting, Briarcliff Asylum (44). Through their careful examination of these institutions, Sakal-Froese and Fawcett demonstrate that "by calling to mind the dangers of institutional influence, *AHS: Asylum* allows us to read the larger establishment through the lens of the monstrous characters who are shaped by and in turn shape the structures they serve" (44). Between individuals and these structural systems are mechanisms of influence; Sakal-Froese and Fawsett call them "authorities," individual characters who serve as metonyms for the institutions (44). When interpreted through an organizational studies perspective, these institutional authorities are leaders, and their behaviors become interpretable through various frames offered by leadership studies. When those leaders' values, behaviors, and goals run in line with the institutions they serve, the institution can "absolve individuals of their responsibilities" and "normalize monstrous behaviour" (45). When these authorities, these leaders, exhibit values, behaviors, and goals that run counter to the institution, we are permitted to examine these leaders as individuals free from the absolution their institutions may have provided them.

Even in the imaginary worlds it creates, *AHS* connects its viewers to real fears and anxieties through characters that remind us of the darker, insidious aspects of human nature. Fictionalizations of leaders in any genre allow viewers to watch them "as they think, worry, hope, hesitate, commit, exult, regret, and reflect" and certainly we bear witness to both Fiona and Elsa doing all of those and more (Badaracco 3). In *Coven* and *Freak Show*, we are asked to reflect doubly on the meaning of *character*: the roles Fiona and Elsa play in their respective seasons as well as the distinctive qualities each of them possesses and by which we judge them as morally corrupt or incorrupt. A close analysis of Fiona and Elsa's strategies and discourses through the perspective of destructive leadership reveals how, as Earle and Clark remark (citing Tim Cresswell and Deborah Dixon), "*AHS* (and visual media more broadly) is not just mere image but should be viewed as the 'temporary embodiment of social processes that continually construct [...] the world as we know it'" (11). For a series that revels in exposing the sinister qualities within human nature and emphasizing the "palpable crises plaguing the contemporary United States," we should not be surprised to see destructive leadership employed as one realistic framework leveraged to guide the behaviors and attitudes of the show's characters (Keetley 90).

Destructive Leadership

Scholars interested in destructive leadership are quick to mention that the majority of their disciplinary colleagues have left the "dark side" of leadership largely unexplored (Clements and Washbush 170). Save for a few spotlights on particular negative qualities (e.g., charisma, narcissism, self-aggrandizement) or practices (e.g., manipulating, lying, bullying) of leaders, the bulk of the available literature focuses on perpetuating the "heroic conceptualization" of leadership (Hunter et al. 437). Although research into negative leader behaviors, derailment, and destructive leadership is "still in its infancy," interest is growing, as evidenced by issues dedicated to exploring bad workplace behaviors in books and in journals like *The Leadership Quarterly*, *Organizational Dynamics*, and the *Journal of Change Management* (Thoroughgood et al. 648).

Although this essay cannot provide a comprehensive review of destructive leadership scholarship, some points hold significance. Attempts at establishing a consistent and universally accepted definition of destructive leadership sits at the center of the debate (Padilla et al. 177). Contributors in the field began by making distinctions between destructive leaders and destructive leadership, where the former focuses on particular inherent characteristics (charisma, narcissism, psychopathy) or behaviors (manipulation, intimidation, coercion) that lead to describing these individuals as destructive leaders. For example, through their work, Robert Hogan and Joyce Hogan sought to identify eleven "dysfunctional dispositions" of managers and the potential these dispositions may have on negative organizational outcomes: excitable, skeptical, cautious, reserved, leisurely, bold, mischievous, colorful, imaginative, diligent, and dutiful (43). Others have researched the ways in which particular socially attractive characteristics, like charisma, can act as catalysts for good or bad leader behaviors. However, examining destructive leadership through only an individual leader's actions, behaviors, or personality traits limits our understanding of how destructive leaders accomplish their goals as well as their influence on their subordinates.

The latter approach to destructive leadership attempts to delineate between destructive leadership qualities, practices, and outcomes. In some cases, scholars look at organizations where abusive, questionable, or unethical practices have become systematically imbedded within institutions so much so that the leadership of the organization itself (as a whole) is destructive. Citing work by Robert Hogan and Robert B. Kaiser, Padilla et al. explain, "Organizational destructiveness occurs when leaders bring misfortune to their followers, including internal and external stakeholders, and to social institutions" (178). This more encompassing perspective of destructive leadership allows us to conceptualize the ways in which destructive leaders not only exert influence on particular individuals within their followership but also on organizations as a whole; at the same time, we can see how some organizations may provide safe haven for destructive leaders because of flaws in their own systems.

Toxic Triangle

While theoretical approaches to destructive leadership vary, this essay adopts Padilla, Hogan, and Kaiser's concept of the "toxic triangle." The three leadership experts are responsible for coining the term to illustrate the three elements necessary for destructive leadership to occur: destructive leaders, susceptible followers, and conducive environments. Through employing the toxic triangle approach, the remainder of this essay (1) establishes the coven and freak show troupe as organizational climates vulnerable to destructive leaders, (2) analyzes a selection of the followership in both seasons using Thoroughgood, Padilla, Hunter, and Tate's "susceptible circle" taxonomy (897), and (3) investigates the attributes, behaviors, and rhetorical strategies of Fiona Goode and Elsa Mars that allow them to flourish as destructive leaders.

The Coven and Troupe as Organizations

Rather than communities, both the coven and troupe operate more akin to informal organizations. The coven's hierarchy, implicit and explicit expectations for member loyalty and acceptable behaviors, communal living/working space, shared organizational goals (i.e., to protect and perpetuate the Salem line), cultural systems and values, and an established leadership all support equating the coven with an organization. We can also liken the freak show troupe to an organization, even if it lacks some of the coven's more established structure. Rather than an explicit hierarchy, the troupe follows an implicit sense of mutual respect. Additionally, those who are less capable of caring for themselves (e.g., Pepper, Salty, Meep, and Ma Petite) enjoy the sibling-like protection of the more able-bodied and/or able-minded. As public display pieces, freak shows have an extensive history in both England and America, and the freaks in Elsa's troupe seem well-versed in the narratives of their elders as well as knowledge that they are, like the coven witches, a dying breed (Grande 23). Although the troupe's cultural diversity makes it a less stable organization, the freaks still retain rules of acceptable behavior, abide by a shared justice system, and maintain a family-like structure designed to ensure the show's survival.

The Coven and Troupe as Environments Conducive to Destructive Leadership

Organizational environments ripe for destructive leader influence are those that embody cultural values complementary to authoritative leadership, experience sudden or persistent instability, believe in the imminent nature of internal or external threats, and lack shared governance or control between leaders and followers. Both the coven and the troupe conform to each of these environmental conditions, opening themselves to the influence of destructive leaders.

Cultural Values

Acting as a social control mechanism, an organization's culture facilitates or constrains member behaviors through a shared understanding of and explicit or implicit agreement to particular norms and values (O'Reilly and Chatman 160). Organizational identification occurs when members connect their own identities to their organizations, because they achieve a sense of belonging; share in the organization's goals, values, and successes; and benefit personally from such a connection (e.g., increase self-esteem or self-worth) (Conroy et al. 185). When members inculcate their organization's values as a part of their own identities, they often make decisions or behave in ways similar to collectivist cultures. Collective cultures "prefer strong leaders to bring people together ... to provide solidarity and group identity," rendering them vulnerable to destructive leaders (Padilla et al. 186). Additionally, organizations with a higher power distance between the leader and her followers are also more apt to tolerate destructive leaders, because followers can often do little to change the power structure. Finally, an organizational culture built upon "dependency and apathy among followers" both reaffirms the power structure and "concentrates power in a leader" (186).

Collectivist

Both the coven and the troupe are collectivist cultures, meeting several criteria Geert Hofstede and Gert Jan Hofstede outline in their book, *Cultures and Organizations*. In collectivist groups, members are born into the in-group (witches are born witches, and freaks are born freaks); these in-groups "continue protecting [members] in exchange for loyalty" (92). In *Coven* and *Freak Show*, the leaders and current members offer new members (e.g., Zoe and Misty Day in *Coven*; Bette and Dot Tattler, Ima Wiggles in *Freak Show*) protection, freedom to be themselves, and a surrogate family. While Hofstede and Hofstede assert, "Children learn to think in terms of 'we,'" the same could be said of the coven and troupe in-group members (92). Members of both groups locate themselves in "we" and "us" references to separate in-group members from out-group members. In *Coven*, for example, Fiona Goode admonishes any witch in her coven who wants to use outsiders to solve their problems: "When strangers come asking questions, *we* close ranks. [...] Even the weakest of *us* are better than the best of *them*" (3:2, my emphasis). Fiona uses *us-them* language to rhetorically locate the witches as a collective, positioning them not only as unified group but also as a unified group separate from others (humans, Marie Laveau's Vodou clan, witch hunters). Elsa Mars' troupe seems well established in their collective identity. At the time of the Tattler sisters' induction at the end of "Monsters Among Us," most of the existing members are well indoctrinated into the notion of the freak show as a "family" in need of shelter from the "monsters ... outside this tent ... in all these little towns" (4:1). Jimmy, his mother Ethel, and Eve and then later, Desiree, the Tattler sisters, and even magician Chester Creb adopt the freaks-as-family language that continuously reinforces its collective identity. Finally, collectivist cultures also share resources, and in the coven and the troupe, members share space, food, assets, and any other resources beneficial to the community's health. While the witches and freaks have personal possessions, they agree to share both the workload and the rewards of their environments to ensure their group members' basic needs are met.

High Power Distance

Organizations rely on systems to achieve its goals; the mere presence of such structures invite debates about how, by whom, and for what purpose power is managed among its members. Hofstede and Hofstede define *power distance* as "the extent to which the less powerful members of institutions and organizations ... expect and accept that power is distributed unequally" (46). In smaller power distance cultures, members experience less dependence on their leaders, and their relationship is collaborative. The coven and troupe, however, are high power distance cultures; that is, a significant power gap exists, and followers are more dependent upon their leaders. Power distance can also influence followership behaviors. In organizations with greater power distance, "subordinates respond by either preferring such dependence ... or rejecting it entirely" (46). Followers who accept the power differential become colluders or conformers, while those who reject it become defectors—typologies we will explore later. First, let us examine how a high power distance structure manifests in the coven and troupe.

In the coven, the Supreme, by its very name, conjures unquestionable authority; furthermore, the function of the Supreme position as one that controls the health of the coven instills a near-single point of failure (save for the Council on Witchcraft). Finally, the Supreme's installation through the Seven Wonders ritual certifies her power. Viewers are privy to the coven's philosophy in the episode, "Go to Hell." In the opening scene, we witness reel footage of long-dead coven witches offset with a series of quotes explaining the purpose of the Seven Wonders ritual: "Guided by ancient tradition, witches survive only if united under a strong, singular authority. Every generation needs its leader. The Supreme. No simple test could ever determine the sovereign among us. We rely upon seven" (3:12). Coven witches are to be *united*, together as one supportive unit. This supportive unit (the followership) serves *under* the rule of a *strong, singular authority*, leaving no allowance for a follower to question her Supreme. Likewise, the coven followers anoint the Supreme, having demonstrated mastery of the Seven Wonders, superior to them in terms of her "gifts" and her authority. This high power distance culture deliberately removes power and autonomy from the lesser coven witches. The age difference between the lesser coven witches (twenty-somethings) and the two older witches, Cordelia and Fiona, agitates an already imbalanced power dynamic within the coven.

Despite the lack of a formal ascension process, the freak show troupe still maintains a high power distance culture. Although the power lines are not so clearly drawn as "one leader to many followers" like the coven, members respect an implicit hierarchy through mutual respect for members and their value to the organization. As the founder of Fräulein Elsa's Cabinet of Curiosities, Elsa sits at the top and remains there through a combination of her actions (presented in detail later) and an organizational climate that fosters the freaks' dependency upon her. She maintains and distributes the show's income, sets the order of the acts, determines if potential members can stay (e.g., Dell and Desiree's contentious admittance into the group), and provides a vision. Several freaks—Meep, Ma Petite, Pepper, and Salty—are incapable of altering the power differential and remain entirely dependent upon Elsa and the other members for protection. Those who could challenge Elsa accept the inequality unquestionably, because they believe she protects the organization's interests and its members. When some members question Elsa's motivation, they fail to rally as a group to take action. Instead, potential defectors like Paul, Ethel, and Jimmy attempt, single-handedly, to hold her accountable for her destructive actions. Their efforts fail because Elsa can disable each traitor, one by one.

Dependency and Apathy

The coven at Miss Robichaux's Academy and Fräulein Elsa's Cabinet of Curiosities both represent physical locations that provide security for each organization's membership and protect the witches and freaks from the normal public. Each organization welcomes those who have been born into a world that seeks to eradicate them, and both represent one of the few remaining refuges in the country. Members may leave if they wish but risk their lives in doing so. In *Coven*, Queenie leaves to join Marie Laveau's Vodou tribe only to find herself one of the two survivors of Hank's massacre. In *Freak Show*, after inmates at the jail murder a falsely arrested Meep, the freaks in Elsa's troupe do not even discuss leaving. By manipulating their organization's limitations of space and place, Elsa and Fiona can centralize their authority over a vulnerable environment and create a "culture of dependency" amongst their followers (Padilla et al. 186).

Organizational Instability and Threats

The greatest vulnerabilities the coven and the troupe experience are the instabilities plaguing them. In traditional organizations, unexpected personnel departures, restructuring, or leadership vision changes can cause instability. Organizational instability might also result from the "perception of imminent threat" (Padilla et al. 185). Threats to an organization can cause members to behave in ways motivated by the fear of uncertainty.

When members operate in fear of external threats and also feel unequipped to respond to moments of instability, they put their faith in leaders to make unilateral decisions, guide them through safely, and stabilize the organization. In moments of sudden and unexpected change, destructive "leaders can enhance their power by advocating for radical change to restore order" (185). The witches and freaks expect their leaders to do the same. Unbeknownst to most of them, Fiona and Elsa are the cause of many of the threats they encounter.

The coven endures attacks from the living and the undead, a reignited war with the Vodou witches, internal power struggles, and the dissolution of the Council on Witchcraft. Amidst these destabilizing events, Fiona's followers are also living under the constant threat of their species' demise. From the moment she enters the coven, Zoe learns witches are a "dying breed." After sharing Misty Day's *auto-da-fé*, Cordelia reminds them: "We are under siege, ladies. Our lives, our very existence, is always at risk. Know this, or face extinction" (3:1). One threat of imminent eradication, however powerfully delivered, would likely not be enough to cause widespread panic amongst an organization's members. Rhetorically, however, these threats come often, change shape, and spill from both Cordelia and Fiona's lips. Outsiders, like the police and the neighbors, are a threat. Competing factions, like the one lead by Marie Laveau, are a threat. Throughout the season, the threat/survival rhetoric circulates amongst the witches, and eventually they begin to repeat it—evidence that the followers have accepted it as an organizational reality. Early in the season, when Fiona mitigates some threats and restores the coven's stability, the fearful younger witches believe her leadership is key to their survival. For example, Fiona enchants the police who have come to speak with Madison and Zoe about the fraternity bus accident (3:2). She also gains their respect when she publicly punishes Madame LaLaurie for her refusal to serve Queenie lunch. "There's nothing I hate more than a racist," Fiona remarks, and the younger witches seem pleased at her response (3:3). By rectifying minor moments of organizational instability, Fiona builds her reputation as a strong, capable leader.

Elsa's troupe also suffers from instability and external threats throughout its temporary residence in Jupiter. While the public is less of an issue for the witches in New Orleans, they represent one of the freaks' central conflicts. In town for less than two months, the troupe already faces eviction. Disgusted by freaks in their diners and shops, the townspeople become suspicious when news spreads of a serial killer. The threat of public condemnation becomes real, destabilizing the troupe. Police visit the grounds four times (resulting in two arrests and Meep's death), a curfew forces them to hold matinees to generate income, and the townspeople—even after branding Jimmy a hero—turn on them after the Tupperware party massacre. The public, however, is not the only destabilizing force at work. In the last few episodes, Elsa sells the show twice, to Chester Creb and Dandy, and disaster follows both. The troupe also encounters internal and external threats, including that of their inevitable demise. "A vanishing breed," Elsa's show is the last haven for people like them (4:2). The troupe must survive threats by the psychotic Dandy and the grifting duo, Stanley and Maggie. As freaks start to disappear or die, the freaks look to Elsa for guidance. Elsa only acts when her own dreams are not in danger and such acts are necessary to restore order. Early in the season, she hides the Tattler sisters from the police to protect them and allows Dell and Desiree to join the show (4:2). She does not, however, block the police from falsely arresting Meep for the detective's murder or oust Dell after he attacks Eve (4:2; 4:7). Instead of powerful actions, Elsa relies on her rhetorical power to reassure her "monsters" amidst the constant barrage of threats, even when she makes decisions in her own interest (4:1).

Lack of Shared Governance

An absence of checks and balances in the power dynamics of an organization can also make them liable to the unbridled dominance of destructive leaders. While the coven's organizational structure includes a system of checks and balances, the system fails. The Council on Witchcraft keeps the Supreme and her coven in "check" when necessary using an objective, independent board of elder witches (Myrtle Snow, Quentin Fleming, and Cecily Pembroke). At Nan's behest, the Council arrives to initiate a formal "inquiry" into Madison's disappearance (4:4). As the murderess responsible for two witches' deaths, Fiona knows her fate should the Council discover her guilt. However, the Council is also an obstacle maintaining her position as Supreme, so Fiona vanquishes it using the illusion of conspiracy within its ranks, forcing it to turn on itself. She even enlists Queenie's help to sell the Council on Myrtle's guilt as Cordelia's attacker (4:5). With the Council in disarray, Fiona can operate without oversight.

While the coven's structure includes a mechanism for shared governance, the troupe possesses no such mechanism. The troupe operates, its members believe, democratically; thus, a formal entity to balance power would be unnecessary. For most of the season, the freaks believe Elsa is devoted to their wellbeing. By the time they realize her motivations are misguided and her decisions are deadly, they are powerless to repair the damage or take control. Because Elsa owns the show, she owns the talent; without a system to regulate her ownership, Elsa is free to transfer control to the highest bidder. When the freaks pool their money to buy the show from Elsa, she has already sold it to the traveling salesman and wannabe magician, Chester Creb (4:11; 4:12). In refusing to transfer ownership to her organization's members, Elsa reduces her monsters to products and not people. And without a system to monitor her, Elsa's destructive behaviors are unstoppable.

Followership

If leadership only exists through its influence on a followership, then the nature and process of influence is equally as important to consider. Drawing from previous research on susceptible individuals, Padilla, Hogan, and Kaiser identify two categories of followers most likely to support destructive leaders: *conformers* and *colluders*. Motivated by fear, conformers comply with a destructive leader, because they believe the consequences of not complying will be worse. Unsure of themselves, conformers are the more vulnerable of the two groups, because they have unmet needs they believe the leader and organization can fill (Padilla et al. 183). The young and impressionable especially are more attracted to dominant, charismatic leaders; in turn, leaders can groom self-doubting conformers into colluders who "become committed to a destructive enterprise" (184). Colluders "actively participate in a destructive leader's agenda" due in part to their own selfish motivations for personal gain (183). According to McClelland, colluders are ambitious individuals who seek status, recognition, or profit and may even act or make choices in a destructive way to please leadership (qtd. in Padilla et al. 185).

Using John E. Barbuto's theory of follower compliance as a framework, Thoroughgood, Padilla, Hunter, and Tate generate five follower subtypes within the conformer and colluder groups, whom they label the "susceptible circle." The five follower types include *Lost Souls* (conformer), *Bystanders* (conformer), *Authoritarians* (conformer), *Opportunists* (colluder), and *Acolytes* (colluder). *Lost souls* are attracted to charismatic leaders because they usually suffer from low self-esteem and a lack of direction; as such, destructive leaders can tap into the lost soul's desire for direction, community, and self-worth (903). *Bystanders* follow destructive leaders because of their passivity and fear of the potential consequences for not complying with a destructive leader's demands. While some bystanders may hold beliefs or values that run counter to their leaders, their fear of punishment prohibits them from acting or speaking out against them (907). *Authoritarians*, the last of the conformer subtypes, are allegiant to their leaders, because a sense of personal and moral obedience to a designated authority compels them (905). *Opportunists* support destructive leaders because they believe they will reap personal power, status, or recognition; that is, they can achieve their own goals by connecting themselves to someone who is already in a position of power and influence (908). The second of the two colluder subtypes, *acolytes*, also willingly follow destructive leaders; unlike opportunists, however, acolytes' personal values and goals align with the leaders. "True believers" in the organization's cause or goals, acolytes require little prodding to comply with leader demands (910). Overall, these different follower subtypes generate ample character material for fictionalized communities within print, film, and television including those in both *Coven* and *Freak Show*.

Followers and Defectors in Coven *and* Freak Show

Colluder and conformers abound in both Fiona's and Elsa's followership. In both seasons of the show, destabilizing organizational structures and mutating follower dynamics accentuate the precariousness of the toxic triangle. Rather than analyzing superficially every follower, this section will examine in detail one prominent follower integral to each season. The more interesting followers are those who do not remain static in one follower type, because change exemplifies the complexity inherent to human nature under influence.

Consider the first character we meet, Zoe, in the *Coven* season, for example. Zoe's vulnerability is evident after she experiences sudden instability in her self-concept when her mother reveals that the teen suffers from the same "genetic affliction" as her maternal grandmother, one that causes both her unnatural powers and her subsequent dismissal from the family home (3:1). Then, the confused young witch undergoes an outsider-to-insider transition that commences upon her initial entry into the coven, as the more established girls at Miss Robichaux's taunt and haze her (3:1). The audience experiences Zoe's discombobulation when it follows her perspective as she is transported from her old life as an insecure teenager to her new one as a similarly insecure witch in the coven all within the first episode. As a new witch lacking a supportive social environment within her family and within the coven, Zoe suffers from low self-efficacy in her powers, and her self-identification as a witch is "vulnerable and raw" (3:1). An initial *lost soul* looking for a community, Zoe is impressionable, "exposed" (an analogy to the people of New Orleans Zoe describes in her voiceover at the conclusion of the first episode), and easily malleable. Initially, Cordelia seems to vie for Zoe's loyalty when the elder witch saves her from her mischievous sister witches, but she is also bewitched by Fiona's charisma and power when she enters the academy, tosses Madison against a wall, and treats the girls to a downtown New Orleans fieldtrip to a sacred place in their history (3:1). Arguably, these same qualities also make her susceptible to Madison's peer pressure when Zoe reluctantly participates in Madison's criminal mishap at the fraternity party (3:1). Quickly in the season, however, Zoe moves from *lost soul* to *bystander*, as she connects to members of the coven and develops a salient fear of Fiona's wrath after she tries to "out" witches to the police (3:2).

During the season, Zoe continues to evolve as a follower. Eventually, she defects from Fiona and aligns herself with Cordelia. Ironically, Zoe's conversion from follower to defector can be directly linked to Fiona's own actions. First, Fiona helps build Zoe's confidence when she tells her, "I like a witch who fights. You've done this coven a great service, Zoe, and I won't forget it" after Zoe helps defeat the walking dead on Halloween night (3:5). Soon after, Zoe's confidence inspires her to lead the effort to locate Madison. In "The Axeman Cometh," Zoe calls Queenie and Nan's attention to the coven's dwindling numbers, remarking, "No one in charge has done shit" (3:6). Zoe's growing self-confidence runs parallel with her growing lack of confidence and trust in both Fiona and Cordelia. When Queenie suggests they take their concerns about Madison to Fiona, Zoe scoffs and tells her, "Last time I checked, she was setting witches on fire. We can't afford to lose a single witch if we want to survive" (3:6). Zoe's comments are evidence of Fiona's second behavior that contributes to Zoe's shifts in follower typology. Fiona casts doubt on her own leadership when she has Myrtle Snow put to death. Miss Robichaux's Academy is not the stable, community-centered, sisterhood that Zoe and her fellow lesser witches were promised. At the season's halfway point, Zoe has taken on the responsibility of leading the lesser coven witches.

Zoe's progression from follower to defector completes when Cordelia approaches Zoe to discuss Madison's killer. Cordelia first warns Zoe that her growing powers are not going unnoticed: "You've got a bullseye on your back, kiddo, and our biggest enemy is locked, loaded, and looking at you" (3:7). Zoe's inclination is to blame Marie Laveau, and she is surprised when Cordelia identifies Fiona as the culprit. "But she's on our side," Zoe counters (3:7). Cordelia reveals the truth to Zoe, and Zoe's choice of phrase reveals her immediate shift of allegiance to Cordelia: "So what do *we* do?" (3:7, my emphasis). Their conversation also cements Zoe's shift from follower to defector, and afterward, Zoe deliberately contradicts Fiona's leadership by helping Cordelia draft the plans for her mother's demise. In a moment of clarity, Zoe tells Nan, "I didn't realize this before, but we can't survive on our own. The sisterhood protects each of us" (3:10). By the latter half of the season, Zoe assumes the position of *acolyte*, and her remaining actions in the season are those designed to support and sustain the coven's organizational mission (providing a safe, nurturing environment for young witches) even if it means putting herself in danger. At the end of the season, Cordelia rewards Zoe's allegiance to the coven by appointing her to the new Council on Witchcraft (3:13).

Freak Show offers a wealth of characters portraying a diversity of follower and defector types, but the freaks closest to Elsa (Ethel, Paul the Illustrated Seal, Amazon Eve, Jimmy Darling, and Legless Suzi) are particularly interesting to watch. Among these, Jimmy Darling wanders through a variety of follower typologies as his allegiance to Elsa waivers. From his opening scene at the diner where he flirts with a waitress, Jimmy strikes us as an *authoritarian*—someone who does not believe in Elsa's approach of keeping freaks in their place to make nice with the locals but who, nonetheless, acknowledges her authority as the troupe's leader. When Elsa scolds him for selfishly risking the show's success, Jimmy tells her, "They don't want us here; you're living in your own dream, Elsa" (4:1). Throughout the season, we realize that Elsa can maintain her control over Jimmy's rebellious spirit with constant reminders that he is not as normal as he pretends to be. Jimmy toys with his position as a follower: he operates a side business of pleasing housewives for cash, violates the town's curfew, talks back to the police, and kills the detective who tries to remove the Tattler sisters from the campgrounds. Like Zoe, Jimmy leads his fellow freaks when Elsa is absent or unwilling to act. In the season opener, Jimmy gathers the other freaks to help dispose of the detective's body and delivers a speech that establishes his vision for the future of his kind:

> All we've ever wanted was a place where we feel safe and be just the way we are, but no one is gonna hand it to us. We're gonna have to rise up and take it. Don't we deserve to be happy? If anyone tries to mess with us, any of us ... they're gonna end up like this pig [4:1].

The freaks' willingness to dismember the detective suggests Jimmy exerts some influence amongst Fiona's followers.

Jimmy spends much of the season in conflict with his own beliefs. On the one hand, he recognizes he is different and hates that Elsa expects him to exploit his deformity to the public for money but stay in camp when he's not on stage. On the other hand, he genuinely believes the public would accept him and other freaks if they learned to see them as people, and acceptance holds the key to happiness. Fiercely protective of his fellow freaks, Jimmy takes upon himself the responsibility of keeping his family safe from harm. Three events endanger Jimmy's allegiance to Elsa: his inability to prevent Meep's death, the Tattler sisters' mysterious disappearance from camp, and Elsa's demands that the freaks demonstrate their devotion to her by sacrificing one of their own to her spinning wheel. Like

Fiona, Elsa's actions and inactions cause questions of loyalty amongst several followers, Jimmy included. After Elsa injures Paul on the spinning wheel, Jimmy is ripe to defect.

Because Jimmy is unable to identify Elsa as the source of the troupe's difficulties, he fails to make personal progress and never defects. Though he is convinced Elsa sold the Tattler twins to Dandy, the twins recant their confession and admit they went to Dandy willingly. Jimmy's relationships with Dell the Strong Man and with Maggie the con artist complicate matters. Finally, Ethel's inexplicable suicide sends Jimmy into a drunken stupor where he remains, a nonthreat to Elsa, until he is arrested for the murder of the housewives attending a Tupperware party. Jimmy's imprisonment, mutilation, and long recovery all prevent him from protecting the freaks in his troupe and from discovering any more of Elsa's indiscretions. Elsa uses Jimmy's vulnerable state to reinstate his allegiance; she offers him the services of the Italian doctor to create his prosthetics and appeals to his loyalty to the troupe. She tells him, "I have seen you grow from a boy to a man, a man to a leader, and we need you now" (4:12). Jimmy never has the opportunity to defect from Elsa's leadership; by the time he recovers and leaves the barn, he is too late. Elsa is gone, Dandy has massacred the remaining freaks (except Desiree), and the Tattler sisters are now Dandy's. All that's left for Jimmy to do is to avenge their deaths, upholding their code. As he, the twins, and Desiree watch Dandy drown to death, Jimmy explains: "We will always win, we will always defend each other to the death, and you want to know why? Because we have no one else to turn to. The freaks shall inherit the earth" (4:13). Rather than defect, Jimmy is set free when the organization crumbles upon itself after Elsa abandons it.

Leader Qualities

The coven and the troupe are filled with members susceptible to dominant, destructive leaders. No doubt, Fiona and Elsa demand the greatest attention as their groups' leaders. Many of their actions have been recounted in previous sections of this analysis, but we have yet to engage directly with the characteristics that define them and the rhetorical strategies they use to assert their power and maintain control. After thorough review of the literature on destructive leader qualities, Padilla and his colleagues suggest five "critical leader factors: charisma, personalized use of power, narcissism, negative life themes, and an ideology of hate" (180). A deeper look into Fiona and Elsa reveals these qualities in both women.

Fiona flaunts the negative qualities most leaders attempt to avoid in themselves: narcissism, bullying, self-aggrandizing, manipulative, deceitful, untrustworthy, and cunning. She is also strategic, influential, and fiercely protective; the same charisma that draws the younger witches to her is the same that perpetuates their fear of disobeying her. Yet, nearly every decision she makes as Supreme is for her own good. If those same decisions happen to benefit the coven as well, it makes covering her malfeasance easier. Fiona's only desire is to maintain her position as Supreme to prevent her death. Unable to cure herself through human means (e.g., experimental drugs, plastic surgery, chemotherapy), she does not hesitate to turn to magic and then to murder to slow her decay. Her narcissism prevents her from choosing the coven's welfare above her own, even in the face of her own daughter's mutilation. While negative life themes are often associated with adverse childhood experiences, we know little about Fiona's childhood except that she spent much of it growing up in the Academy. Nevertheless, Fiona's self-absorption and belief in her destiny to become Supreme is clear even from an early age when she murders then-Supreme Anna Leigh Leighton. We know that internally, Fiona is beleaguered by her own inadequacies as a mother. She vocalizes regret for how she's handled her relationship with Cordelia (to Delphine, to Madison, and to the Axeman), accuses Myrtle of "latch[ing] on" to Cordelia, and even regenerates a dead baby for a stranger (3:5). However unrelenting her guilt, Fiona still adopts and spreads an ideology of hate amongst her followers. Padilla and his colleagues explain, "The rhetoric, vision, and worldview of destructive leaders contain images of hate—vanquishing rivals and destroying despised enemies" (182). Fiona supports her ideology amongst her followers by leading them in acts or encouraging them to commit acts of violence against those who might attempt to destroy them. Examining the rhetoric of Fiona's leadership exposes a conflation of her narcissism and insecurity.

Fiona's rhetoric follows several trajectories to maintain follower compliance: simulated protection, manipulations of grandeur, and public shaming. By creating the allusion of security, Fiona gains her followers' confidence when they are at their most vulnerable. Repeatedly, she tells the other witches that they will handle their threats "internally" rather than going to the police, instilling confidence that she can lead them into doing so (3:4). Fiona also acquires loyalty by manipulating her followers into believing they are the next Supreme. She uses this strategy first with Madison, after learning Madison has the ability of *pyrokinesis* when she sets the neighbor's curtains ablaze. When Madison refuses to apologize for her behavior, Fiona assures her, "People in our position have no need to apologize; our actions speak for themselves" (3:3). By suggesting to Madison that the two of them are in the same group ("our position"; "our actions"), Fiona manipulates her into showing Fiona evidence of her growing abilities. Fiona feigns vulnerability and reveals her failure as a mother in front of Madison, telling her, "I have so much to teach," Madison falls for it and asks Fiona to "teach" her (3:3). Fiona employs the same strategy with Queenie when she manipulates her into framing Myrtle for the acid attack on Cordelia. When Queenie expresses her discomfort with helping her "roast" a fellow witch, Fiona attempts to flatter her by citing the strength of her mind and of her powers—under Fiona's "tutelage" of course (3:5). Fiona dangles the idea of Supreme in front of her: "Maybe that's what this coven needs: a supreme of color" (3:5). Bait accepted; Queenie admits she has been "feeling stronger" and that she could be a good Supreme. In exchange, Fiona tells Queenie, "You have to trust me. Follow my instruction to the letter, and you'll be fine" (3:5). If she's not manipulating her follower witches, Fiona is publicly shaming those whom she sees as competition. Cordelia is often the victim. During the season, Fiona berates Cordelia several times, labeling her teaching approach "an abject failure" (3:1), chiding her for "undermining" her authority when Cordelia visits Marie Laveau (3:4), and slapping and accusing her of bringing "a viper into this sacred house" when Hank's identity as a witch hunter is revealed (3:10). Fiona uses the same public shaming on Zoe early in the season, on Myrtle Snow, on Queenie, and on Misty Day. By creating a false sense of security, appealing to vulnerable followers' notions of self-worth, and insulting those who dare contradict or undermine her, Fiona's bark is just as bad as her bite.

Like Fiona, Elsa Mars is a delusional narcissist whose actions as the troupe's leader are guided almost entirely by her selfish desire to recapture the short-lived fame she once enjoyed. She loathes the thought of television but learns to embrace it as the only way she might be the star she knows she was born to be. For her, leading the freak show is temporary—a means to an end. In confidence, she admits to Ethel that bringing the two-headed Tattler sisters into the show was only to entice audience members to hear her sing. Elsa is charismatic—full of energy and passion to give the people the best show they can imagine if she remains the star. After Dot's delightful cover of Fiona Apple's "Criminal" suggests the sisters might steal her spotlight, Elsa responds by feeding off Bette's vulnerability and resentment. To preserve her spot as the headliner, Elsa tries to convince Bette that Dot is trying to steal her star power and that she "mustn't allow it" to happen (4:2). While we are privy to few details of Elsa's childhood, we know that she has undergone a life filled with trauma: her parents had her to replace the baby they lost, she was disfigured for a sadomasochistic snuff film by a Nazi, and she was left to die alone. Her past fuels a psychological compulsion to "be loved" while allowing her to sacrifice anyone in her way (4:6). Elsa's voiceover monologue in the opening scene of "Bullseye" reveals her true nature:

> I know how to stay off the wheel. I control my fate. I have survived, because I know one must be willing to destroy anyone or anything—even the ones you love—to keep the gods in check [4:6].

Elsa may not spread an ideology of hate, but she is willing to commit violence to protect her potential for stardom; she stabs Paul and kills Ethel to protect her sins against the troupe. She is also willing to encourage others to use violence as a way to make their problems disappear; in so doing, she gathers additional power to bribe or manipulate others.

Elsa also employs consistent rhetorical strategies to keep her monsters under control, the most pervasive of which are the family and savior rhetorics. Throughout the season, Elsa maintains that the freaks in her show are a "family" (4:1). She fashions this family rhetoric for several purposes. First, she uses it to allure potential newcomers into the organization, as she does with the Tattler sisters in the season opener and, later, to lure Barbara (a.k.a. Ima Wiggles) away from the weight loss camp and into the freak show. She also juxtaposes family with abandonment when followers leave (willingly or unwillingly). For example, when she sells the Tattler sisters to Dandy, Elsa claims the twins simply left: "We bring them in, we give them a home, a family, and how do they repay us? By disappearing into the night" (4:6). Those who abandon the family are worthless to the organization and endanger the troupe and its members. In addition to acting as the matriarch of her monster family, Elsa also leverages a savior rhetoric to generate member loyalty. In the first episode, as Elsa persuades the twins to join her troupe, she tells them that her only intention is to "save" them, savior language Bette mimics in her diary entry when she says she feels "free" and describes her arrival into the troupe as one of "glorious freedom" (4:1). Elsa then combines her family rhetoric with her savior rhetoric as persuasive devices when her members question her loyalty or trust. After Paul confronts her about the twins' real whereabouts, Elsa explodes and calls all of her monsters into the big tent to chastise them. One by one, she reminds them in what "filth" they would be without her intervention:

> You ungrateful ingrates! I rescue you from the squalor of your miserable existences, and this is how you repay me: with accusations, disgusting rumors. […] You should be ashamed. After everything that I have done for you, everything that I have sacrificed for us, for our family. And I still am not one you trust [4:6].

Tapping into her followers' feelings of guilt, fear of abandonment, shame, and gratitude, Elsa maintains control over her family. When her deceits finally catch up with her, Elsa has enough favor with the Tattler sisters to buy herself a head start, escaping the troupe before they can kill her.

A View from the Inside: The Toxic Triangle in Cult

Cult offers a compelling look into the toxic triangle at work throughout the full lifecycle—existence, survival, success, renewal, and decline—of a community at the hands of its dynamic and volatile leader, Kai Anderson (Lester et al. 342). A compendious look into the seventh season's depiction of cult behavior illustrates *AHS'* desire to continue riding the line between absurdity and terror, this time, by leveraging the political fears and curiosities of its viewers through characters who experience crippling phobias, violence, and terrorism (Chaney). In both *Coven* and *Freak Show*, the communities have formed themselves prior to the audience's arrival, so viewers piece together segments of their histories throughout the season. *Cult*, however, offers an insider view into a community from its formation that comprises individuals who do not share explicit points of connection (like freaks or witches). Nonetheless, they fall in unison, recruited systematically and strategically by Kai Anderson. Kai's appeal to the Brookfield Heights, Michigan City Council sets the tone for the season:

> [People] want to be scared. They yearned to be so scared that they don't have to think anymore, that they don't have to want for anything anymore. Fear will release them from their desires and their ambitions and their bullshit needs. And then they will come running to us like children in a feverish nightmare, and the chosen few who are not afraid of the seas and the heights and the beasts of the world will return at the head of the evolutionary table to shepherd the weak into the chosen promise land of truth and freedom [7:1].

Empowered by Donald Trump's recent election as President, Kai moves to capitalize on the collective fear among citizens while perpetuating his own motivation for personal political power through an overthrow of the current system. His plan is to harness enough followers willing to commit violence (specifically against the pregnant women and their unborn) in order to provoke others (namely women) to rise up and overthrow the nation's current political leaders. After the "Night of 100 Tates," Kai and his followers plan to use the subsequent chaos to "[surf] an electoral bloodbath straight to Capitol Hill" (7:11). The season, then, is the journey toward, and eventual thwarting of, that plan at the hands of the scorned follower-turned-defector, Ally Mayfair-Richards.

The cult—like the coven and troupe—functions as an organization ideal for a destructive leader like Kai Anderson. During its initial formation, the group operates more akin to a community, where each member shares interests, goals, and decision making. Although we do not see the faces behind the masked clown killers at first, viewers eventually learn their identities: Kai, his sister Winter, his brother Dr. Rudy Vincent, Detective

Jack Samuels, Beverly Hope, Harrison and Meadow Wilton, Gary Longstreet, and Ivy Mayfair-Richards. Together, they form an elite inner circle, working together as vested co-leaders (or so they each believe) in the larger movement. While recruiting, Kai offers to share major decision making with others in the inner circle, like television reporter Beverly Hope. Kai recruits Beverly when he plays into her rage about her mistreatment at work (7:4). Despite his repeated promises of "equal power," Beverly initially rebuffs Kai: "I don't believe in you or anyone, not even myself" (7:4). Kai has to prove himself, and he does by coordinating the brutal murder of her rival, Serena Belinda. However, Kai's quest for personal political domination grows; he evolves (ideologically and physically) from narcissist to messiah, gathering a second group of followers when he begins sensing "resistance" and "dissention in the ranks" of his inner circle (7:5). Viewers watch the community transform into a cult, and a hierarchy between the inner circle and the followership emerges. Initially, the two groups work together, but as their common goals start to fracture, suspicion, disruption, and then violence ensue.

Communal living space, increased authoritarianism, and decreased shared governance perpetuate Kai's movement of the group from community to cult. As the cult grows in strength and in commitment to the cause, members begin living with Kai—an arrangement that satisfies the group's need for cohesion and Kai's desire to watch his flock. Taking lessons from other cult leaders, Kai tests member loyalty in both his inner circle and his followership. Absurd pinky-swear honesty sessions progress into demonstrations of fealty. In "Holes," Kai convinces the inner circle to murder one of their own, RJ, whom Kai decides "should have never been a part of this" (7:5). Convinced RJ will turn on them, they commit murder by nail gun to protect themselves against the threat of exposure. In the meantime, Kai has ensured that each member knows the price for betrayal. Later, viewers witness the very moment at which the group becomes a cult through the experiences of Kai's followers. In a scene that mimics story time for sadists, Kai explains, "Real power is having people loyal enough to you that if you ask them to, they will kill themselves. They will override their natural survival instinct in service of your needs and will." When a member questions if the group is a "cult" or a "political movement," Kai tells him, "All politics is a personality cult now" (7:9). Story time ends as members pledge their devotion, solidifying the high power distance between Divine Ruler and his new family. "The cult group itself is often inserted as a member's new and by implication, 'Superior family,'" and in Kai's family, members with questionable loyalty or who fail to uphold group expectations are punished in increasingly violent ways (Olsson 41).

Like the coven and troupe, the cult faces internal and external threats.

Some of these threats are real while others are suggested by Kai's design, spreading fear and reaffirming member loyalty. When Meadow Wilton outs the cult's existence and Ivy's involvement to Ally, she is promptly disposed of. Fear of an internal conspiracy to destroy the cult plagues Kai to the point of madness. When a member, like Speed Wagon in "Great Again," for example, goes missing, Kai is apoplectic and fearful: "My sister probably turned him into the feds, the goddamn rat!" Ally uses Kai's fear of exposure against him, concocting a story that Speed Wagon was compromised and sent to infiltrate the cult to avoid prison time and that she murdered the traitor to protect him (7:11). Kai's instincts about this particular internal threat are not wholly without merit, but he leaves himself susceptible to the manipulation of the season's primary follower of interest, Ally Mayfield-Richards.

Ally is an entertaining character to watch, because her journey from a paralyzed polyphobic to a manipulative, vengeful whistleblower is fascinating. One could argue that Ally is never genuinely a cult follower in the traditional susceptible follower typology (*lost soul, bystander, authoritarian, opportunist,* or *acolyte*), because she does not join the cult with a genuine intention for serving its leadership. Rather, her primary goal is to reclaim her son and take down Kai and her wife in the process. What makes Ally so captivating is that, at one point or another, she exhibits or feigns the traits of nearly all the susceptible follower types. When Kai tries to win Ally's support for his run for City Council, she is so shaken because of the constant plague from her phobias she could easily be the *lost soul* who needs direction, community, and self-worth (Thoroughgood et al. 903). When Kai provokes her for preaching rhetoric that supports diversity, peace, and bridge-building when she lives in a house with "bars on the windows," Ally is visibly disturbed (7:2). Ally credits her non-voluntary committal into the psychiatric hospital for catalyzing her transformation, a stay during which she confesses she "fills the hole" left by her fears with revenge against Ivy (7:9). From a woman who respects diversity and human life to someone capable of murdering her own wife, Ally assumes the "dark personality" of the *opportunist,* someone with the capability "to display cunning, manipulation, deception, and forceful persuasion to gain personal power and control" (Thoroughgood et al. 909). By joining Kai and the cult, Ally can grow close enough to her wife to carry out her own deadly agenda. Capable of incredible manipulation, Ally transforms herself into whatever follower type she needs to be to retain her cover in the cult while accomplishing her own goals. For example, she simulates traits of both the *bystander* and *acolyte* rolls upon entering the cult in an effort to persuade Kai of her loyalty; she falsifies her son's donor records to convince Kai of the illusion that he is the boy's father and, thus, the three of them are divinely connected (7:9). Later, she supports his story about the reason for Ivy's disappearance, reaffirms his delusions of a federal investigation, and assassinates Bebe Babbitt without even knowing who she is (7:10). By these actions—and by Kai's hallucinatory Charles Manson who confirms, "That one definitely ain't no mole"—Ally safeguards Kai's trust in her (7:10). When Beverly grows so dissatisfied with the cult's new hierarchical structure—one that renders her powerless and leaves her chopping salad for Kai's followers—Ally discourages her from seeing death as the answer. When Ally tells Beverly, "We did what we had to do, and we still are," her message suggests blind support of Kai's leadership and the forthcoming "Night of 100 Tates" (7:11). Instead, we learn that what Ally "had to do" was turn federal informant and destroy the group she's infiltrated. A socioemotional chameleon, Ally's character exemplifies the susceptible followers, in both the colluder and conformer dimensions, providing us with a blueprint of human psychological responses to fear, uncertainty, and rage.

Complexity and Uncertainty in Fiction and Reality

Rather than hiding their monstrous qualities, Fiona, Elsa, and Kai put them on display for all to see and admonish. The more difficult task for us, then, is to consider how they might also be acting constructively even during some of their more insidious moments. Although we may typecast them early in their respective seasons as leaders driven entirely by their own desires, they make decisions during their tenures that complicate these stereotypes. Fiona struggles with trying to protect her coven while preserving her own position. Elsa wrestles with keeping her monsters safe from harm while pursuing her own dreams of stardom. Kai grapples with effecting political change while achieving his own desire for validation and self-worth. Their inner conflicts are genuine and often painful to witness. While Badaracco insists most fictionalized leaders are "one-dimensional people, dominated or ruined by the pursuit of wealth and power," Fiona, Elsa, and Kai offer viewers greater depth of character (5).

People are just as captivated by stories of failure, corruption, and a profound darkness of heart and mind as they are stories of success and heroism. We are captivated by the abnormal, and "without the American cultural obsession with the dark and depraved, *AHS* would not work" (Earle and Clark 7). *AHS* exploits our fascination with the grotesque, offering narratives drawn from the deep wells of Gothic fiction and a sordid American history and hoisted into air filled with anxieties and fears about an uncertain future amid current political, financial, and social unrest. We may have rid our society of Madame Delphine LaLaurie and Charles Manson, but we remain concerned about those who will be victimized by the next serial killer or cult leader. What is perhaps most frightening is the near certainty that the destructive leaders hiding truths, extorting politicians, pocketing millions, and destroying the lives of others today will live and die in the darkness, untouched and untouchable.

Works Cited

Auvinen, Tommi P., et al. "Leadership Manipulation and Ethics in Storytelling." *Journal of Business Ethics*, vol. 116, no. 2, Aug. 2013, pp. 415–31.
Badaracco, Joseph L. *Questions of Character: Illuminating the Heart of Leadership Through Literature.* Harvard Business School Press, 2006.
Chaney, Jen. "*American Horror Story: Cult* Is a Fascinating Take on Our Political Moment." *Vulture*, 1 Sep. 2017, www.vulture.com/2017/09/american-horror-story-cult-review.html.
Christian, Tiffany A. "Using the Past to Recuperate the Present: The Authentic Evil of Madame Delphine Lalaurie in *American Horror Story: Coven*." *The Journal of Popular Culture*, vol. 52, no. 5, 2019, pp. 1101–19.
Clements, Christine, and John Washbush. "The Two Faces of Leadership: Considering the Dark Side of Leader-follower Dynamics." *Journal of Workplace Learning*, vol. 11, no. 5, 1999, pp. 170–75.
Conroy, Samantha, et al. "Where There Is Light, There Is Dark: A Review of the Detrimental Outcomes of High Organizational Identification." *Journal of Organizational Behavior*, vol. 38, 2017, pp. 184–203.
Costa, Stevi. "*American Horror Story*: Capital, Counterculture, and the Freak." *European Journal of American Culture*, vol. 38, no. 1, 2019, pp. 71–82.
Earle, Harriet E.H. "'A Convenient Place for Inconvenient People': Madness, Sex and the Asylum in *American Horror Story*." *The Journal of Popular Culture*, vol. 50, no. 2, 2017, pp. 259–75.
Earle, Harriet, and Jessica Clark. "Telling National Stories in *American Horror Story*." Introduction. *European Journal of American Culture*, vol. 38, no. 1, 2019, pp. 5–13.
Geller, Theresa L., and Anna Marie Banker. "'That Magic Box Lies': Queer Theory, Seriality, and *American Horror Story*." *The Velvet Light Trap*, no. 79, Spring 2017, pp. 36–49.
Grande, Laura. "Strange and Bizarre: The History of Freak Shows." *History Magazine*, vol. 12, no. 1, Oct. 2010, pp. 19–23.
Hofstede, Geert, and Gert Jan Hofstede. *Cultures and Organizations: Software of the Mind.* 2nd ed., McGraw-Hill, 2005.
Hogan, Robert, and Joyce Hogan. "Assessing Leadership: A View from the Dark Side." *International Journal of Selection and Assessment*, vol. 9, no. 1–2, Mar. 2001, pp. 40–51.
Howell, Jane M., and Bruce J. Avolio. "The Ethics of Charismatic Leadership: Submission or Liberation?" *The Executive*, vol. 6, no. 2, May 1992, pp. 43–54.
Hunter, Samuel T., et al. "The Typical Leadership Study: Assumptions, Implications, and Potential Remedies" *The Leadership Quarterly*, vol. 18, no. 5, Oct. 2007, pp. 435–46.
Keetley, Dawn. "Stillborn: The Entropic Gothic of *American Horror Story*." *Gothic Studies*, vol. 15, no. 2, Nov. 2013, pp. 89–107.
King, Amy K. "A Monstrous(ly-Feminine) Whiteness: Gender, Genre, and the Abject Horror of the Past in *American Horror Story: Coven*." *Women's Studies*, vol. 46, no 6, 2017, pp. 557–73.
LeBlanc, Amanda Kay. "'There's Nothing I Hate More Than a Racist': (Re)centering Whiteness in *American Horror Story: Coven*." *Critical Studies in Media Communication*, vol. 35, no. 3, 2018, pp. 273–285.
Lester, Donald L., et al. "Organizational Life Cycle: A Five-Stage Empirical Scale." *The International Journal of Organizational Analysis*, vol. 11, no. 4, 2003, pp. 339–54.
Lopes, Elisabete. "The Season of the Witch: Gender Trouble in *American Horror Story-Coven*."

Re-visiting Female Evil: Power, Purity and Desire. At the Interface / Probing the Boundaries, vol. 90, 2017, pp. 116–139.

O'Reilly, Charles A., and Jennifer A. Chatman. "Culture as Social Control: Corporations, Cults, and Commitment." *Research in Organizational Behavior*, vol. 18, 1996, pp. 157–200.

O'Reilly, Jennifer. "'We're more than just pins and dolls and seeing the future in chicken parts': Race, Magic and Religion in *American Horror Story: Coven*." *European Journal of American Culture*, vol. 38, no. 1, 2019, pp. 29–41.

Olsson, Peter Alan. "'Normal' Compared to Abnormal Leaders and Groups." *Journal of Psychohistory*, vol. 41, no. 1, Summer 2013, pp. 39–43.

Padilla, Art, et al. "The Toxic Triangle: Destructive Leaders, Susceptible Followers, and Conducive Environments." *The Leadership Quarterly*, vol. 18, no. 3, June 2007, pp. 176–94.

Sakal-Froese, Jocelyn, and Christina Fawcett. "White Coat, White Alb, White Mic: Institutions of Truth in America in *American Horror Story: Asylum*." *European Journal of American Culture*, vol. 38, no. 1, 2019, pp. 43–55.

Thoroughgood, Christian N., et al. "Bad Apples, Bad Barrels, and Broken Followers? An Empirical Examination of Contextual Influences on Follower Perceptions and Reactions to Aversive Leadership." *Journal of Business Ethics*, vol. 100, no.4, June 2011, pp. 647–72.

Thoroughgood, Christian N., Art Padilla, et al. "The Susceptible Circle: A Taxonomy of Followers Associated with Destructive Leadership." *The Leadership Quarterly*, vol. 23, no. 5, Oct. 2012, pp. 897–917.

The Lesbian Gothic in *Asylum* and *Hotel*

Tosha R. Taylor

American Horror Story boasts a complicated relationship with sexual aberration. The first episode of its first season prominently depicted a woman's rape by a ghost in a rubber BDSM suit, and this instance now seems rather tame when compared to subsequent depictions of sex-based deviance as the series has continued. It is, of course, natural that a television show preoccupied with sexuality and otherness would address and even focus upon queerness. Yet as a "horror story," it cannot be expected to normalize queer identities even as they are increasingly recognized and even accepted by mainstream American society. The queerness of men (or those whose biology causes them to initially be perceived as men) is a prominent theme in the series' exploration of the grotesque, and its tendency to depict gay and bisexual men being violently harmed or even killed by anal penetration has received criticism. Queer women, however, have been given prominence in two seasons at the time of this writing: its second season, entitled *Asylum*, and its fifth, *Hotel*. In these seasons, nonheterosexual women emerge not only as lead characters but also as embodiments of Gothic lesbian histories. Their sexualities, far from being incidental, tie them inextricably to the Gothic and position them at the center of these seasons' establishment of horror.

In *Asylum*, lesbian journalist Lana Winters enters the sanitarium Briarcliff Manor in 1964 intending to write an exposé on the treatment of its patients (with an initial focus on the serial killer known as Bloody Face) but is soon committed there as a deviant for her sexual orientation. She is subjected to a number of horrors historically faced by lesbians in mental institutions, then abducted by her psychiatrist, Oliver Thredson, who reveals himself to be the actual Bloody Face. In captivity, Lana is sexually abused and impregnated by Thredson as he imposes his own Oedipal desire for

189

the mother who abandoned him. After she escapes, she is briefly returned to Briarcliff, where she endures a failed abortion attempt, before being released, at which point she kills Thredson and resumes her career as journalist, eventually writing a bestselling memoir of her experience. As the season ends, present-day Lana, now a celebrity who seems an amalgamation of the Maysles brothers, Geraldo Rivera, and Barbara Walters, learns that her son by Thredson has taken up his father's mantle and must kill him in a final confrontation. Rather than depicting a queer woman forced into a Gothic narrative, *Hotel* posits her as a supernatural Gothic entity herself. The Countess, whose name is given as Elizabeth in a conspicuous reference to Erzsébet—popularly anglicized as Elizabeth—Báthory (as will be discussed in detail later in this essay), rules the Hotel Cortez with literal bejeweled glove instead of the figurative iron fist. An undefined disorder requires the Countess to drink blood for sustenance and imbues her with seeming immortality. Over the course of the twentieth and twenty-first centuries, she entertains a series of high-profile lovers of both sexes and kidnaps children to make them her own. As the season draws to a close, several of her wronged lovers unite in a plot to at long last kill her; their success, however, traps her within the hotel as a ghost. In both instances, queerness is an essential facet of these characters' experiences and their construction within a Gothic narrative.

The significance of the queer woman—and of her queerness itself—is clear in both seasons. Lana's imprisonment speaks to the pathologization and criminalization of homosexuality in modern history. By establishing her as distinctly lesbian, *Asylum* places abuses perpetrated against queer women in institutions alongside acts of murder, rape, necrophilia, Nazi human experimentation, and even alien abductions as horror phenomena. The Countess is primarily depicted engaging sexually with men, but her queerness aligns her with the Gothic traditions of haunting, vampirism, betrayal, and repression that characterize the hotel and in this way suggests that she (rather than the hotel's psychopathic architect) is the hotel's embodiment, a treacherous site made flesh in a treacherous woman. As with Lana, furthermore, her sexual inclinations have roots in discourses of queerness that have historically been deployed to malign and subjugate sexual Others.

This essay will explore the relationship of the queer woman to the Gothic and more specifically the lesbian Gothic as it manifests through *Asylum* and *Hotel*. The use of "lesbian" in this essay will not always correspond to the word's common usage, which typically indicates a woman who, at the point of application, exclusively experiences romantic or sexual attraction to other women and/or who, furthermore and in the twenty-first-century context, adopts the label as a designation of her own sexual identity.[1] Rather, it will at times be applied in a more adjectival sense to refer to sexual relationships between queer women, and will also partly invoke Adrienne Rich's *lesbian continuum* "of woman-identified experience" that includes "forms of primary intensity between and among women" that are as intimate as they are subversive of compulsory heterosexuality (135). The relationship between the Countess and Ramona Royale, for instance, will be referred to as a lesbian one even though the women themselves are not exclusively lesbian-identified. By examining both Lana Winters and the Countess through the lens of the lesbian Gothic, this essay elucidates the ways in which *AHS* both challenges and upholds historical discourses of queer women's sexuality.

Lesbian Gothic

The Gothic and queerness are intrinsically linked. For such reasons, Mair Rigby argues that queer studies itself owes "a debt to the Gothic" (54).[2] If, as Harry Benshoff writes, "queerness disrupts narrative equilibrium and sets in motion a questioning of the status quo, and […] the nature of reality itself," the Gothic presents a ready home for its literary and cinematic exploration (5). Uncanny doubling and repression, both prominent features of the Gothic, are easily translated into a queer context, where, in addition to their literal Gothic manifestations, they find echoes in queer experience. Paulina Palmer, who has written extensively of the Gothic's lesbian potential, emphasizes such a link: "Repressed desires and anxieties are, of course, of central importance to the lesbian subject who, lacking a history and a language to articulate her sexual orientation, may feel haunted by emotions which she cannot or dare not articulate" (119). The early unspeakability of women's same-sex desire, according to Palmer, "carries connotations of the abject" and eventually, through a paradoxical cultural anxiety over that which is repressed to the point of near-invisibility, "returns us to the topic of the Gothic" (120). Describing the Gothic as a "twilight realm of unconscious fantasies and forbidden desires," Sarah Parker similarly credits its ability to give space and voice to lesbian experience (4). The grotesque imagery and relations frequently found in the Gothic enable embodied manifestations of the unspeakable and the forbidden. The risk of spiritual and bodily destruction, or even death, in the Gothic text mirrors the danger of queer discovery. Reproduction is deemed impossible yet occurs nonetheless via doubling or transmission if not literal procreative childbirth. Like the Gothic creatures found in the ghost and the vampire, queer sex exists as "an unlive practice that was consequently unnatural, or queer, and, as that which was unlive, without the right to life"

(Case 4).[3] The lesbian Gothic, then, locates that which *should not be* within that which *is*: flesh-and-blood women or apparitions of such who subvert the roles that would otherwise be assigned to them. Their desire, even if it destroys them as is typical in both the Gothic genre and the non–Gothic texts that address queerness, overturns heteronormative prescriptions in favor of the forbidden and the repressed.

Terry Castle describes the lesbian in terms evocative of a Gothic apparition, for she "is never with us, it seems, but always somewhere else: in the shadows, in the margins, hidden from history, out of sight, out of mind, a wanderer in the dark, a lost soul, a tragic mistake, a pale denizen of the night" (2). A tradition of lesbian erasure makes her into a historical ghost even apart from her Gothic manifestations; she exists only on the periphery, often unrecognized as real or condemned as an abomination when acknowledged. Until quite recently, her romantic and/or sexual partnerships have not been deemed valid, so she has not been a wife or properly a lover (and she is certainly not a mother). Her navigations of experiences that are better acknowledged when concerning heterosexual women (such as violence and bodily autonomy) are rendered lesser or invisible. Rhetoric arguing that queer women are simply "confused," in need of a specific man to extinguish their same-sex desires, or that they have only turned to same-sex love after suffering abuse continue to proliferate in the twenty-first century, thus maintaining the sense that a truly queer woman, save for in rare occasions, is something of a shadow, the unliving, unproductive, and unreproductive being of which Sue-Ellen Case and, respectively, Benshoff write. It is here that the lesbian Gothic readily intersects with the discourses and practices of that entity that has variously been termed the sanitarium, the insane asylum, and the mental institution, the setting of *Asylum* and the structure which physically entraps Lana Winters within the Gothic architectural landscape.

Asylum

In her study of the lesbian Gothic, Parker suggests that we should not rely upon the common tropes in identifying the Gothic but instead look for a "fluid 'organizing principle'" that is expressed through patriarchal relations and physical space (7). Using this approach, we may posit *Asylum* as the most traditionally Gothic installment of the series up to this point and further recognize its place within the lesbian Gothic. *AHS* has thus far typically paid little attention to the paternal relationship or patriarchal governance, yet *Asylum* boasts a rigid patriarchal rule that distinguishes it from other seasons.[4] With its heavy focus upon female sexuality, historical gender inequality, and pregnancy, *Asylum* may at first (mis)lead the viewer into interpreting the asylum itself as a rare site in which women hold ultimate power. Superficially, Sister Jude appears the true authority in Briarcliff. It is she who meets with the press regarding the asylum, she who oversees day-to-day affairs, and she administers punishments to the inmates, often via caning but, in the cases of Kit Walker and Grace Bertrand, ordering sterilization and thus implying a complete control over her wards' bodies. Although her sex and station leave her beholden to Dr. Arden and Monsignor Timothy Howard, she voices conviction in her own power when she tells Arden, "I'll always win against the patriarchal male" (2:1). Jude is assisted by a younger woman, Sister Mary Eunice, who is equally pious but restrained by her own timidity. Kit Walker remains the only prominently featured male patient throughout the season, save for two featured but limited appearances in *Asylum* by Ian McShane as a Santa-themed serial killer. The other featured patients—Grace, Shelley, Pepper, "the Mexican"—are female. Even Shachath, the Angel of Death who acts as counselor to many characters, appears as a woman in a black dress and veil. The illusion of gynarchy, however, is quickly put to rout in the season's first half. Jude's authority is steadily compromised by the same male colleagues against whom she expected to "win," resulting in accusations that she has "lost [her] credibility at Briarcliff" and ultimately her own involuntary commitment to the asylum (2:8). The Mary Eunice who comes to rule the asylum when Jude is deposed is not truly Mary Eunice herself but rather a demon who possesses the young nun in the second episode, "Tricks and Treats," after leaving the body of its male victim. While Shachath uses the feminine pronoun to refer to the demon, its first appearance suggests a masculine alignment. When the demon speaks through Mary Eunice, it uses her own, unaltered voice as if to invite the question of whether or not this is simply mental illness manifesting in Mary Eunice herself, but when speaking through the young man, the demon uses a deep, distorted male voice not necessarily belonging to its host. Briarcliff's existence as a truly Gothic space is thus guaranteed by the revelation of a shadowy patriarchy in which the lesbian Gothic must unfold.

Lana enters Briarcliff two years after the Roman Catholic Church has purchased it to house and rehabilitate the criminally insane. As the physical intersection of religious dogma and psychiatry, Briarcliff embodies the typical Foucauldian mental institution in which it is believed that "[t]here are aspects of evil that have such a power of contagion, such a force of scandal that any publicity multiplies them infinitely. Only oblivion can suppress them" (*Madness and Civilization* 67). The residents of Briarcliff, who double as prison inmates and mental patients, have been deemed criminally insane for acts that violate both religious and secular law. Their containment in the asylum, though nominally for curative purposes, is clearly designed not only to prevent further criminal actions (an imperative at which Briarcliff fails spectacularly) but to curb the spread of spiritual, physiological, and mental flaws that, the keepers of the madhouse believe, may otherwise be transmitted. Thus, Briarcliff resembles the rebuilt Salpetriere where, Michel Foucault writes, "evil could vegetate [...] where it would have all the powers of example and none of the risks of contagion" (207). The inmates' criminal actions and conditions (homicide, nymphomania, homosexuality) continue but are directed only against other inmates and their caretakers.

Historically, the asylum has readily lent itself to the imprisonment of those who experience or enact queer desire. Foucault identifies "the brothel and the mental institution" as the two sites to which "illegitimate sexualities" could be confined in the modern age (*History of Sexuality* 4). The pathologization of sexuality in the nineteenth century allowed "sexual irregularity" (which included adultery, rape, homosexuality, and bestiality) to be "annexed to mental illness" and thus brought under the power of the nascent field of psychiatry (36). Ultimately, the establishment of a pathological queerness led to what Foucault calls the "psychiatrization of perverse pleasure" in which sexuality could be rendered distinct from identity and thus made subject to "corrective technology" via treatments devised by medical professionals who viewed queer inclinations as psychological "anomalies" (105). John D'Emilio and Estelle B. Freedman date the 1880s as the point at which American physicians became especially concerned with what they termed "contrary sexual impulse[s]" (226). Among them, homosexuality was often characterized as a "degenerative disease, an acquired form of insanity" (226). Further acquisition could be prevented and treated through total confinement within an institution, whose administrators and physicians were given authority to exercise complete power over their patients.

Most studies of queerness within the mental institution focus on men's sexuality. As the early discourses of homosexuality largely concerned biologically defined men, so, too, did many of the laws that criminalized same-sex attraction and behavior; women's homosexuality has often undergone systematic erasure and invalidation. Indeed, Castle warns that the "singularity of [lesbian] experience [...] tends to become obscured" by studies that presume queer women have undergone identical treatments as queer men (12). However, while documentation of lesbian experiences within the mental institution is comparatively lacking, existing records do not indicate that lesbians and other same-sex attracted women avoided the same pathologization and subsequent medical treatment that have been more thoroughly documented as pertaining to their male counterparts. Institutionalized lesbians were often subjected to similar treatments as those women committed for nymphomania (Ussher 395). Tamsin Wilton identifies invasive surgery, female circumcision, lobotomy, and even "therapeutic rape" as historical treatments for lesbian attraction in the institution system (79). D'Emilio further lists electroshock and aversion therapy as common treatments (both of which are depicted in *Asylum*), as well as experimental drug usage (18). For such practices, Ronald Bayer draws a comparison between the institutional church's abuses of those deemed to be witches and early psychiatry's treatment of queer patients; both, he argues, caused extensive harm to their subject in the guise of "saving" them (59). The diagnoses of secular psychiatry intersect with religious dogma to condemn, subjugate, and even torment those afflicted with queerness.

Such a confluence is readily visible in *Asylum* as members of the clergy and a representative of modern psychiatry compete to successfully rid patients of real or perceived ailments. Jude signals this conflict to Lana in their first meeting when she shares her belief that "mental illness is the fashionable explanation for sin" (2:1). Monsignor Timothy Howard, Father Malachi, and Sister Jude participate in an exorcism of the possessed youth; meanwhile, Oliver Thredson disavows this treatment. He alone in Briarcliff's staff appears to be a voice of reason, opposing the religion-based treatments proffered by Sister Jude and the Monsignor in favor of newer, more progressive solutions. He is further aligned with notions of progress when he criticizes Jude's prescription of electroshock therapy for Lana, calling it "barbaric" and identifying behavior modification as the approved method of curing her homosexual inclinations. In both cases, however, the outcome is only trauma. Indeed, while Lana's resistance against the attendants who restrain her for the electroshock treatment visually resembles that of a rape victim, Thredson's prescribed treatment invokes more literal sexual abuse and heralds her eventual rape. In a scene that conspicuously invokes the Kristevan abject with its associations with nausea and vomiting (Kristeva 3), Lana must not only view photographs of female models as an emetic is administered to her, she must also look at a candid photograph of her lover Wendy, who is topless but covered in a bedsheet and smoking a cigarette in a common postcoital image (2:4). When Lana requests a break from the emetic treatment, Thredson begins a *con*version therapy session by presenting Lana with a nude male patient who has allegedly voiced attraction to Lana and has thus agreed to "participate in anything that might liberate" her. Lana is first directed to study the male patient's body then to touch his penis, all the while masturbating as Thredson observes. It is only when Lana's weeping gives way to vomiting that Thredson ends the session. His apparent sympathy, however, is soon revealed as false when he orchestrates an escape for her, only to then take her captive in his home (2:5).

In the context of his painful, abject aversion therapy sessions with her, Thredson's rape of Lana may also be read as an attempt at corrective rape despite, or in addition to, its basis in his Oedipal desires. As a lesbian living in a committed relationship prior to her commitment to Briarcliff, Lana has rejected heterosexual relations outright. She has already voiced this rejection to Thredson during their first private conversation, telling him "I have been this way since ... since I can remember. There is no cure" (2:4). Her inability to feel attraction to the male patient emphasizes the innateness of her homosexuality. Thredson believes he is raping her to satisfy his longing for a mother. Indeed, his (and later, his son's) fear of disempowerment and fixation on breastfeeding recalls Kristeva's "gradation within modalities of separation: a real *deprivation* of the breast, an imaginary *frustration* of the gift as maternal relation, and, to conclude, a symbolic *castration* inscribed in the Oedipus complex" (32–3). Thredson's anger is explicitly directed at the mother who placed him into the foster system at birth, but, when viewed within the context of the lesbian Gothic and lesbian history, it finds an implicit target in Lana's failure to engage in heterosexuality. As a Gothic lesbian, Lana remains on the periphery, in the shadows; she cannot join the heteronormative center, nor can she be elucidated in such a way that her captors (both the administration of Briarcliff and Thredson-as-Bloody-Face) may understand her nature and reconcile it with their own. She remains to Thredson an abomination apart from anxieties of the maternal.

Moreover, Lana's abuse at Thredson's hands functions as an obliteration of the self, a common (and commonly criticized) theme both in the Gothic and in texts depicting lesbians. Torture, according to Lynne S. Arnault, extends beyond the products of physical violence to see "the victim undergoing the destruction (or near destruction) of meaning, the loss of dignity and agency, and the fragmentation and disintegration of subjectivity" (160). This destruction mirrors the birth of the Kristevan abject we see during the aversion therapy scene: "I give birth to myself my condition as a living being. My body extricates itself, as being alive, from that border" (3).[5] In being relocated physically and spiritually into Thredson's Oedipal fantasy, Lana is temporarily at loss of self. She is no longer Wendy's lover; she is Thredson's rape and torture victim. She is no longer a reporter; she is a slave. She no longer wields any control over her own body; instead, it is subject to her captor's abusive whims. She is forced into the role of the mother, first symbolically as depicted onscreen, then literally when she and the spectator learn that she has been impregnated. Placed against her will into heterosexual coupling and the role of mother (a role which, Lana herself reports later, she believed prohibited to lesbians at the time), Lana experiences the Gothic in a way that simultaneously denies and underscores her queerness.

Gothic repression and disruption continue after Lana escapes Thredson's home and, after a car accident, is returned to Briarcliff; now, however, Lana navigates her confinement as a more knowledgeable witness, granted clarity by her survival of all but the greatest abjection.[6] Here, Lana finds the old power structures upended. Sister Jude's investigation into Dr. Arden's Nazi past has brought her under clerical and demonic scrutiny, and as the possessed Mary Eunice seizes power, Jude is committed as a patient and forced to undergo traumatic electroshock therapy. Grace's death is literally undone by the extraterrestrial beings that have haunted Kit Walker and within mere days, her newly conceived child grows to full term. Dr. Arden's authority is compromised by his continued desire for the real Mary Eunice, which the demon possessing her uses to torment him. Monsignor Timothy Howard, too, is compromised when the demon rapes him. At no point, however, do these Gothic undoings truly ally Lana's previous tormentors with her; she remains a peripheral figure. Jude's newfound sympathies for Lana do not extend to acceptance of her sexuality. Now made equals in their confinement, Lana and Jude are still not fully reconciled. In one of her final moments of lucidity, Jude petitions Mother Claudia to arrange Lana's escape from Briarcliff, but never does she voice any absolution of Lana for perceived wrongdoing. Rather, Jude accepts responsibility for Lana's commitment ("She doesn't belong here. I put her here.") without naming its cause (2:10). Lana's second tenure at Briarcliff sees queerness acknowledged only by those who are closely aligned with the abject (a demon and a Nazi) and who torment the asylum's patients (Kristeva 4, 107). True to Gothic form, queerness remains unspeakable as anything other than disorder or abomination.

Lana eventually triumphs over the asylum, beginning with an escape facilitated by Mother Claudia and then, soon afterward, killing Thredson. With Wendy dead at Thredson's hands, she is in less danger of unsympathetic public scrutiny and thus resumes her career as a journalist, eventually bringing about Briarcliff's end through a documentary exposé reminiscent of *Titticut Follies* and a memoir of her experience as a patient. The memoir that secures her fame, however, is *Maniac: One Woman's Story of Survival*, which details her captivity by Thredson, now publicly identified as Bloody Face. Yet even in her personal writing, Lana participates in the repression of queerness. Despite Thredson's use of Wendy's photos and her physical corpse in Lana's torture, Lana does not acknowledge the truth of their relationship as her fame initially develops. Wendy's role in Lana's life is de-romanticized and de-eroticized as Lana's memoirs convert her from lover to "roommate." Appearing as the hallucinated product of Lana's guilty conscience, Wendy herself accuses Lana of "cover[ing]" her "in a cloak of asexuality" (2:12). In this manner, the Lana who emerges from

Gothic captivity has subscribed—albeit temporarily—to the heteronormative patriarchal order that Gothic resists.

Lana does not, however, truly remove herself from embodying resistance. In its last but perhaps most significant Gothic upending, *Asylum*'s final scene suggests that, just as Lana has manipulated narratives of her life in order to create a more palatable persona, her depiction within the show itself has manipulated the viewer into accepting a similar narrative. Lana's transformation from innocent lesbian imprisoned and tortured for her sexuality to celebrity journalist challenges both the literary/cinematic tradition of lesbian destruction and the spectator's understanding of her as a contemporary Gothic heroine. In this way, *Asylum* subverts a number of expectations yet also invokes Gothic unknowability in a new context. In *Asylum*'s final two episodes, which are framed within a present-day interview with Lana, we are presented with the possibility that even our own knowledge of Lana has been illusory.

Through multiple instances, *Asylum* reminds the viewer of Lana's ambition in her pursuit of the Briarcliff story and at first, these instances do not challenge our expectations of her. Rather, they uphold a heteronormative narrative in which a woman's ambition takes her away from home and family and leads her to harm while simultaneously guiding us to interpret Lana as a career woman who, though ambitious, could not have known the true risks of her work. In their first and only scene together, Lana and Wendy discuss Lana's plan; at the scene's conclusion, Wendy asks Lana how she intends to gain access to the asylum. In response, Lana, in closeup, merely smiles (2:1). Her plan, like her sexuality, is unspeakable. Long afterward, as she gathers with friends in the mausoleum housing Wendy's remains, Lana blames her ambition for all that has befallen her (and Wendy) in language that evokes sympathy: "It was the story. I was going to do anything to get that story. I just didn't realize how much it was going to cost" (2:13). Yet here the viewer is invited to consider that Lana's navigation of these traumatic, abject experiences is even more self-serving than previously realized. When reporters who have learned of her sexual orientation inquire if she has indeed been "cured" of it, Lana responds, "All I can say is read my book," seemingly *before* the book has been published (2:11). Surprised by her interest in achieving Hollywood recognition over exposing the conditions at Briarcliff, Kit Walker accuses Lana of having become a "cheap celebrity" (2:11). His accusation earns more validity when we see Lana in the present day, surrounded by awards, artwork of herself, and an admiring film crew. However, heralding *Asylum*'s final disruptive scene, Lana admits to the interviewer that the popular image of her as a "crusader" is simply a carefully constructed "myth" that has hidden a more selfish ambition.

In *Asylum*'s final minutes, Lana is confronted by Thredson's son, whom she (like Thredson's mother), gave up at birth. Johnny Thredson arrives as his father's Gothic doppelganger, disguising himself amongst the film crew and lingering after they have gone with the intention of killing Lana. When Lana instead kills him, the narrative returns to the day she arrived at Briarcliff as a reporter in 1964 and her first encounter with Sister Jude. This disorienting return to the past creates further unease with the viewer's realization that what we now see is a conversation that was deliberately hidden in the first episode. Lana's meeting with Jude, previously appearing complete, in fact included one more exchange that *Asylum* has reserved for the final revelation (2:13). Warning Lana that her ambition is "dangerous," Jude continues, "I do hope you know what you're in for. The loneliness, the heartbreak, the sacrifice you'll face as a woman with a dream on her own." Lana counters, "You don't have any idea what I'm capable of." Had the episode, and thus *Asylum* itself, ended here, the viewer might continue to interpret this line as a retroactive sign of Lana's strength. Yet as the shot transitions to an extreme close-up of Jude's face, Jude admonishes, "Just remember, if you look in the face of evil, evil's gonna look right back at you." Following this line, a disorienting jump cut zooms in on Lana's face as she smiles. This moment visually hearkens back to Lana's first conversation with Wendy but now in another context. Here, Lana does not respond to a concerned lover but to the suggestion that she invites contact with a greater and unknowable evil. Indeed, although the shot is focused upon Jude as she says "face of evil," the campy cut-and-zoom to Lana's smile raises the possibility that, in light of her own emphasis on cutthroat ambition, it is she and not Jude whom the line frames. As the season's final shot locates the viewer above Briarcliff's foyer and "Dominique," the song used to torture its patients, begins once more to play, the episode presents a cycle in which the viewer is invited to reconsider all that transpired after this previously unspoken scene in the context of this exchange.

Through its final scene, *Asylum* disrupts a narrative identification that has thus far been particularly significant for a lesbian Gothic reading. *Asylum* has, up to this point, created a rare instance in which a potentially diverse audience's perspective is aligned with that of a lesbian. Noël Carroll writes of the implicit trust between the spectator and the protagonistic character, whose perspective "we (mistakenly) accept (or confusedly take) [...] to be our own" (90). He further argues that in the horror text especially, "the emotions of the audience are supposed to mirror those of the positive human characters [...] to parallel those of the characters [...] to converge (but not exactly duplicate) those of the characters" (18). The assumption of spectatorial identification with the main protagonist has garnered much debate in film criticism, especially from feminist approaches, and while we should be careful of such assumptions, there is little room for doubt that Lana's perspective, as that of the primary focalization, is offered up as a truthful one until she, and the narrative itself, challenges it. Lana presents such a conundrum for spectatorial identification that Kat Rosenfield of MTV describes her as "marvelously morally ambiguous [...] she's not a bad person, exactly, but she's too opportunistic and grasping to be among the innocents." While Rosenfield's description may perhaps be too charitable (*did* Lana place her lover into Thredson's trajectory? *Did* she willingly let Jude languish in confinement? *Did* she know far more about the risk she took by becoming confined to Briarcliff than both Jude and the viewer realized?), it points toward popular recognition of Lana's Gothic unknowability. If Lana has indeed manipulated her confinement and its consequences to an even more extreme degree, she may join the literary Gothic heroine who first appears "as blameless victim of a corrupt and oppressive society while utilising passive-aggressive and masochistic strategies to triumph over that system" (Smith and Wallace 2). Rather than the anticipated damsel, Lana emerges from *Asylum*'s finale as the architect of her own Gothic experience.

As a self-identified lesbian committed to a mental institution for her sexuality and there subjected to actual abuses historically perpetrated against queer women in asylums, Lana's embodiment of the lesbian Gothic is highly conspicuous. Moreover, she currently remains *AHS*' most visible queer woman (as her reappearance in the show's sixth season, *Roanoke*, reminds the viewer). More conspicuously Gothic but less conspicuously belonging to the *lesbian Gothic* is the Countess, one of the chief antagonists of *Hotel*. Yet she, like Lana, occupies a significant place on a queer Gothic continuum. The next section of this essay will locate the Countess, and *Hotel*'s narrative around her, within the lesbian Gothic.

HOTEL

For most of *Hotel*'s narrative, the Countess exists in stark contrast to Lana. Where Lana's lesbianism avoids a sexual realization onscreen, the Countess is hypersexual. She is frequently depicted in graphic sexual encounters. Even her most basic interactions carry an erotic charge. When not dressed in a patient's shift or a captive's nightgown, Lana dresses with modish practicality; the Countess, conversely, embodies a high fashion fantasy. While Lana is primarily contained within the asylum, the Countess comes and goes freely from the Hotel Cortez, which (like the eponymous Murder House) entraps the souls of those who die within its walls. Where Lana finds freedom from Briarcliff, the Countess is finally imprisoned in the hotel when she dies. Lana is exclusively lesbian, depicted in heterosexual sex only through rape, while the Countess engages in both heterosexual and lesbian sex, with the vast majority of her depicted encounters occurring with male partners.

Their greatest difference, however, lies in their relationship to the monster, a key figure in the Gothic and horror texts that has not yet been discussed here.[7] Even if we allow for a less virtuous interpretation of Lana in light of *Asylum*'s final scene, she cannot be said to be a monster, least of all in the supernatural sense that some Gothic and horror scholars deem necessary (Carroll 4). According to Carroll, the monster of the horror text must be supernatural, and while his argument is challenged by the prominence of human figures who function as figurative monsters in the genre, it is useful for locating the Countess along a lesbian Gothic continuum (57). The Countess, though also appearing human, transcends the natural human state. A rare, transmittable "blood disorder" transforms the Countess into a vampiric murderess who feasts on the blood of the living and who, when she chooses, creates similar creatures in victims she wants as her lovers. Beautiful and theoretically immortal, she is distinguished from the common image of vampire primarily through her method of killing; lacking the classical fangs, she instead penetrates her victims with the sharpened finger of a glove. Although it challenges the conventional image of the vampire, the glove does not humanize her; rather, when coupled with her portrayal by pop fashion icon Lady Gaga and in the context of the Hotel Cortez's ties to the fashion industry, it emphasizes her separation from humanity. Her reliance on the glove indicates a "transubstantiation of the fleshy, organic substance of the body [...] into the artificial, synthetic substance of the fashion garment" (de Perthuis 409). Her human physicality is, in fact, compromised by the addition of the weapon by which she draws the blood that sustains her. The monster is critically characterized in terms reminiscent of the queer woman. Edward Ingebretsen writes that

> Monsters have, or seem to have, freedoms we lack. They transgress, cross over, do not stay put where—for the convenience of our categories of sex, race, class or creed—we would like them to stay. Sometimes it is their painful beauty, or untrammelled individuality; other times it is simply the liberties they take (and *that* they take them in the first place) that so astonish us. They get away with murder and that fascinates us. Monsters are supposed to do just what they desire, and that frightens us [5].

As a beautiful woman who crosses the borders of natural/unnatural, life/death, and murder/creation, the Countess queers the typical categories of existence itself as the classical vampire does.

It is her connection to vampirism, rather than her same-sex affairs, that best locates the Countess within the lesbian Gothic and even queer horror. The horror genre has traditionally not allotted lesbians the same attention as queer monsters aligned with biological maleness; however, when she does appear, the queer woman of horror has often been linked to vampirism (Benshoff 7). Writing of this tradition (but focusing upon lesbian rather than bisexual women), Andrew Weiss argues that the queer woman "is a complex and ambiguous figure, at once an image of death and an object of desire, drawing on profound subconscious fears that the living have toward the dead and that men have toward women, while serving as a focus for repressed fantasies" (84). Tanya Krzywinska expands upon the queer woman/vampire link, noting that she poses a challenge to both notions of patriarchy and feminist readings due to her problematic invocation of the heterosexual male gaze in her eroticism and simultaneous subversion through her undeath (108–12). The Countess' title and even her given name further align her with the lesbian Gothic, for they serve as a conspicuous homage to the Erzsébet Báthory, the infamous seventeenth-century "Blood Countess," who has appeared in numerous twentieth- and twenty-first-century texts as a queer vampire. Literal or symbolic links between Báthory, lesbians, and vampirism occur, for instance in *The Hunger* (1983) and *Hostel: Part II* (2007). Like the lesbian who haunts the female Gothic, Báthory remains a longstanding specter in modern queer vampirism.

While the Countess engages in only one lesbian relationship that does not include a third, male figure, her name and nature prohibit her removal from the lesbian Gothic. Indeed, Hanson argues for the appropriateness of the term "bisexual" for even vampiric women who are initially figured as lesbian due to the traditional inevitability of male intrusion into women's same-sex relationships (184). These intrusions, Ellis Hanson notes, typically see the queer woman spurning her female lover in favor of the man (216). Such betrayal occurs in the Countess' decades-long relationship with former Blaxploitation actress Ramona Royale. After their first meeting in 1977 that is initially forged when the Countess subtly saves Royale from a predatory producer, the Countess and Royale engage in a passionate love affair (5:3). The affair ends, however, when Royale becomes disillusioned with the Countess' need for co-dependency and ultimately leaves her for a male lover. The Countess inverts the lesbian-turned-heterosexual trope in her seduction of gay fashion magnate Will Drake, who at first voices disgust with female genitalia but eventually succumbs to the Countess' administrations. Through her, queerness itself is queered.

Returning to Castle's characterization of the lesbian as "in the shadows, in the margins, […] out of sight, out of mind, a wanderer in the dark, a lost soul, a tragic mistake, a pale denizen of the night," we are able to recognize the bisexual Countess as a similar figure. Through a "tragic mistake," her early years as an Old Hollywood actress opposite Rudolph Valentino enable her transformation from unremarkable mortal to vampiric nobility (5:7). The Hotel Cortez serves as a potential feeding ground for her but also as a false haven for transients, who, dying there, become forever trapped within its walls. She, however, is permitted to wander through geographic space as she simultaneously seduces and feeds. Most significantly, Castle's description could aptly be applied to the Countess' position within the Hotel Cortez itself. Contact with her is not a daily occurrence for most of the hotel's ghostly occupants or its living guests; indeed, after the Countess' death, many years pass before she is seen again. Yet those who are aware of the hotel's true nature fear her, alternately working to appease her bloodlust by supplying victims or concealing themselves from her notice. A conspicuous lack of interaction between the Countess and the ghost known as Hypodermic Sally culminates in an encounter that is rife with lesbian potential when the Countess is grievously injured in an attempted murder and Sally appears to nurse her (5:11). This period of recovery facilitates a flashback that reveals Sally in a past bisexual love triangle (similar to the Countess' own triangle with Valentino and Natacha Rambova); the viewer soon sees that she has placed the Countess' body in the same spot where she and her lovers engaged sexually. While Sally does not similarly engage the Countess, her ministrations invite an erotic reading. The act of penetrative lesbian sex itself, which has gone unseen and unacknowledged even in the Countess' trysts, is here suggested by images of Sally using her fingers to remove bullets from the Countess' wounds. Here, sex itself becomes a peripheral entity, lingering at the edges of the scene but never being realized in a way that resists heteronormative prescription.

Conclusion

From its first episode, *AHS* has been predicated upon Gothic depictions of deviance and aberration. Its consistent main title invites us to consider these phenomena not simply as general Gothic entities and events but as aberrations within a cultural context. Therefore, as stated earlier in this essay, it is inevitable that the series has taken queerness as a prominent subject. Its engagement with the lesbian Gothic in *Asylum* and *Hotel* has particular resonance for queer scholarship and its intersection with horror scholarship, as both have often focused on depictions of queer men. While Lana Winters and the Countess are hardly similar characters, they serve as significant embodiments of the lesbian Gothic tradition. Through these women, *AHS* navigates historical abuses and cultural anxieties traditionally associated with women's same-sex desire and behaviors. Lana's experience at Briarcliff, even if it is far more artfully engineered than the narrative at first leads the viewer to believe, enables *Asylum* to explore the treatment of lesbian and sexually aberrant women in the context of pathologized sexuality. Demonic possession, Nazi experimentation, and alien abductions notwithstanding, the show's second season exposes the traumatic histories of women committed to the institution system, whose experiences (as this essay has noted) are often either overlooked or conflated with those of male patients. Lana's place amongst Briarcliff's inmates, most of whom have been arrested (at times wrongfully) for murder, further reminds us of the modern criminalization of queer sexualities that accompanied their pathologization. Lana's role as a lesbian Gothic figure forcibly confined within a Gothic space reveals a significance beyond her pop cultural value as a lesbian leading lady. The Countess of *Hotel* traffics in tropes of the lesbian Gothic that have clear roots in queer media histories, including both those that create a Gothic empowerment for queer women and those that, conversely, perpetuate ideas based in heteronormative, patriarchal culture. Through both women, *Asylum* and *Hotel* establish themselves as texts within the lesbian Gothic corpus.

This is not to say, of course, that these are model depictions of queer women. As is common in the lesbian Gothic, both Lana and the Countess exist as ambivalent figures that defy total spectatorial identification or admiration. Lana's ambition, to some degree, costs Wendy her life and Lana's own loss of autonomy. Furthermore, it encourages Lana to participate in the same patriarchal system of repression that enabled her confinement at Briarcliff. As discussed above, *Asylum*'s final scene goes as far as to suggest that the spectator has only seen Lana in carefully revealed moments that may not be entirely representative of her intentions. The Countess' queerness, on one hand, acknowledges bisexual women who primarily engage in heterosexual relationships, yet, even if we make some allowances for its camp nature, it also conforms to heterosexist discourses of women's same-sex love as temporary or incomplete without male inclusion. For all its powers of subversion, *AHS* does not fully transcend the homophobic discourses that govern queer monsters in the Countess' case or that render the lesbian a shifting and thus suspicious entity in Lana's. Yet what it does provide are contemporary installments within the greater lesbian Gothic continuum, and even its own ambivalence as a text, while perhaps resisting progressive idealism, largely upholds this Gothic as its main discursive guide.

Notes

1. Some debate has been offered regarding the nature of "exclusivity" and the label of *lesbian*. It is not, however, within the scope of this paper to discuss their semantic relationship in further detail.
2. To further support this argument, Mair Rigby notes that queer theorists such as Eve Kosofsky Sedgwick and Jack Halberstam began their scholarly careers working with the Gothic (47).
3. See also Harry Benshoff (5).

4. Fathers *are* depicted in the series, but rarely with much narrative or iconographic concern. When they do receive attention, however, it is typically as failed patriarchs. Ben Harmon of *Murder House*, for instance, is first characterized as a failed husband when his sexual compulsions lead him to habitual adultery, then again when he fails to protect his wife from rape in their new home, and yet again when he fails to acknowledge the rape. He similarly appears to fail as a father when he does not notice that his daughter has committed suicide and is now physically trapped within the home as a ghost. Rule of women is realized or suggested through both Nora Montgomery and Constance Langdon in *Murder House*, through Sister Jude in *Asylum* (as discussed in this essay), the Supreme witch Fiona Goode and her daughter, Cordelia Foxx, in *Coven*, Elsa Mars in *Freak Show*, and the Countess in *Hotel* (as discussed in this essay).

5. Kristeva's description of the abject self-birth here is first explicitly linked to food loathing. I would argue, however, that the use of an emetic invites a similar reading as food loathing, and that the visual objects with which Lana is confronted during her therapy simply take the place of the abjected food to which Kristeva figuratively reacts here.

6. Kristeva identifies the corpse as "the utmost of abjection" (4).

7. As some critics, such as Carroll, call for a separation within the Gothic and horror partly based upon the existence of a supernatural monster, I employ this separation here.

Works Cited

Arnault, Lynne S. "Cruelty, Horror, and the Will to Redemption." *Hypatia*, vol. 18, no. 2, 2003, pp. 155–88.
Bayer, Ronald. *Homosexuality and American Psychiatry: The Politics of Diagnosis*. Princeton UP, 1987.
Benshoff, Harry. *Monsters in the Closet: Homosexuality and the Horror Film*, Manchester UP, 1997.
Carroll, Noël. *The Philosophy of Horror: Or, Paradoxes of the Heart*. Routledge, 1990.
Case, Sue-Ellen. "Tracking the Vampire." *Differences: A Journal of Feminist Cultural Studies*, vol. 5, no. 2, 1991, pp. 1–20.
Castle, Terry. *The Apparitional Lesbian: Female Homosexuality and Modern Culture*, Columbia UP, 1993.
D'Emilio, John. *Sexual Politics, Sexual Communities: The Making of a Homosexual Minority in the United States, 1940–1970*. U of Chicago P, 1983.
D'Emilio, John, and Estelle B. Freedman. *Intimate Matters: A History of Sexuality in America*. Harper & Row, 1988.
De Perthuis, Karen. "The Synthetic Ideal: The Fashion Model and Photographic Manipulation." *Fashion Theory*, vol. 9, no. 4, 2005, pp. 407–24.
Foucault, Michel. *The History of Sexuality Volume I: An Introduction*. Translated by Robert Hurley, Pantheon Books, 1978.
_____. *Madness and Civilization: A History of Insanity in the Age of Reason*. Translated by Richard Howard, Vintage Books, 1988.
Hanson, Ellis. "Lesbians Who Bite." *Out Takes: Essays on Queer Theory and Film*, edited by Ellis Hanson, Duke UP, 1999.
Ingebretsen, Edward. *At Stake: Monsters and Rhetoric of Fear in Public Culture*. U of Chicago P, 2001.
Kristeva, Julia. *Powers of Horror: An Essay on Abjection*. Translated by Leon S. Roudiez, Columbia UP, 1982.
Krzywinska, Tanya. "La Belle Dame Sans Merci." *A Queer Romance: Lesbians, Gay Men and Popular Culture*, edited by Paul Burston and Colin Richardson, Routledge, 1995, pp. 99–110.
Palmer, Paulina. "Lesbian Gothic: Genre, Transformation, Transgression." *Gothic Studies*, vol. 6, no. 1, 2004, pp. 118–30.
Parker, Sarah. "'The darkness is the closet in which your lover roosts her heart': Lesbians,

Desire, and the Gothic Genre." *Journal of International Women's Studies*, vol. 9, no. 2, 2008, pp. 4–19.

Rich, Adrienne. "Compulsory Heterosexuality and Lesbian Existence." *Feminism and Sexuality: A Reader*, edited by Stevi Jackson and Sue Scott, Columbia UP, 1996, pp. 130–41.

Rigby, Mair. "Uncanny Recognition: Queer Theory's Debt to the Gothic." *Gothic Studies*, vol. 11, no. 1, 2009, pp. 46–57.

Rosenfield, Kat. "45 '*American Horror Story*' Characters Ranked in Order of Absolute Evilness." *MTV*, 24 Dec. 2014, www.mtv.com/news/2007463/american-horror-story-evil-ranked/. Accessed 1 Feb. 2017.

Smith, Andrew, and Diana Wallace. "The Female Gothic: Then and Now." *Gothic Studies*, vol. 6, no. 1, 2004, pp. 1–7.

Ussher, Jane M. "Sexual Science and the Law." *Sex, Gender, and Sexuality: The New Basics*, edited by Abby L. Ferber, Kimberly Holcomb, and Tre Wentling, Oxford UP, 2009, pp. 377–416.

Weiss, Andrea. *Vampires and Violets: Lesbians in Film*. Penguin Books, 1993.

Wilton, Tamsin. *Lesbian Studies: Setting an Agenda*. Routledge, 1995.

Appendix I
List of Episodes

Season 1: Murder House

1:1 "Pilot." *American Horror Story: Murder House*, written by Ryan Murphy and Brad Falchuck, directed by Ryan Murphy, 20th Century Fox, 5 Oct. 2011.

1:2 "Home Invasion." *American Horror Story: Murder House*, written by Ryan Murphy and Brad Falchuck, directed by Alfonso Gomez-Rejon, 20th Century Fox, 12 Oct. 2011.

1:3 "Murder House." *American Horror Story: Murder House*, written by Jennifer Salt, directed by Bradley Buecker, 20th Century Fox, 19 Oct. 2011.

1:4 "Halloween (Part 1)." *American Horror Story: Murder House*, written by James Wong, directed by David Semel, 20th Century Fox, 26 Oct. 2011.

1:5 "Halloween (Part 2)." *American Horror Story: Murder House*, written by Tim Minear, directed by David Semel, 20th Century Fox, 2 Nov. 2011.

1:6 "Piggy Piggy." *American Horror Story: Murder House*, written by Jessica Sharzer, directed by Michael Uppendahl, 20th Century Fox, 9 Nov. 2011.

1:7 "Open House." *American Horror Story: Murder House*, written by Brad Falchuck, directed by Tim Hunter, 20th Century Fox, 16 Nov. 2011.

1:8 "Rubber Man." *American Horror Story: Murder House*, written by Ryan Murphy, directed by Miguel Arteta, 20th Century Fox, 23 Nov. 2011.

1:9 "Spooky Little Girl." *American Horror Story: Murder House*, written by Jennifer Salt, directed by John Scott, 20th Century Fox, 30 Nov. 2011.

1:10 "Smoldering Children." *American Horror Story: Murder House*, written by James Wong, directed by Michael Lehmann, 20th Century Fox, 7 Dec. 2011.

1:11 "Birth." *American Horror Story: Murder House*, written by Tim Minear, directed by Alfonso Gomez-Rejon, 20th Century Fox, 14 Dec. 2011.

1:12 "Afterbirth." *American Horror Story: Murder House*, written by Jessica Sharzer, directed by Bradley Buecker, 20th Century Fox, 21 Dec. 2011.

Season 2: Asylum

2:1 "Welcome to Briarcliff." *American Horror Story: Asylum*, written by Tim Minear, directed by Bradley Buecker, 20th Century Fox, 17 Oct. 2012.

2:2 "Tricks and Treats." *American Horror Story: Asylum*, written by James Wong, directed by Bradley Buecker, 20th Century Fox, 24 Oct. 2012.

2:3 "Nor'easter." *American Horror Story: Asylum*, written by Jennifer Salt, directed by Michael Uppendahl, 20th Century Fox, 31 Oct. 2012.

2:4 "I Am Anne Frank (Part 1)." *American Horror Story: Asylum*, written by Jessica Sharzer, directed by Bradley Buecker, 20th Century Fox, 7 Nov. 2012.

2:5 "I Am Anne Frank (Part 2)." *American Horror Story: Asylum*, written by Brad Falchuk, directed by Alfonso Gomez-Rejon, 20th Century Fox, 14 Nov. 2012.

2:6 "The Origins of Monstrosity." *American Horror Story: Asylum*, written by Ryan Murphy, directed by David Semel, 20th Century Fox, 21 Nov. 2012.

2:7 "Dark Cousin." *American Horror Story: Asylum*, written by Tim Minear, directed by Michael Rymer, 20th Century Fox, 28 Nov. 2012.

2:8 "Unholy Night." *American Horror Story: Asylum*, written by James Wong, directed by Michael Lehmann, 20th Century Fox, 5 Dec. 2012.

2:9 "The Coat Hanger." *American Horror Story: Asylum*, written by Jennifer Salt, directed by Jeremy Podeswa, 20th Century Fox, 12 Dec. 2012.

2:10 "The Name Game." *American Horror Story: Asylum*, written by Jessica Sharzer, directed by Michael Lehmann, 20th Century Fox, 2 Jan. 2013.

2:11 "Spilt Milk." *American Horror Story: Asylum*, written by Brad Falchuk, directed by Alfonso Gomez-Rejon, 20th Century Fox, 9 Jan. 2013.

2:12 "Continuum." *American Horror Story: Asylum*, written by Ryan Murphy, directed by Craig Zisk, 20th Century Fox, 16 Jan. 2013.

2:13 "Madness Ends." *American Horror Story: Asylum*, written by Tim Minear, directed by Alfonso Gomez-Rejon, 20th Century Fox, 23 Jan. 2013.

Season 3: Coven

3:1 "Bitchcraft." *American Horror Story: Coven*, written by Ryan Murphy and Brad Falchuk, directed by Alfonso Gomez-Rejon, 20th Century Fox, 9 Oct. 2013.

3:2 "Boy Parts." *American Horror Story: Coven*, written by Tim Minear, directed by Michael Rymer, 20th Century Fox, 16 Oct. 2013.

3:3 "The Replacements." *American Horror Story: Coven*, written by James Wong, directed by Alfonso Gomez-Rejon, 20th Century Fox, 23 Oct. 2013.

3:4 "Fearful Pranks Ensue." *American Horror Story: Coven*, written by Jennifer Salt, directed by Michael Uppendahl, 20th Century Fox, 30 Oct. 2013.

3:5 "Burn, Witch, Burn!" *American Horror Story: Coven*, written by Jessica Sharzer, directed by Jeremy Podeswa, 20th Century Fox, 6 Nov. 2013.

3:6 "The Axeman Cometh." *American Horror Story: Coven*, written by Douglas Petrie, directed by Michael Uppendahl, 20th Century Fox, 13 Nov. 2013.

3:7 "The Dead." *American Horror Story: Coven*, written by Brad Falchuk, directed by Bradley Buecker, 20th Century Fox, 20 Nov. 2013.

3:8 "The Sacred Taking." *American Horror Story: Coven*, written by Ryan Murphy, directed by Alfonso Gomez-Rejon, 20th Century Fox, 4 Dec. 2013.

3:9 "Head." *American Horror Story: Coven*, written by Tim Minear, directed by Howard Deutch, 20th Century Fox, 11 Dec. 2013.

3:10 "The Magical Delights of Stevie Nicks." *American Horror Story: Coven*, written by James Wong, directed by Alfonso Gomez-Rejon, 20th Century Fox, 8 Jan. 2014.

3:11 "Protect the Coven." *American Horror Story: Coven*, written by Jennifer Salt, directed by Bradley Buecker, 20th Century Fox, 15 Jan. 2014.

3:12 "Go to Hell." *American Horror Story: Coven*, written by Jessica Sharzer, directed by Alfonso Gomez-Rejon, 20th Century Fox, 22 Jan. 2014.
3:13 "The Seven Wonders." *American Horror Story: Coven*, written by Douglas Petrie, directed by Alfonso Gomez-Rejon, 20th Century Fox, 29 Jan. 2014.

Season 4: Freak Show

4:1 "Monsters Among Us." *American Horror Story: Freak Show*, written by Ryan Murphy and Brad Falchuk, directed by Ryan Murphy, 20th Century Fox, 8 Oct. 2014.
4:2 "Massacres and Matinees." *American Horror Story: Freak Show*, written by Tim Minear, directed by Alfonso Gomez-Rejon, 20th Century Fox, 15 Oct. 2014.
4:3 "Edward Mordrake (Part 1)." *American Horror Story: Freak Show*, written by James Wong, directed by Michael Uppendahl, 20th Century Fox, 22 Oct. 2014.
4:4 "Edward Mordrake (Part 2)." *American Horror Story: Freak Show*, written by Jennifer Salt, directed by Howard Deutch, 20th Century Fox, 29 Oct. 2014.
4:5 "Pink Cupcakes." *American Horror Story: Freak Show*, written by Jessica Sharzer, directed by Michael Uppendahl, 20th Century Fox, 5 Nov. 2014.
4:6 "Bullseye." *American Horror Story: Freak Show*, written by John J. Gray, directed by Howard Deutch, 20th Century Fox, 12 Nov. 2014.
4:7 "Test of Strength." *American Horror Story: Freak Show*, written by Crystal Liu, directed by Anthony Hemingway, 20th Century Fox, 19 Nov. 2014.
4:8 "Blood Bath." *American Horror Story: Freak Show*, written by Ryan Murphy, directed by Bradley Buecker, 20th Century Fox, 3 Dec. 2014.
4:9 "Tupperware Party Massacre." *American Horror Story: Freak Show*, written by Brad Falchuk, directed by Loni Peristere, 20th Century Fox, 10 Dec. 2014.
4:10 "Orphans." *American Horror Story: Freak Show*, written by James Wong, directed by Bradley Buecker, 20th Century Fox, 17 Dec. 2014.
4:11 "Magical Thinking." *American Horror Story: Freak Show*, written by Jennifer Salt, directed by Michael Goi, 20th Century Fox, 7 Jan. 2015.
4:12 "Show Stoppers." *American Horror Story: Freak Show*, written by Jessica Sharzer, directed by Loni Peristere, 20th Century Fox, 14 Jan. 2015.
4:13 "Curtain Call." *American Horror Story: Freak Show*, written by John J. Gray, directed by Bradley Buecker, 20th Century Fox, 21 Jan. 2015.

Season 5: Hotel

5:1 "Checking In." *American Horror Story: Hotel*, written by Ryan Murphy and Brad Falchuk, directed by Ryan Murphy, 20th Century Fox, 7 Oct. 2015.
5:2 "Chutes and Ladders." *American Horror Story: Hotel*, written by Tim Minear, directed by Bradley Buecker, 20th Century Fox, 14 Oct. 2015.
5:3 "Mommy." *American Horror Story: Hotel*, written by James Wong, directed by Bradley Buecker, 20th Century Fox, 21 Oct. 2015.
5:4 "Devil's Night." *American Horror Story: Hotel*, written by Jennifer Salt, directed by Loni Peristere, 20th Century Fox, 28 Oct. 2015.
5:5 "Room Service." *American Horror Story: Hotel*, written by Ned Martel, directed by Michael Goi, 20th Century Fox, 4 Nov. 2015.

5:6 "Room 33." *American Horror Story: Hotel*, written by John J. Gray, directed by Loni Peristere, 20th Century Fox, 11 Nov. 2015.

5:7 "Flicker." *American Horror Story: Hotel*, written by Crystal Lui, directed by Michael Goi, 20th Century Fox, 18 Nov. 2015.

5:8 "The Ten Commandments Killer." *American Horror Story: Hotel*, written by Ryan Murphy, directed by Loni Peristere, 20th Century Fox, 2 Dec. 2015.

5:9 "She Wants Revenge." *American Horror Story: Hotel*, written by Brad Falchuck, directed by Michael Uppendahl, 20th Century Fox, 9 Dec. 2015.

5:10 "She Gets Revenge." *American Horror Story: Hotel*, written by James Wong, directed by Bradley Buecker, 20th Century Fox, 16 Dec. 2015.

5:11 "Battle Royale." *American Horror Story: Hotel*, written by Ned Martel, directed by Michael Uppendahl, 20th Century Fox, 6 Jan. 2016.

5:12 "Be Our Guest." *American Horror Story: Hotel*, written by John J. Gray, directed by Bradley Buecker, 20th Century Fox, 13 Jan. 2016.

Season 6: Roanoke

6:1 "Chapter 1." *American Horror Story: Roanoke*, written by Ryan Murphy and Brad Falchuck, directed by Bradley Buecker, 20th Century Fox, 14 Sep. 2016.

6:2 "Chapter 2." *American Horror Story: Roanoke*, written by Tim Minear, directed by Michael Goi, 20th Century Fox, 21 Sep. 2016.

6:3 "Chapter 3." *American Horror Story: Roanoke*, written by James Wong, directed by Jennifer Lynch, 20th Century Fox, 28 Sep. 2016.

6:4 "Chapter 4." *American Horror Story: Roanoke*, written by John J. Gray, directed by Marita Grabiak, 20th Century Fox, 5 Oct. 2016.

6:5 "Chapter 5." *American Horror Story: Roanoke*, written by Akela Cooper, directed by Nelson Cragg, 20th Century Fox, 12 Oct. 2016.

6:6 "Chapter 6." *American Horror Story: Roanoke*, written by Ned Martel, directed by Angela Bassett, 20th Century Fox, 19 Oct. 2016.

6:7 "Chapter 7." *American Horror Story: Roanoke*, written by Crystal Liu, directed by Elodie Keene, 20th Century Fox, 26 Oct. 2016.

6:8 "Chapter 8." *American Horror Story: Roanoke*, written by Todd Kubrack, directed by Gwyneth Horder-Payton, 20th Century Fox, 2 Nov. 2016.

6:9 "Chapter 9." *American Horror Story: Roanoke*, written by Tim Minear, directed by Alexis O. Korycinski, 20th Century Fox, 9 Nov. 2016.

6:10 "Chapter 10." *American Horror Story: Roanoke*, written by Ryan Murphy and Brad Falchuck, directed by Bradley Buecker, 20th Century Fox, 16 Nov. 2016.

Season 7: Cult

7:1 "Election Night." *American Horror Story: Cult*, written by Ryan Murphy and Brad Falchuck, directed by Bradley Buecker, 20th Century Fox, 5 Sep. 2017.

7:2 "Don't Be Afraid of the Dark." *American Horror Story: Cult*, written by Tim Minear, directed by Liza Johnson, 20th Century Fox, 12 Sep. 2017.

7:3 "Neighbors from Hell." *American Horror Story: Cult*, written by James Wong, directed by Gwyneth Horder-Payton, 20th Century Fox, 19 Sep. 2017.

7:4 "11/9." *American Horror Story: Cult*, written by John J. Gray, directed by Gwyneth Horder-Payton, 20th Century Fox, 26 Sep. 2017.

7:5 "Holes." *American Horror Story: Cult*, written by Crystal Liu, directed by Maggie Kiley, 20th Century Fox, 3 Oct. 2017.

7:6 "Mid-Western Assassin." *American Horror Story: Cult*, written by Todd Kubrack, directed by Bradley Buecker, 20th Century Fox, 10 Oct. 2017.

7:7 "Valerie Solanas Died for Your Sins: Scumbag." *American Horror Story: Cult*, written by Crystal Liu, directed by Rachel Goldberg, 20th Century Fox, 17 Oct. 2017.

7:8 "Winter of Our Discontent." *American Horror Story: Cult*, written by Joshua Green, directed by Barbara Brown, 20th Century Fox, 24 Oct. 2017.

7:9 "Drink the Kool-Aid." *American Horror Story: Cult*, written by Adam Penn, directed by Angela Bassett, 20th Century Fox, 31 Oct. 2017.

7:10 "Charles (Manson) in Charge." *American Horror Story: Cult*, written by Ryan Murphy and Brad Falchuk, directed by Bradley Buecker, 20th Century Fox, 7 Nov. 2017.

7:11 "Great Again." *American Horror Story: Cult*, written by Tim Minear, directed by Jennifer Lynch, 20th Century Fox, 14 Nov. 2017.

Season 8: Apocalypse

8:1 "The End." *American Horror Story: Apocalypse*, written by Ryan Murphy and Brad Falchuk, directed by Bradley Buecker, 20th Century Fox, 12 Sep. 2018.

8:2 "The Morning After." *American Horror Story: Apocalypse*, written by James Wong, directed by Jennifer Lynch, 20th Century Fox, 19 Sep. 2018.

8:3 "Forbidden Fruit." *American Horror Story: Apocalypse*, written by Manny Coto, directed by Loni Peristere, 20th Century Fox, 26 Sep. 2018.

8:4 "Could It Be... Satan?" *American Horror Story: Apocalypse*, written by Tim Minear, directed by Sheree Folkson, 20th Century Fox, 3 Oct. 2018.

8:5 "Boy Wonder." *American Horror Story: Apocalypse*, written by John J. Gray, directed by Gwyneth Horder-Payton, 20th Century Fox, 10 Oct. 2018.

8:6 "Return to Murder House." *American Horror Story: Apocalypse*, written by Crystal Liu, directed by Sarah Paulson, 20th Century Fox, 17 Oct. 2018.

8:7 "Traitor." *American Horror Story: Apocalypse*, written by Adam Penn, directed by Jennifer Lynch, 20th Century Fox, 24 Oct. 2018.

8:8 "Sojourn." *American Horror Story: Apocalypse*, written by Josh Green, directed by Bradley Buecker, 20th Century Fox, 31 Oct. 2018.

8:9 "Fire and Reign." *American Horror Story: Apocalypse*, written by Asha Michelle Wilson, directed by Jennifer Arnold, 20th Century Fox, 7 Nov. 2018.

8:10 "Apocalypse Then." *American Horror Story: Apocalypse*, written by Ryan Murphy and Brad Falchuk, directed by Bradley Buecker, 20th Century Fox, 14 Nov. 2018.

Appendix II
List of Major Characters

Season 1: Murder House

Vivien Harmon	Connie Britton
Ben Harmon	Dylan McDermott
Violet Harmon	Taissa Farmiga
Constance Langdon	Jessica Lange
Tate Langdon	Evan Peters
Addie Langdon	Jamie Brewer
Moira O'Hara	Frances Conroy
Young Moira	Alexandra Breckenridge
Hayden McClaine	Kate Mara
Dr. Charles Montgomery	Matt Ross
Nora Montgomery	Lily Rabe
Chad Warwick	Zachary Quinto
Patrick	Teddy Sears
Billie Dean Howard	Sarah Paulson

Season 2: Asylum

Lana Winters	Sarah Paulson
Kit Walker	Evan Peters
Alma Walker	Britne Oldford
Sister Jude Martin	Jessica Lange
Sister Mary Eunice	McKee Lily Rabe
Dr. Oliver Thredson	Zachary Quinto
Dr. Arthur Arden	James Cromwell
Monsignor Timothy Howard	Joseph Fiennes
Grace Bertrand	Lizzie Broncheré
Pepper	Naomi Grossman
Shelley	Chloë Sevigny
Wendy Peyser	Clea DuVall
Johnny Morgan	Dylan McDermott

Shachath — Frances Conroy
Anne Frank/Charlotte Brown — Franka Potente
Leigh Emerson — Ian McShane

Season 3: Coven

Cordelia Foxx — Sarah Paulson
Fiona Goode — Jessica Lange
Zoe Benson — Taissa Farmiga
Madison Montgomery — Emma Roberts
Queenie — Gabourey Sidibe
Nan — Jamie Brewer
Misty Day — Lily Rabe
Myrtle Snow — Frances Conroy
Marie Laveau — Angela Bassett
Delphine LaLaurie — Kathy Bates
Kyle Spencer — Evan Peters
Spalding — Denis O'Hare
Hank Foxx — Josh Hamilton
Bastien the Minotaur — Ameer Baraka
Papa Legba — Lance Reddick

Season 4: Freak Show

Elsa Mars — Jessica Lange
Bette and Dot Tattler — Sarah Paulson
Jimmy Darling — Evan Peters
Ethel Darling — Kathy Bates
Desiree Dupree — Angela Bassett
Dell Toledo — Michael Chiklis
Pepper — Naomi Grossman
Paul the Illustrated Seal — Mat Fraser
Amazon Eve — Erika Ervin
Ma Petite — Jyoti Amge
Legless Suzi — Rose Siggins
Toulouse — Drew Rin Varick
Salty — Christopher Neiman
Penny — Grace Gummer
Barbara/Ima Wiggles — Chrissy Metz
Meep — Ben Woolf
Stanley — Denis O'Hare
Maggie Esmerelda — Emma Roberts
Dandy Mott — Finn Witrock
Gloria Mott — Frances Conroy
Dora Ross — Patti LaBelle
Twisty the Clown — John Carroll Lynch
Bonnie Lipton — Skyler Samuels

Corey Bachman   Major Dodson
Mike   Dalton E. Gray
Chester Creb   Neil Patrick Harris

Season 5: Hotel

Detective John Lowe	Wes Bentley
Dr. Alex Lowe	Chloë Sevigny
The Countess/Elizabeth Johnson	Lady Gaga
Will Drake	Cheyenne Jackson
James Patrick March	Evan Peters
Ramona Royale	Angela Bassett
Donovan	Matt Bomer
Iris	Kathy Bates
Liz Taylor	Denis O'Hare
Sally McKenna	Sarah Paulson
Tristan Duffy	Finn Wittrock

Season 6: Roanoke

Shelby Miller	Lily Rabe
Matt Miller	André Holland
Lee Harris	Adina Porter
Audrey Tindall	Sarah Paulson
Dominic Banks	Cuba Gooding, Jr.
Rory Monahan	Evan Peters
Monet Tumusiime	Angela Bassett
Thomasin White/The Butcher	Kathy Bates
Ambrose White	Wes Bentley
Scáthach	Lady Gaga
Mama Polk	Frances Conroy
Jether Polk	Finn Wittrock
Lot Polk	Chaz Bono
Nurse Miranda Jane	Maya Rose Berko
Nurse Bridget Jane	Kristen Rakes
Dr. Elias Cunningham	Denis O'Hare
Cricket Marlowe	Leslie Jordan
Edward Phillipe Mott	Evan Peters

Season 7: Cult

Ally Mayfair-Richards	Sarah Paulson
Ivy Mayfair-Richards	Alison Pill
Ozymandias "Oz" Mayfair-Richards	Cooper Dodson
Dr. Rudy Vincent	Cheyenne Jackson
Kai Anderson	Evan Peters
Winter Anderson	Billie Lourd

Harrison Wilton   Billy Eichner
Meadow Wilton   Leslie Grossman
Gary Longstreet   Chaz Bono
Beverly Hope   Adina Porter
Detective Jack Samuels   Colton Haynes

Season 8: Apocalypse

Michael Langdon   Cody Fern
Jeff Pfister   Evan Peters
Tate Langdon   Evan Peters
Wilhemina Venable   Sarah Paulson
Mr. Gallant   Evan Peters
Miriam Mead   Kathy Bates
Behold Chablis   Billy Porter
John Henry Moore   Cheyenne Jackson
Anton LaVey   Carlo Rota
Mutt Nutter   Billy Eichner
Timothy Campbell   Kyle Allen
Emily Campbell   Ash Santos
Mallory   Billie Lourd
Cordelia Goode   Sarah Paulson
Madison Montgomery   Emma Roberts
Misty Day   Lily Rabe
Queenie   Gabourey Sidibe
Zoe Benson   Taissa Farmiga
Nan   Jamie Brewer
Dr. Ben Harmon   Dylan McDermott
Vivien Harmon   Connie Britton
Violet Harmon   Taissa Farmiga
Constance Langdon   Jessica Lange

About the Contributors

Erin Guydish **Buchholz** earned a Ph.D. from Indiana University of Pennsylvania. She teaches at an all girls' boarding school in Western Pennsylvania, where she focuses on empowering women, studying American literature and culture, as well as encouraging girls to grow into conscientious global citizens.

Leverett **Butts** received his Ph.D. in twentieth-century American/Southern literature from Georgia State University. He is an associate professor at the University of North Georgia in Gainesville. His critical work has been published in *The Robert Penn Warren Review*, *The Eudora Welty Newsletter*, and *Literary Matters*. He is the editor of *H.P. Lovecraft: Selected Works, Critical Perspectives and Interviews on His Influence* (McFarland, 2018). His creative work has appeared in *Weird Tales*, *The Georgia State University Review*, and several anthologies.

Jennifer K. **Cox** is a Ph.D. candidate at Idaho State University. Her dissertation theorizes the Dark Carnival in American fantasy literature. She has served as the editorial assistant for the *Journal of the Fantastic in the Arts* and her work includes articles on medieval posthuman configurations in *Quidditas*; on Neil Gaiman's strategies for adapting *Mr. Punch* in *JFA*; and an essay on pop culture's killer clowns.

Cameron Williams **Crawford** received her a Ph.D. in twentieth- and twenty-first-century American/Southern literature from Florida State University. She is a senior lecturer at the University of North Georgia in Gainesville. Her work has been published in *The Southern Quarterly* (56.1, Fall 2018), *True Detective: Critical Essays on the HBO Series* (Lexington, 2018) and *Constructing the Literary Self* (Cambridge, 2013).

Jonathan **Greenaway** is an independent researcher. He has Ph.D. from the Manchester Centre for Gothic Studies. He is founding editor of the *Dark Arts Journal* and coeditor of *Horror and Religion: New Literary Approaches to Theology, Race and Sexuality* (UWP, 2019).

Corrine E. **Hinton** is an associate professor of English at Texas A&M University–Texarkana. Her work examines social influence, rhetorical manipulation, and Gothic realism in television drama and includes publications on *Wentworth*, and "'God Decreed it So': The Rhetoric of Destiny in 1963" with T.S. Hill in *Living Legacies* (Routledge, 2018).

Tammie **Jenkins** received a doctorate from Louisiana State University in curriculum and instruction. Her publications include "Culture, Identity, and Otherness:

An Analysis of Kino's Songs in John Steinbeck's *The Pearl* and Pilate's Melody in Toni Morrison's *Song of Solomon*" (Salem Press). She is an associate editor for *The Criterion* and is a special education teacher in her local public school system.

Rita **Mookerjee** is an assistant teaching professor at Iowa State University. Her critical work has been featured in the *Bloomsbury Handbook to Literary and Cultural Theory*, the *Bloomsbury Handbook of Twenty-First Century Feminist Theory*, and the *Routledge Companion to Food and Literature*. She is the author of *Becoming the Bronze Idol* (Bone Ink Press, 2019) and is poetry staff reader for *[PANK]*.

Michelle L. **Pribbernow** is a Ph.D. candidate in comparative literature and cultural studies at the University of Arkansas. She is interested in critical cultural studies, and her dissertation focuses on the shifting representations of gender, sexuality and women's agency in possession horror films. Her work has appeared in *Critical Insights: Isaac Asimov* (2017) and *Science Fiction Film and Television*.

Antonio **Sanna** (Ph.D., University of Westminster) has published widely on English literature, Gothic literature, horror films and TV series, epic films and cinematic adaptations. He is the coeditor of the Lexington Books' series *Critical Companions to Popular Directors* and has also edited the volumes *Pirates in History and Popular Culture* (2018) and *Critical Essays on Twin Peaks: The Return* (2019).

Tosha R. **Taylor** is a lecturer at Manhattanville College. Her publications include work on violence and queer bodies in horror media, extreme horror, media fandoms, and gender performance in popular music. She holds a Ph.D. from Loughborough University, where her doctoral research concerned the captivity of Americans in contemporary horror films.

Sarah Foust **Vinson**, Ph.D., is an associate professor at Cardinal Stritch University in Milwaukee, Wisconsin. She teaches many literature courses, including contemporary literature, women's literature, global literature, science fiction and fantasy, African American literature, and first year composition. She has published on Gloria Naylor, Dorothy Allison, Tim O'Brien, Cheryl Strayed, and Ruth Reichl.

Index

Addie Langdon (character) 67, 212
"Afterbirth" (episode 1:12) 75, 77, 207
Alma Walker (character) 23, 91, 95, 212
Ally Mayfair-Richards (character) 183, 185–6, 214
Amazon Eve (character) 122, 170, 174, 178, 213
Ambrose White (character) 214
Anne Frank/Charlotte Brown (character) 9–10, 94, 213
Anton LaVey (character) 62, 215
Apocalypse 1, 4, 54–64, 211
"Apocalypse Then" (episode 8:10) 55, 58, 211
Asylum 1, 3–5, 8–25, 54, 78, 81–99, 106, 112, 164–6, 189–208, 212–3
Audrey Tindall (character) 214
"The Axeman Cometh" (episode 3:6) 46, 48, 177, 208

Barbara/Ima Wiggles (character) 170, 182, 213
Bastien the Minotaur (character) 32, 46–7, 49–51, 139, 213
"Battle Royale" (episode 5:11) 203, 210
"Be Our Guest" (episode 5:12) 210
Behold Chablis (character) 58, 62, 215
Ben Harmon (character) 62, 63, 68, 69, 74–6, 78, 205n4, 212, 215
Bette and Dot Tattler (character) 104, 106, 115–7, 119–20, 124–5, 127–9, 131n6, 170, 181–2, 213
Beverly Hope (character) 184, 186, 215
Billie Dean Howard (character) 75, 212
"Birth" (episode 1:11) 75–7, 207
"Bitchcraft" (episode 3:1) 44, 46, 48, 137–41, 146n1, 154–5, 159, 173, 176–7, 181 208
"Blood Bath" (episode 4:8) 125–7, 129, 209
Bonnie Lipton (character) 104–5, 213
"Boy Parts" (episode 3:2) 32, 138, 142–3, 145, 170, 173, 177, 208
"Boy Wonder" (episode 8:5) 56, 58, 211
"Bullseye" (episode 4:6) 107, 121, 123, 181–2, 209
"Burn, Witch, Burn!" (episode 3:5) 44, 46, 48, 141, 143, 177, 180–1, 208

Chad Warwick (character) 70, 72–6, 79n8, 212

"Chapter 1" (episode 6.1) 210
"Chapter 2" (episode 6.2) 109, 210
"Chapter 3" (episode 6.3) 108, 210
"Chapter 4" (episode 6.4) 210
"Chapter 5" (episode 6.5) 101, 210
"Chapter 6" (episode 6.6) 210
"Chapter 7" (episode 6.7) 210
"Chapter 8" (episode 6.8) 210
"Chapter 9" (episode 6.9) 210
"Chapter 10" (episode 6.10) 210
Charles Manson (character) 186
"Charles (Manson) in Charge" (episode 7:10) 186, 211
Charles Montgomery (character) 75, 212
"Checking In" (episode 5:1) 209
Chester Creb (character) 170, 174, 175, 214
"Chutes and Ladders" (episode 5:2) 209
"The Coat Hanger" (episode 2:9) 15, 208
Constance Langdon (character) 61–4, 68, 70, 71, 75, 77, 205n4, 212, 215
"Continuum" (episode 2:12) 22, 97, 197, 208
Cordelia Foxx/Goode (character) 5, 54–5, 57–8, 61, 63, 134–47, 153, 159, 164, 171, 176–8, 180–1, 205n4, 213, 215
Corey Bachman (character) 105, 214
"Could It Be… Satan?" (episode 8:4) 57–8, 211
The Countess/Elizabeth Johnson (character) 55, 190–1, 200–5, 214
Coven 1, 3–5, 26–38, 39–53, 54–64, 112, 134–47, 148–63, 164–88, 205n4, 208–9, 213
Cricket Marlowe (character) 107–8, 214
Cult 1–5, 54, 164–88, 210–1, 214–6, 213
"Curtain Call" (episode 4:13) 127, 179, 209

Dandy Mott (character) 101, 105–6, 109–10, 124–7, 174, 179, 182, 213
"Dark Cousin" (episode 2:7) 95–6, 208
"The Dead" (episode 3:7) 34, 50, 140, 177, 208
Dell Toledo (character) 128–9, 172, 174, 179, 213
Delphine LaLaurie (character) 4,, 32, 39–53, 138, 143, 180, 186, 213
Desiree Dupree (character) 127–8, 170, 172, 174, 179, 213

Detective Jack Samuels (character) 184, 215
Detective John Lowe (character) 214
"Devil's Night" (episode 5:4) 209
Dr. Alex Lowe (character) 214
Dr. Arthur Arden (character) 9–10, 13–14, 69, 89–90, 93–4, 193, 197, 212
Dr. Elias Cunningham (character) 108–9, 214
Dr. Oliver Thredson (character) 10–1, 18, 20–1, 23, 96, 189, 195, 212
Dr. Rudy Vincent (character) 183, 214
Dominic Banks (character) 214
Donovan (character) 214
"Don't Be Afraid of the Dark" (episode 7:2) 185, 210
Dora Ross (character) 124–6, 213
"Drink the Kool-Aid" (episode 7:9) 184, 185, 211

"Edward Mordrake (Part 1)" (episode 4:3) 105, 122, 129, 209
"Edward Mordrake (Part 2)" (episode 4:4) 106, 121, 174, 209
Edward Philipe Mott (character) 100–1, 108, 110, 216
"Election Night" (episode 7:1) 183, 210
"11/9" (episode 7:4) 184, 210
Elsa Mars (character) 5, 101, 103–6, 114–5, 117–23, 127–30, 151, 164–70, 172–6, 178–82, 186, 205n4, 213
Emily Campbell (character) 57, 215
"The End" (episode 8:1) 56, 211
Ethel Darling (character) 106, 114–5, 121, 127–30, 170–1, 178–9, 181–2, 213

Falchuk, Brad 1–3, 114
"Fearful Pranks Ensue" (episode 3:4) 31, 34–5, 139, 159, 180–1,
Fiona Goode (character) 5, 31–2, 37, 44, 134–47, 152–5, 159, 161, 164–8, 170–4, 176–81, 186, 205n4, 213
"Fire and Reign" (episode 8:9) 61–2, 211
"Flicker" (episode 5:7) 202, 210
"Forbidden Fruit" (episode 8:3) 55, 57, 211
Freak Show 1, 3–5, 54, 100–11, 112–32, 164–88, 209, 213–4

Gary Longstreet (character) 184, 215
Gloria Mott (character) 105, 114–5, 123–7, 213
"Go to Hell" (episode 3:12) 51, 57, 146, 153, 171, 209
Grace Bertrand (character) 4, 23, 90–2, 94–6, 193, 197, 212
"Great Again" (episode 7:11) 183, 185–6, 211

"Halloween (Part 1)" (episode 1:4) 70–1, 73, 207
"Halloween (Part 2)" (episode 1:5) 70–1, 74, 207
Hank Foxx (character) 141, 145, 153, 172, 181, 213

Harrison Wilton (character) 184, 215
Hayden McClaine (character) 69, 74–5, 212
"Head" (episode 3:9) 144, 208
"Holes" (episode 7:5) 184, 211
"Home Invasion" (episode 1:2) 69, 207
Hotel 1, 3, 5, 54–5, 57, 152, 164, 166, 189–206, 209–10, 214

"I Am Anne Frank (Part 1)" (episode 2:4) 9, 11, 19–20, 56, 94, 195–6, 208
"I Am Anne Frank (Part 2)" (episode 2:5) 91, 96, 195, 208
Iris (character) 214
Ivy Mayfair-Richards (character) 184–5, 214

James Patrick March (character) 214
Jeff Pfister (character) 56, 61–2, 215
Jether Polk (character) 109, 214
Jimmy Darling (character) 106–7, 110, 117–8, 127–9, 131n4, 170, 172, 174, 178–9, 213
John Henry Moore (character) 55, 215
Johnny Morgan/Thredson (character) 17, 91, 199, 212

Kai Anderson (character) 5, 165, 183–6, 214
Kit Walker (character) 9, 21, 23–4, 88, 90–7, 193, 197–8, 212
Kyle Spencer (character) 55, 138, 146, 153, 213

Lana Winters (character) 9, 11, 16–23, 88, 90–1, 93–4, 96–7, 189–93, 195–201, 203–4, 205n5, 212
Lee Harris (character) 107–8, 143, 214
Legless Suzi (character) 178, 213
Leigh Emerson (character) 14–5, 213
Liz Taylor (character) 214
Lot Polk (character) 109, 214

Ma Petite (character) 120–1, 169, 172, 213
Madison Montgomery (character) 57–8, 62, 138–9, 141, 143, 153, 173–4, 177, 180–1, 213, 215
"Madness Ends" (episode 2:13) 17–9, 21, 23–4, 91, 95, 97, 198–9, 208
Maggie Esmerelda (character) 106, 174, 179, 213
"The Magical Delights of Stevie Nicks" (episode 3:10) 44, 51, 140, 142–3, 177, 181, 208
"Magical Thinking" (episode 4:11) 128, 175, 209
Mallory (character) 55, 64, 215
Mama Polk (character) 109–10, 214
Marie Laveau (character) 4, 26–38, 39–53, 140, 142, 145, 152, 156, 172–3, 177, 181, 213
"Massacres and Matinees" (episode 4:2) 105, 124–5, 174, 181,
Matt Miller (character) 100, 107, 214
Meadow Wilton (character) 184–5, 215
Meep (character) 169, 172–4, 178, 213

Index   221

Michael Langdon (character) 54–64, 215
"Mid-Western Assassin" (episode 7:6) 211
Mike (character) 105, 214
Miriam Mead (character) 61–3, 215
Mr. Gallant (character) 57, 215
Misty Day (character) 58, 139, 145, 146n1, 153, 170, 173, 181, 213, 215
Moira O'Hara (character) 70, 212
"Mommy" (episode 5:3) 202, 209
Monet Tumusiime (character) 214
Monsignor Timothy Howard (character) 10, 14, 23, 94–5, 193, 195, 197, 212
"Monsters Among Us" (episode 4:1) 104–7, 115, 117–20, 124, 128–9, 170, 174, 178, 182, 209
"The Morning After" (episode 8:2) 57, 61, 211
Murder House 1, 3–4, 54–64, 66–80, 112, 152, 164, 165, 166, 200, 205n4, 206–7, 212
"Murder House" (episode 1:3) 69–70, 207
Murphy, Ryan 1–3, 10–11, 13–4, 103, 110, 112, 114, 134, 137, 152–3, 207–11
Mutt Nutter (character) 56, 61–2, 215
Myrtle Snow (character) 139, 141, 144–5, 153, 174, 177, 180–1, 213

"The Name Game" (episode 2:10) 14–5, 22, 197, 208
Nan (character) 139, 142, 153, 174, 177, 213, 215
"Neighbors from Hell" (episode 7:3) 210
Nora Montgomery (character) 73–4, 77, 139, 205n4, 212
"Nor'easter" (episode 2:3) 89–91, 208
Nurse Bridget Jane (character) 108, 214
Nurse Miranda Jane (character) 108, 214

"Open House" (episode 1:7) 68, 77, 207
"The Origins of Monstrosity" (episode 2:6) 14, 96, 208
"Orphans" (episode 4:10) 121, 209
Ozymandias "Oz" Mayfair-Richards (character) 214

Papa Legba (character) 27, 44, 51, 140, 142–3, 146, 213
Patrick (character) 70, 72, 74–7, 79n8, 212
Paul the Illustrated Seal (character) 106, 121, 123, 172, 178–9, 182, 213
Penny (character) 106, 213
Pepper (character) 14–6, 54, 121, 169, 172, 193, 212–3
"Piggy Piggy" (episode 1:6) 207
"Pilot" (episode 1:1) 67, 72, 94, 207
"Pink Cupcakes" (episode 4:5) 106, 125–6, 174, 209
"Protect the Coven" (episode 3:11) 48, 145, 153, 208

Queenie (character) 34, 54, 57, 138–9, 153, 156, 172–4, 177, 181, 213, 215

Ramona Royale (character) 191, 202, 214

"The Replacements" (episode 3:3) 46, 139–41, 143, 153, 173, 180–1, 208
"Return to Murder House" (episode 8:6) 55, 57–8, 60–3, 211
Roanoke 1, 3–5, 100–11, 164, 166, 200, 210, 214
"Room Service" (episode 5:5) 209
"Room 33" (episode 5:6) 210
Rory Monahan (character) 214
"Rubber Man" (episode 1:8) 207

"The Sacred Taking" (episode 3:8) 138, 141–2, 145, 208
Sally McKenna (character) 203, 214
Salty (character) 169, 172, 213
Scáthach (character) 214
"The Seven Wonders" (episode 3:13) 134, 144–5, 153, 178, 209
Shachath (character) 193, 213
"She Gets Revenge" (episode 5:10) 210
"She Wants Revenge" (episode 5:9) 210
Shelby Miller (character) 100, 109, 214
Shelley (character) 12–3, 89, 94–5, 193, 212
"Show Stoppers" (episode 4:12) 175, 179, 209
Sister Jude Martin (character) 9–10, 22–4, 89–90, 92–7, 193, 195, 197, 199–200, 205, 212
Sister Mary Eunice (character) 87, 94–5, 193, 197, 212
"Smoldering Children" (episode 1:10) 207
"Sojourn" (episode 8:8) 56, 61, 63, 211
Spalding (character) 153, 213
"Spilt Milk" (episode 2:11) 17, 22–3, 198, 208
"Spooky Little Girl" (episode 1:9) 75, 207
Stanley (character) 106, 129, 174, 213
Stevie Nicks (character) 5, 148, 151, 153, 208

Tate Langdon (character) 54, 62, 70–3, 75, 77–8, 175, 212, 215
"The Ten Commandments Killer" (episode 5:8) 210,
"Test of Strength" (episode 4:7) 174, 209
Thomasin White/The Butcher (character) 107–10, 214
Timothy Campbell (character) 57, 215
Toulouse (character) 121, 213
"Traitor" (episode 8:7) 211
"Tricks and Treats" (episode 2:2) 10, 13, 89–90, 94, 96, 193, 207
Tristan Duffy (character) 214
"Tupperware Party Massacre" (episode 4:9) 118, 209
Twisty the Clown (character) 54, 104–7, 109, 125, 131n3, 131n6, 213

"Unholy Night" (episode 2:8) 90, 193, 208

"Valerie Solanas Died for Your Sins: Scumbag" (episode 7:7)
Violet Harmon (character) 63, 67–8, 71, 76–7, 119, 212, 215
Vivien Harmon (character) 212, 214

"Welcome to Briarcliff" (episode 2:1) 12, 92, 96, 193, 195, 198, 207
Wendy Peyser (character) 18–9, 195–9, 204, 212
Wilhemina Venable (character) 56–7, 215
Will Drake (character) 202, 214

Winter Anderson (character) 183, 214
"Winter of Our Discontent" 211

Zoe Benson (character) 138–9, 153, 159, 170, 173, 176–8, 181, 213, 215

www.ingramcontent.com/pod-product-compliance
Lightning Source LLC
Chambersburg PA
CBHW032041300426
44117CB00009B/1140